Mac Runciman

A Life in the Grain Trade

Mac Runciman

A Life in the grain trade

Paul D. Earl

THE UNIVERSITY OF MANITOBA PRESS

The University of Manitoba Press

Winnipeg, Manitoba Canada R3T 5V6

www.umanitoba.ca/uofmpress

Printed in Canada on recycled, acid-free paper

Cover and text design: Karen Armstrong

Frontispiece: portrait of Mac Runciman reproduced by permission of Yousuf Karsh.

Cover: Mac Runciman, c. 1934.

Photographs: Unless otherwise indicated, all photographs are from the collection of Mac Runciman.

Canadian Cataloguing-in-Publication Data

Earl, Paul D. (Paul David), 1941–

    Mac Runciman

    Includes bibliographical references and index.

    ISBN 0-88755-666-3

1. Runciman, Mac, 1914– 2. Farmers—Saskatchewan—
Biography. 3. Grain trade—Prairie Provinces—History—
20th century. 4. United Grain Growers—Biography.
I. Title.

HD9044.C22E37 2000   380.1'4131'092   C00-920129-7

The University of Manitoba Press gratefully acknowledges the financial support for its publishing program provided by the Government of Canada through the Book Publishing Industry Development Program (BPIDP); the Manitoba Arts Council; and the Manitoba Department of Culture, Heritage and Tourism.

Special assistance for the publication of this book was also provided by the United Grain Growers and the Canadian Pacific Railway.

Contents

To Pat
who was always there for me.

Preface

This book, to begin with, tells the story of Alexander McInnes (Mac) Runciman, a man who is best known as a former president of United Grain Growers (UGG). However, the book is more than Mac's story. It also provides an analysis of one of the most difficult public policy issues faced by the federal government, farmers, the grain industry, and the railways in the last half-century: the modernization of grain handling and transportation in western Canada over the 1960s and 1970s. Moreover, it chronicles a major paradigm shift in farm opinion in western Canada, in which the wisdom of maintaining the highly centralized and regulated grain marketing and transportation systems came under increasing criticism within the rural community. A word about each of these stories is in order, beginning with Mac's.

Mac played his most prominent role in public life as the president of United Grain Growers from 1961 to 1981, and as an outstanding leader in western Canadian agriculture. However, he was much more than that, and others will remember him as a director of a number of major Canadian companies, as the founding president of the Rapeseed Association of Canada (now the Canola Council of Canada), as a former chair of the University of Manitoba Board of Governors, as an appointee to the Order of Canada, or as filling one of several prominent roles he played in Canadian affairs.

Mac was born in Scotland in 1914, and emigrated to Canada when he was thirteen years old, in 1928. His family had farmed in Scotland and they took up holdings in Saskatchewan, not far from Balcarres, shortly after they arrived. Mac first farmed with his father and continued to live on the family farm until the war. However, in 1934, in addition to his responsibilities at home, he began to work, on his own, a quarter section that had been purchased by his grandfather for him (Mac) and six other grandchildren (his brother and sister and their cousins).

In 1940, he joined the Canadian Army (Ordnance Corps) and served overseas until the spring of 1945. It was during the war that his leadership abilities began to emerge in a substantive way. He started his military career as a private and, by the end of the war, had attained the highest non-commissioned officer rank. He was selected for officer training, but a curious quirk of fate prevented him from taking it.

The family farm was given up during the war, but Mac was determined to resume farming and so he purchased property near Abernethy, Saskatchewan, shortly after his return. He then became interested in United Grain Growers and was elected secretary of the UGG "local board" in Abernethy in the early 1950s. This brought him to the attention of the company's directors and in 1955 he was asked to join the board. It seems likely (although Mac himself does not know for sure, and hard evidence is lacking) that he was former president John Brownlee's choice as successor. Regardless, when Mr. Brownlee resigned from office due to illness, the UGG board selected Mac as the company's new president.

In 1961, therefore, Mac left farming a second time and moved to Winnipeg. The presidency of UGG was the first step in what became a distinguished career in corporate and public life. Over the following twenty years, he assumed a broad range of public service responsibilities – in industry, government, and the community at large – and emerged as an outstanding leader who was often spoken of as standing "head and shoulders above his peers."

After retirement from UGG in 1981, he became chairman of the board of governors of the University of Manitoba, and continued what was eventually to be more than two decades of involvement with Victoria General Hospital and the Victoria Hospital Foundation in Winnipeg. He finally stepped down from the board of the foundation in 1999. In 1983, he was invited to become one of the founding directors of Power Financial Corporation.

The formal positions and honours are indicative of Mac's stature, but convey little of the admiration in which he was held. Everyone who was involved in the western Canadian grain industry trusted and respected him. He was often consulted by the grain industry's senior leaders on critical issues or at critical decision points in their own lives and careers. He was the kind of man who attracted such confidences, and to whom people would turn for advice.

His leadership abilities were formally recognized on many occasions. He was asked by the federal government to be the founding chairman of the Canada Grains Council; he was selected by his peers in the industry to be the founding president of the Rapeseed Association (now the Canola Council); and at one point he was asked by the Trudeau government to take a cabinet post, which he refused.

As this biography was coming to completion, Mac was eighty-five years old, and had, only one year earlier, stepped down as president of the condominium complex in which he resided. In this role, he had been involved for several years in a difficult legal case, which the complex had advanced against the construction companies that built the condominium. This was no trivial legal matter. Part of the legal proceedings had been taken earlier to the Supreme Court, and, if the matter had not been settled out of court, he would have to be the condominium's prime witness as the case returned to a lower court to move through its next step.

It is not only the details of Mac's life that merit some public record, but also the way he exercised the leadership role into which he was thrust. He governed himself by a set of values he absorbed from his family, and from which he never wavered: honesty, fair play, justice, and respect for others.

Despite his accomplishments, Mac has remained a very down-to-earth person. He is at home in whatever company he finds himself, and possesses the rare knack of putting anyone – regardless of their personal position, wealth, or rank – at ease. One former employee of United Grain Growers once very aptly described him as "courtly." And while he is not without criticism of others when it is called for, he does not criticize unjustly, and one has to be fairly close to him before one will hear harsh judgements from his lips. As he put it in 1976, speaking to an audience at Knox United Church in Winnipeg on ethics and business, "my standard of judgement is fairness, not softness, and the judgements are mine."[1]

It was during his presidency of United Grain Growers that the other events recorded in this book unfolded: government and industry attempts to deal with the grain handling and transportation problems, and the shifting tide of farm opinion.

When Mac assumed the presidency, the grain industry was just beginning to come to grips with the issue that absorbed more of his time and energy than any other: the need to rationalize and modernize the grain handling and transportation system. Even as late as 1970, this system had changed little from the 1930s, when farmers hauled grain to market with horses and wagons. What was not widely understood in 1961 was the way a tightly woven web of institutional constraints, arising from well-intentioned but questionable policies, combined to frustrate the development of a modern and efficient system. Nor was there a willingness to acknowledge the role of railway freight rates on grain – the Crow's Nest Pass Rates[2] – in the arrested development of the system. These rates were looked on as the Magna Carta of the west, a view that was simply not open to examination or discussion.

In the late 1960s and early 1970s, however, the transportation system faltered and came close to a total breakdown. An intense examination of these problems was undertaken and many previously unquestioned assumptions came under scrutiny.

Mac was one of a handful of people who found themselves in the forefront as the grain industry worked through the protracted and often stormy debates that ensued, and he was one of the first western agricultural leaders to call for an examination of the economic effects of the Crow Rates. Over the course of the 1970s, he continually urged the grain industry and farmers to accept the need for change on this very thorny issue.

The story of how an entire system, serving one of Canada's most important industries (grain farming in western Canada), became so stagnated has not been told before, and certainly has not been told by anyone as intimately involved in the grain industry as was Mac.

Through the course of his presidency of UGG, Mac also saw another major change in western agriculture: the birth and growth of farmer dissatisfaction with the centralized marketing policies of The Canadian Wheat Board and with stringent regulation of the industry. These policies, which earlier generations had fought hard to implement, were increasingly found wanting in the post-war world. Mac's view of this "sea change" in opinion is the third major theme of this book. This is explored through his speeches and reports to the UGG board of directors at the time.

Accordingly, this book is not only about Mac, but also about the grain industry and the major challenges it faced during his presidency. It does not present a complete analysis of these issues, but it presents the views of one prominent and highly respected man. It is a contribution towards understanding and interpreting both a volatile period of western agricultural history, and some of the issues that continue to bedevil farmers, industry people, politicians, and civil servants.

When Mac retired from United Grain Growers, he acquired a computer, and many people hoped he would write his "presidential memoirs." However, it is not in his nature to do so. While he writes beautifully when he sets his mind to it, he does not take naturally to writing a work of this length, and he most certainly is not the sort of person who would write an account of his own professional life and times. He is a modest man who finds it difficult to understand why his life and work would be of interest to anyone other than himself and his family. However, he does recognize the turbulent times through which he led UGG, and believes there is a story about those times that should be told. On this point he is quite right.

After 1981, little progress was made on what came to be called, in a few circles, "the Runciman memoirs." Then, early in 1994, while I was working with UGG, the president of the company, Ted Allen, decided that something should be done to record the company's history. No work had been done on this since 1957, with the publication of R.D. Colquette's *The First Fifty Years*. This task was headed up by John Clark, the man who managed UGG's public affairs functions while Mac was president. Mac was asked to provide his own recollections, and since I was working for UGG at that time, I became involved because of my own interest in the history of the industry, and because I had earlier worked under Mac.

My part in the project was to create a record of his life and his presidency of UGG, and over the following months, I conducted more than twenty taped interviews with him. As resource material for our discussions, Mac and I used the minutes of UGG board meetings, and the written reports he had given to the UGG directors at each and every board meeting over his twenty years as president. These interviews formed one of the prime sources from which this book was developed. Although I left the company before these interviews were finished, I continued to work with him, and UGG was kind enough to give me access to the tapes when they were completed. The present book is the outcome.

This volume is not a full-fledged biography, in that it uses a limited number of sources. It follows a format which takes quotations from Mac and links them through paragraphs that provide context and background. There were three main sources for the quotations. The interviews we conducted were the most frequently used source, particularly in the earlier chapters. His reports to the UGG board of directors were the second and in some ways the most important source. These come into use in chapters 5 to 7, which cover the years of his presidency. The third major source is the speeches that Mac gave as president of UGG.

It should be noted that, throughout the book, quotations from Mac which are not footnoted are taken from the interviews. The referenced quotations are either from the autobiographical notes Mac wrote himself, or from his board reports or his speeches.

The importance of Mac's reports as an historical source can scarcely be overemphasized, because they contain a perspective difficult to find elsewhere. The portions of the reports used in this book provide Mac's contemporary comments on the issues and events of the time, and the juxtaposition of these quotations with his comments today forms a kind of dialogue between past and present, which is rare in a work of this nature. While copies of these reports will eventually find their way into the UGG records at the University of Manitoba archives, they will not likely be open for examination in their entirety for more than another decade. The access to them for purposes of this book was, therefore, simply invaluable.

A few other sources are used in minor ways: a few extracts are taken from UGG annual reports; a few letters in Mac's possession have been quoted; and, since he did write a few autobiographical pages, mostly about his personal life, some of what he wrote is also incorporated.

Secondary sources were consulted to clarify some facts, but they are cited in only a very few instances. Between us, Mac and I felt we knew the ground well, and did not require a great deal of background research. However, C.F. Wilson's well-known works,[3] the annual reports of The Canadian Wheat Board, and UGG annual reports were all consulted to provide necessary detail on a number of points.

The format of the book – quotations interspersed with background and contextual material written by me – gives it two "voices": Mac's and mine. However, as far as possible, we sought to have the two voices tell the same story. First of all, both voices express a particular point of view, which is sharply critical of the very heavy regulation and centralization which has characterized the western Canadian grain industry. Accordingly, the book is not a completely objective account of the events of its time, because this philosophical standpoint colours the book and the way events are portrayed.

Moreover, in writing the book, I very deliberately sought to ensure that the background portions reflected Mac's position: his experience, his knowledge, his recollections, and his philosophy. There are some events I would have portrayed differently if the book were to represent only my views. A major example is the description of the Grains Group, a small government body that existed in the 1970s. I was part of this Group, and it was only after I left it and had worked in the west for a time that I realized just how arrogant and threatening it had been to many in the industry. There was, however, another side to the story of the Grains Group, because within it were those who opposed any extension of Ottawa's control over the western grain industry. All in all, I think the Grains Group deserves rather more credit than it gets in these pages. The account of the Grains Group, therefore, is not as complete as it could be, but it is an accurate account in that it portrays this body very much as Mac and many others in the grain industry saw and experienced it. There were other events that he and I discussed, where I was aware of facts he had not known or had no recollection of today, but these are not included because they are not part of his story.

The book, therefore, presents the story of Mac's life and times as he himself has told it, or would have told it if he had been inclined to do so. In philosophy and historic detail, the book speaks with only one voice.

The first four chapters follow his life chronologically. The subsequent three take a slightly different approach, covering the major events and issues he was involved in during his presidency of UGG. A glance at his curriculum vitae in the Appendix will reveal that, in order to keep this book to a manageable length, we had to choose between treating a few of the many things he was involved with in some depth, or covering them all superficially. We opted for a selection, choosing five areas of his career for attention: the changes he wanted to make to UGG itself; his activities in the world of farm organizations and their role in national agricultural policy; his founding presidency of the Rapeseed Association of Canada; his founding chairmanship of the Canada Grains Council; and the leadership he and UGG exercised in the debate on grain handling and transportation during the 1970s. These matters are dealt with in chapters 5 to 7, and while they more or less followed each other in sequence, there was a great deal of overlap. It is for this reason that these chapters do not quite follow the same chronological pattern as the earlier four. The eighth and final chapter deals very briefly with Mac's life since he retired, but, more importantly, also describes the values and beliefs that guided him throughout his life and career.

The book is not, by any stretch of the imagination, my project alone. Mac was very much part of the creative process. As the work progressed, we followed a pattern in which I would prepare an initial draft of each chapter, and then he and I would meet to review it. Since the tape recorder was always at hand during these sessions, Mac quite often added material, which became incorporated in subsequent drafts. Each chapter has gone through three or four such reviews and editings. In at least one of these review sessions we read the entire chapter aloud, giving us an excellent sense of how it read as a story.

There is one further point of key importance for historians and others who may eventually have access to the taped interviews. The quotations from the interviews will not, in general, be found verbatim on the tapes. There are several reasons for this. First of all, the spoken word contains a great deal of "oral punctuation" – pauses, voice inflections, asides in the middle of sentences – which must be heard to be understood. Some editing, therefore, was necessary to make the transcript understandable. Second, because we did a lot of what Mac used to call "rambling," many subjects were discussed more than once. Accordingly, some quotations are also taken from more than one place and, often, more than one interview.

The third and most important reason that the quotations are not verbatim from the interviews is that Mac himself changed them. As described above, every word of this book has been read and commented on by him. More frequently than I can cite, he found the original quotation was not what he had intended to say, or was not an accurate description of events, or misrepresented his views, or was simply said in an awkward or ambiguous way. While we tried to preserve the spontaneity of the spoken word, he made numerous alterations to the wording in the interests of clarity and accuracy.

In addition to reviewing the text with Mac in this manner, I also formed an advisory committee of three people. The first was Dr. Gerry Friesen, an eminent western Canadian historian. Gerry did not know Mac personally, but knew the background and the times. Gerry's personal point of view on regulation, centralized marketing, and legislated freight rates is contrary to the one in this book. He, therefore, provided a much-appreciated balance to the critical position Mac and I share on these issues. The second was the late Dr. Clay Gilson, Professor Emeritus in Agricultural Economics at the University of Manitoba, who knew Mac well and whose career largely coincided with his. Clay was, among many things, the person who eventually headed up the Crow Rate negotiations with the industry that Mac was at one point approached to lead. The third was Frank Rowan, a retired senior executive from The Canadian Wheat Board, a person with a deep interest in the history of the grain industry and one who experienced many of the events described in the book.

The committee met several times, and gave me their invaluable advice on the content, structure, and presentation of the material. It was gratifying to find, as they reviewed the manuscript, that they found it informative and interesting, and judged it to be a worthwhile contribution to the written history of the grain industry and agriculture.

Gerry Friesen was also kind enough to write an insightful Foreword to this book, bringing to light things which Mac and I, in Gerry's terms, "left in the shadows." My association with Gerry started some years ago when I completed a doctoral degree, and he was my primary advisor on my thesis work. Over three degrees and almost fifty years, I have to single Gerry out as the best teacher I have ever had, so I was enormously gratified when he agreed to make this contribution to the work.

A word now about myself as the prime author of the contextual and background material, and the position from which I have provided this detail about the Canadian grain industry.

I am not a westerner by birth and upbringing, but was raised and educated in the east, receiving a Master's degree in transportation planning from the University of Toronto. This took me to Ottawa in 1970, where I first became involved in the grain industry, working on transportation issues in the Grains Group, the small, interdepartmental advisory body referred to above. In 1975 I took a position as Director of Corporate Planning with UGG, where I had the responsibility of preparing and presenting the company's positions before a series of commissions of inquiry and formal investigations into grain transportation issues. Several of these, including the Hall and Snavely commissions, are described in Chapter 7. I left UGG in 1979 and worked for eight years at the Grain Transportation Authority (later, the Grain Transportation Agency, or GTA), which was partly responsible for the central coordination of grain movement. My work, over these years, lay mostly in the research and policy analysis area, largely, but not exclusively, in transportation.

In 1986, I took educational leave from the GTA, and began working on a doctoral degree. My goal was to study the historical roots of the institutions that had so dominated the Canadian grain industry since the 1920s: the provincial Wheat Pools and The Canadian Wheat Board. Through this work I gained a deeper understanding of the seemingly unbridgeable divide between those who believe grain marketing, handling, and transportation should be centralized and regulated, and those who believe that the entire industry should be commercialized and allowed to operate in a free market.

After completing this degree, I returned to the GTA, but shortly thereafter rejoined UGG for a further five years, working both in operations and policy. The last four years I have spent with the Western Canadian Wheat Growers Association.

My experience in the grain industry overlaps about half of Mac's own career as UGG president. In my own professional work in the industry, I have been intimately involved with the issues that are addressed in this book.

Between us, therefore, Mac and I represent over fifty years of experience in the business, with our combined backgrounds covering farming, government, industry, regulatory bodies, and farm organizations. As Mac said, there are few teams who can claim such qualifications in preparing such a work as this.

There are many people and organizations whom I must acknowledge for their direct and indirect contribution to this work.

To Mac, first of all, for several years of work with me, for endless hours poring over UGG documents and his own records, for spending so much time recording his recollections, and finally for agonizing with me over every line of this book.

To my wife Pat, who has been unfailingly supportive, for reading every chapter of the book as it was produced and encouraging me as the work slowly came to fruition.

To United Grain Growers for a very generous financial contribution to the publication of this book. Also to UGG for access to the taped interviews with Mac, for access to the documents Mac and I used, and for starting the whole process in the first place.

To Canadian Pacific Railway, which also made a significant financial contribution which not only aided in publication, but enabled the book to be launched in a manner which was appropriate to the worthy record of Mac's achievements.

To the Royal Bank of Canada, which provided financial support for the writing of this book. And to the members of the now-disbanded Agricultural Diversification Alliance, which likewise made a financial contribution to the production of the book. The Alliance was a group of western agricultural industry and producer organizations that came together to lobby for the end of the legislated freight rates under the Western Grain Transportation Act. Its members were the Alberta Cattle Commission, Alberta Pork, Canadian National Millers Association, Cargill Grain, Feedrite Mills, the Manitoba Cattle Producers, the Manitoba Feed Grain Users, Manitoba Pork, Saskatchewan Pork International, United Grain Growers, and the Western Canadian Wheat Growers Association.

To the members of my advisory committee, Gerry Friesen, Clay Gilson, and Frank Rowan, for their advice, encouragement, and help.

To my employers, the Western Canadian Wheat Growers Association, for providing photocopying services, for giving me considerable flexibility in the management of my time between the book and the duties they required me to perform, and for the encouragement of their staff and directors in the progress of the work. In particular, to the Executive Director of the Wheat Growers, Alanna Koch, who was not only instrumental in providing all the assistance from the organization, but who also proofread the final draft and picked up dozens of errors Mac and I had made.

The faults in the book are mine alone.

Foreword

Fourteen years in Scotland, eleven Depression years on his immigrant family's Saskatchewan farm, six war years, fifteen years establishing his own farm family during the era of mechanization and electrification between 1945 and 1960, twenty years at the helm of a large grain company and at the centre of agricultural policy-making, nearly twenty more in an active semi-retirement and still going strong as this is written: Mac Runciman has enjoyed a full life and met many responsibilities during his four score years and more. This book is testimony to the regard in which he is held by his colleagues. It also testifies to his perseverance and to that of his co-author, Paul Earl. It is, most of all, a valuable document on the history of western Canada.

Though a memoir, the following narrative is uncanny in the way that it recapitulates the history of prairie Canada in the twentieth century. Mac Runciman was one of the last to sail the great immigrant wave that peopled – or more properly, re-peopled – the prairies between 1870 and 1930. He started out in the age of horse and wagon and the day-long haul to the country elevator. He could say with feeling, from personal experience, that no one in a wealthy society "should have been subjected to the hardships that people were subjected to in Saskatchewan in the '30s, it's as simple as that." He enlisted in Canada's army early in the Second World War and, as his leadership qualities became evident, rose steadily through the ranks. And then, almost by accident, or so it seemed to Mac, he was picked out from the crowd of ordinary citizens, those who surrounded him at the curling rink and the elevator local, and invited to accept greater responsibility. Within the span of a few years, he rose to the presidency of the United Grain Growers. For the next two decades, he managed this large organization and participated in the debates that accompanied the restructuring of Canada's agricultural economy and prairie Canada's rural society. Protesting all the way that he was just a farmer doing what was best for farming, Mac contributed a great deal during this extraordinary historical moment. He emerged from the crucible with reputation enhanced and his feet planted on the ground as firmly as they had been when he was an Abernethy farmer.

The book is unusual in that it has two voices, one speaking in oral interviews, and the other setting scenes and linking the reminiscences. However, it should be seen as a memoir, not a history, because it seeks to record only the main character's point of view. The two authors, Runciman and Earl, share strong opinions about their topic and even many experiences in the grain trade. Both favour self-reliance and personal independence. They distrust government intervention in the workings of the market. The primary obligation of cooperatives, they believe, is to secure local economic advantage, not greater social justice. They are inclined to accept the rules of the global capitalist system and the restrictions on local action that it imposes. They are a little impatient with those who fail to see the juggernaut's overpowering logic or who seek to postpone its advance. All of this will be evident in the pages that follow.

And yet there is also a silence in this narrative that must be taken into account. What could be harder than that? I admit that my admonition is odd. Yet I urge you to think about what is not said, about the actors who are not present, as Mac's story unfolds. As you travel along with the two storytellers, consider the shadows cast by their tale – because in those shadows you will find the people who are opponents of the UGG and of industry "rationalization." These were the individuals who, as Paul Earl designates them, opposed the "more thoughtful and active farmers." His phrase hints at a certain bias in favour of the rationalizers: were the UGG's critics actually thoughtless and sluggish? Who were they and what moved them? On such matters the book is silent, though one can be certain that Mac Runciman treated with consideration and politeness all those with whom he discussed the evolution of prairie agriculture, whether friend or foe.

By the 1960s, one learns, the handling and transportation of grain had reached a critical juncture. The rules and institutions established earlier in the century required renewal. Paul Earl's explanation of the situation emphasizes the "antiquated" elevators, boxcars, and branch rail lines. It also excoriates the government regulatory framework that allegedly prevented market signals reaching farmers. And, it complains, The Canadian Wheat Board remained aloof from economic realities. Then, at the end of this list of obstacles in the way of progress, Earl adds another important consideration: "Arguably, however, the most profound impediment to change was the attitudes among the farmers and residents of smaller towns, who vigorously opposed any changes to the elevator or rail line system." With this suggestion, the uninstructed reader begins to see why Mac Runciman's story possesses historical significance: Mac was a central figure in the drive to change the prairie grain economy. And many, perhaps most, of the people with whom he worked – the farm families and townspeople of prairie Canada – did not embrace this cause enthusiastically. The reader is also discovering that this narrative is not attempting to balance all sides of the debate. Rather, it is elaborating on the perspective held by a principal in this historic transition.

Mac Runciman stood in one camp during the great "market vs. government" debate. He saw his chief business competitors, the prairie Pools – especially the Saskatchewan Wheat Pool – and his chief policy antagonists, the National Farmers Union, as belonging to the other camp. He did not approve of The Canadian Wheat Board's role in the industry. He regarded the New Democratic Party, the governing party in Manitoba (1969-1977) and Saskatchewan (1971-1982), as a symptom of the larger problem. The NDP favoured government intervention in the market and refused to distinguish economic from social considerations when it made policy choices – precisely the attitudes that had to be changed, in Mac's view. One should also remember, however, that the picture is always clearer in retrospect. When Mac was living with these great debates, principles and profits and efficiency were his only guides.

Mac does not devote much time to partisan politics in his memoir. The absence is significant and cannot be attributed solely to his strong sense of personal privacy. It was a requirement of his job that he get along with leaders of all stripes. Yet, there is something more in this absence. Let me illustrate by referring to a story that Mac tells on himself. The one great promotion Mac refused in his career was the invitation to join Pierre Elliott Trudeau's last Cabinet in 1980. Why? Did he feel that he had made his contributions and, at the age of 66, had a right to slow down? Not likely, as will become plain. Was he so private a man that he could not have abided the demands of public life in the television age? Possibly, but people learn to adjust to such things. No, something more was afoot. It must be remembered that Mac was a profoundly democratic and public-spirited citizen. He had accepted comparable responsibilities in the past. Why not now?

Mac has told me that the invitation arrived out of the blue. In a brief telephone call from the office of the Prime Minister, Jim Coutts, one of Trudeau's staff, proposed that Mac become the minister responsible for The Canadian Wheat Board. Mac's refusal was a small thing at the time, an instant response to a last-minute call late in the evening, and was made on the spot. His resistance was not due to the fact that the call was unexpected – after all, governments are always cobbled together on the run. Rather, a decisive factor in his choice was what the invitation revealed about the character of the new government. Trudeau seemed to rely on appointed power-brokers and was proposing to solve a prairie political problem by means of a non-elected Senator, a stop-gap measure that a thoroughgoing democrat such as Mac could not accept. Besides, if he had had time to reflect, what would he have thought about the likely path of the new administration? Could he have influenced the National Economic Policy or the Crow Rate discussions? Would he have been asked to compromise his own principles, including views that were contributing to rapid changes in prairie agriculture? These are history's might-have-beens. What we can say is that Mac was, at heart, a democrat and an economic determinist. As he put it: "I'm a great believer in the inevitability of ... economics. And whether it takes ten years or thirty years or fifty years, economic forces will finally prevail."

Aside from its strengths as a personal memoir, this book outlines one business leader's experience of a profound cultural shift in the last half of the twentieth century. Every reader will be aware of the revolution in political economy associated with Margaret Thatcher and Ronald Reagan and their acolytes, who adopted a version of monetarist policies in the 1980s and 1990s. But were Thatcher and Reagan actually driving the process? Or were they recognizing the power of technological, economic, and social forces that had already been unleashed in the world? Here is an answer from the Canadian prairies. Mac Runciman and many others involved in the prairie grain industry perceived the advantages of a stream-lined system during the 1960s. They launched their campaign to realize their goals before the end of that decade. In short, the market-government debate became intense long before the political revolutions of the 1980s.

Mac Runciman and Paul Earl have written an insightful and useful book. They have provided readers with valuable lessons in life as well as an important memoir concerning a pivotal era in prairie agriculture.

Gerald Friesen
University of Manitoba

Mac Runciman

The Boy: Scotland, 1914 – 1928

1

A hazard of growing old is that one may be smitten by the urge to write a personal or family history. It is debatable whether this affliction arises from a desire to inform present and future generations about the life and times of the author, or is merely an ego trip based on a belief that the experiences of one's life were significant enough to merit recording. Let the cause be what it may, the onset of this affliction can be regarded as a sure sign that the victim has reached old age. Having qualified in that respect, and succumbed to the malady, my course will now be along the well-trodden path of countless previous sufferers.[1]

On this modest and almost apologetic note, Mac Runciman began to write his autobiography. The somewhat old-fashioned style of these opening lines reminds me of nothing so much as the first pages of Dickens's *David Copperfield*: the same elegance, the same cadence and rhythm, the same way of gently insinuating the reader into the story. It is apparent from this introductory paragraph that, when he sets his mind to it, Mac writes so beautifully that the reader will no doubt wish the whole work might have come from his pen alone. Unfortunately, when Mac first gave me a copy of his nascent autobiography, it had progressed to only seven pages.

What he did record contained, with characteristic modesty, a good deal about his forebears, but only the barest minimum about himself. "It is normal," Mac wrote, "in projects of this kind for the opening statement to record that the writer was born, followed by date and place, so who am I to differ? However, in recording my birth at Invergordon, Ross and Cromarty, Scotland, on October 8, 1914, it occurred to me that since the event was not entirely of my own doing, it would be fitting to start the story with some information about my ancestors and relatives, particularly my mother and father, who had such significant roles in my arrival."[2]

Although he has spent some time tracing his ancestry, nothing like a complete genealogy has yet been erected. On his father's side, the first generation of which he has any extensive knowledge is his own grandparents'. His paternal grandfather, after whom Mac was named, was born in Perthshire, Scotland, in 1856. We know nothing of his grandfather's background, schooling, or upbringing, but we do know that he must have been skilled at clerical work and record-keeping, because in about 1878, he commenced a lifelong career at The Register House in Edinburgh. In 1881 the elder Alexander McInnes married the woman who was to become Mac's grandmother, Jemima Paterson, also of Perthshire. Two years later, in 1883, their first-born, Mac's father, entered the world.

Grandfather Runciman must have commuted to Edinburgh during his first few years at The Register House, because the place of his son's birth is recorded as Errol Village, County of Perth.[3] We know that the couple moved to Edinburgh a short time later and resided there until after Alexander McInnes retired.

His career was a successful one, and Mac still has his grandfather's gold watch with the inscription:

Presented to
A.M. RUNCIMAN Esq[re]
Depute Keeper
H.M. General Register of Sasines[4] Edinburgh
By His Colleagues
At His Retirement
After Nearly 43 Years Service
on
27th August 1921

Alexander and Jemima were, in Mac's words, "a rather typical middle-class late-Victorian couple; neat and tidy and as controlled in respectable behaviour as in dress,"[5] and so they appear in the only surviving photograph of the couple together. Mac chose the word "controlled" deliberately. He recalls that his grandfather, who smoked a pipe, would periodically knock the ashes out and place the pipe carefully on the mantelpiece, saying, "Enough of that for now; you will rest up there for a while." And so it would, not to be smoked for a month or so, lest the habit become uncontrollable. It was, Mac recalls, an act of personal discipline.

Alexander McInnes senior was an influential figure in his grandson's life, instilling by example many of the values – discipline included – that Mac himself later bodied forth. He recalls his grandfather as being "a strong advocate of honesty, fair play, good sportsmanship and other commendable attributes," and tells of how grandfather Runciman inculcated these qualities in his grandson.

> Three incidents in my association with my grandfather come easily to mind as I think about him. They say something about what he was like and perhaps some of him rubbed off on me. On a fine summer day I was walking around the Braid Hills golf course in Edinburgh with him as he played with an acquaintance. An errant drive by his opponent went into a clump of whin bushes - which are still a feature of that course - and came to rest in a difficult, but playable, lie. As we approached unnoticed, we both saw him furtively pick up the ball and move it to a much more favourable lie from which to play it. Grandfather, who had been losing to this man, didn't say a word, but with a look of grim determination on his face proceeded to play faultless golf all the way to the clubhouse, and left his opponent without a word of farewell. Not until we were home did Grandfather unwind enough to tell me that what I had seen was cheating, and that cheating at golf or any other sport was, well, "not cricket."[6]

Over seventy years later, in one of our often-meandering conversations, Mac spoke of what he called the "mayhem" of the playoff season in the National Hockey League and, in a voice of grim determination that I cannot convey with the written word, described how "poor sportsmanship just grinds my gears." The lessons from his grandfather clearly stuck with him.

The other two incidents that stayed in his mind in relation to his grandfather were no less powerful in their influence.

> Grandfather and I were walking along the south side of Princes Street in Edinburgh, and as we turned towards an entrance to Princes Street Gardens to view the well-known floral clock, he reached down to pick up a six-penny piece from the sidewalk. I never had much in the way of spending money and the thought went through my mind, Perhaps he will give it to me. Slim hope! What he gave me was a kind lecture on the virtues and benefits of being alert at all times as there were benefits from that such as I had just seen, and with that the sixpence went into his pocket and stayed there!

> The third item of this trilogy occurred when I had gone to church with Grandfather in Edinburgh on a Sunday morning. After the service, as we were leaving the church, Grandfather stopped for a word with his minister, who introduced his son standing beside him. That was the highlight of my life up until that time and for long after. The young man was Eric

Liddell, whose story was so effectively told in the movie of a few years back, *Chariots of Fire*. At that time Eric Liddell was the Wayne Gretzky of British rugby and track and field. So fast could he run that when the ball was passed to him, no one in the game in those days could catch him. At that particular time, however, he was principally in the public eye because, although he had seemed to be a shoo-in to win the hundred-metre dash at a recent Olympic games, having won all his heats easily, he refused to compete in the finals because they were to be run on a Sunday. As it happened, Lord Burleigh won that race for Britain and to show that Liddell had the right stuff, he won the two-hundred metre event when it was run on a subsequent day. As we talked about the matter on the way home, I can remember Grandfather saying, "It just goes to show you that he is a young man of principle." I'm not sure that I knew at the time exactly what that meant but I think I have figured it out since.[7]

Of his grandmother, Jemima Runciman, Mac's recollections are far less vivid. She was a great knitter and would, from time to time, get her grandson to help roll skeins of wool into balls. Mac wrote, "I can recall her then sitting by the kitchen fire knitting socks. Knitting, always knitting and reading the *People's Friend*, a popular household magazine of those days. I never ceased to marvel at how she could knit like fury and never miss a stitch while her eyes were fixed on her story. Except, that is, when performing the tricky procedure of 'turning a heel'. She must have been a quiet, unassuming, unassertive person and I cannot recall the content of any conversation I may have had with her."[8]

About a year after the birth of Mac's father, Alexander, the Runcimans moved to Edinburgh. There, the senior Runciman continued his lengthy career at The Register House, and young Alexander grew to maturity, later joined by two brothers and one sister. One of the brothers, James, later preceded Mac and his family to Canada.

Although he was raised in the city, Alexander aspired to a life in agriculture, and so "became educated in a peculiar sort of way," Mac said. At a variety of colleges in Edinburgh, he pursued a course of study designed to fit him for the career of estate factor, the professional manager hired by large landowners to administer their holdings. He mastered his subjects with distinction: a medal in agricultural bookkeeping "for passing with 99% of the possible marks"; designation of "student of distinction" in elementary building construction (which in those days included stonemasonry); and a "certificate of merit" in elementary agriculture. During his studies, he also worked for a time in a law office in Edinburgh. In 1905, having completed all his coursework, he became estate clerk for the Earl of

Morton at Hatton Mains, Midlothian, and in 1910 became estate clerk and then factor for Sir Hector McLeod of Cadboll at Invergordon, County of Ross and Cromarty.

Although they were studious, Alexander and his brothers did not neglect other aspects of their lives. They were active in the Cluny rugby club, which proved to be a fateful connection. Through the club, he met the Anderson brothers, whose sister Evelyn later became Alexander's wife and Mac's mother.

Mac's genealogy on his mother's side of the family is better documented. Four of his maternal great-great-great-grandparents are known to have resided in the Scottish Border Counties, and one of these, Charlotte Hope, was the granddaughter of Sir Walter Scott. Charlotte's daughter Joan married Andrew Scott (unrelated to Sir Walter) and their son George Scott fathered, with Elizabeth Fraser, Mac's maternal grandmother, Joanna Hope Scott. Unfortunately, no record has been found of the marriage of George and Elizabeth, and without such a record, the Scottish genealogical authorities hold that the legitimacy of the lineage back to Sir Walter is clouded.

His maternal grandfather's line is known only back to his great–grandfather, William Anderson, who founded a tailoring business in Edinburgh in 1868. Mac's grandmother, Joanna, married Andrew Hislop Anderson, one of two sons of William, who together carried on the tailoring enterprise under the name of "William Anderson and Sons." Joanna and Andrew produced fourteen children, of whom eleven – seven girls and four boys - survived to adulthood. Mac's mother, Evelyn Hope Anderson, entered the world in 1884, one of the younger daughters in the family.

The tailoring business did well, allowing the family to live in relative comfort and to enjoy some luxuries. Mac still has in his possession an oil painting of his mother, commissioned when she was five years old.

"However, in the Edinburgh of those days," Mac wrote, "people in the professions tended to look down their noses at people engaged in the 'crass commercialism' of trade, and for that reason the Andersons were not accorded a high social standing. But emphasis was placed on providing good educations for their family."[9]

They were taught music - theory and instrumental - and Evelyn went to a private school, St. Margaret's College for Girls, which still exists, where she studied French, Latin, and German.

While the tailoring business supported the growing family well, it provided a career for only two of the next generation of Andersons. The eldest and the second youngest sons of Andrew Hislop entered the business, but the younger of these was subsequently killed in the Great War, and thus the eldest son became the sole member of the third generation to carry on the enterprise. As for the rest, wrote Mac, "the Anderson brood was turned loose on an unsuspecting world to fend for itself."[10]

They were an adventurous lot. Several emigrated to North America. The second youngest son, Herbert, came first to Regina, where he was employed as secretary to the lieutenant governor. He eventually went with another brother, Andrew, to Los Angeles, where both resided for the remainder of their lives. Mac still has cousins in the US.

The seven sisters – of whom only three ever married – were no less venturesome than the boys. Three emigrated to Canada and joined their brother in Regina, where one worked as a clerk in Government House. The Regina trio eventually travelled further west and lived out the rest of their lives in Portland, Oregon.

One of those who stayed in Britain was postmistress in a succession of small towns, first in Scotland and later in England. The eldest girl, Elizabeth (always known as Cissie), worked on a poultry farm outside Edinburgh for some time, but for many years - until the end of her life, in fact - managed the Scottish Youth Hostel at Broadmeadows in the Borders area of Scotland. Mac visited "Auntie Cissie" at the hostel on more than one occasion during the war, the last time just before her death. "We saw her in June, and in August, I got a letter saying she was dead. She had cancer when we saw her in June and she never said a thing about it." A gritty lady from a gritty family.

Ambition and accomplishment ran on into the next generations, too. One of Evelyn's grandnephews, Eric, became headmaster at Eton College. This caused quite a stir when, after his appointment, it was found he was a Scottish Presbyterian, while Eton's articles of incorporation quite explicitly required its headmaster to be a member of the Church of England. By this time, the importance accorded to such things had changed and therefore, the school's constitution was amended.

Evelyn, like many of her siblings, was an adventurous traveller, using her education to secure several postings as a governess. In this capacity, she worked first in the United States, where she was employed by a family associated with the Armor Packing empire. Later, she came to visit family members in Saskatchewan and, having decided to stay for a while, served from about 1906 to 1908 as governess to a family in the Qu'Appelle Valley north of Grenfell. She went back to Scotland for a couple of years thereafter, but apparently liked Canada so much, she returned to work as a governess on a farm near Craven, just north of Regina.

Here, the past caught up with her. By this time, Alexander had established himself in his career and decided the time had come to start a family. "Dad wired her a proposal of marriage – which she accepted – and came back to Scotland to be married in December of 1913, which was quite a thing in itself." Indeed it was, for, as Mac put it, "the stage was set for my arrival in this world," an event which occurred on October the 8th of the following year. And thus begins the real story of this book.

"My place of birth," Mac wrote, "was Seabank Cottage, a sturdy stone structure set in a pleasant garden above the Saltburn road and in command of a magnificent view across the Cromarty Firth to the Black Isle." He was too young to remember that it also provided a view of the British warships that used the harbour during the Great War. Here he spent the earliest years of his life.

> My knowledge of events in that period has to be based on hearsay from my parents, who often spoke in later years of their life there and took pleasure in recounting a variety of my escapades while learning to walk and talk and get into mischief.
>
> Of these I recall that, apparently, in a bright red coat, I had a running battle with a large turkey gobbler that chased me whenever he had an opportunity. Then, it seems, at a very early age, without my parents being aware of it, I started chatting up the girls on the local telephone exchange, much to their amusement.
>
> But the development that caused most concern for my parents was my early schooling in Gaelic from the Hebridean fishermen who came around to Invergordon at a particular season of the year to fish in the North Sea. Father and Mother were quite impressed with the progress I was making in picking up this new tongue until they found out from local enquiry that the words being learned were the richest swear words of the language. That discovery brought an abrupt end to the possibility of my becoming bilingual at an early age.[11]

Mac's life might have taken an entirely different turn in late 1915 when a tragic event occurred in which his parents were very nearly involved. Just as the year was drawing to a close, his parents were invited to a New Year's entertainment aboard a naval cruiser, the *HMS Natal*.

> They fully intended to accept the invitation but it seems that I developed a tummy-ache during the afternoon and the decision was made to remain at home with me. As it happened, the *Natal* blew up and sank late

that evening with the loss of hundreds of lives. Had they accepted the invitation, my parents would almost certainly have added to that number. Such are the quirks of fate that can change the course of a lifetime.

I tell the story of the *Natal* in some detail because one of my prized possessions is a heavy brass ring inscribed "Main Steam Shutoff," which was salvaged from the wreck of the *Natal* many years later. It was presented me by Mr. Joe Harris, who was at the time chairman of the board of directors of The Great West Life Assurance Company. Knowing that Joe was going to be in the neighbourhood of Invergordon on a trip to Scotland, I told him the story of my parents and the *Natal*, which I suspect he took with a grain of salt. The impression lingers with me that the plate - handsomely mounted with an explanatory plaque – was perhaps his way of apologising for any scepticism he may originally have harboured about the truth of my story.[12]

Mac's father joined the British army on November 28th, 1915, but his contribution to the war actually began before that. Invergordon lay on the shores of the Cromarty Firth, a beautiful landlocked harbour, which became the home base for the British naval fleet. As factor of the Cadboll estate, he spent the year prior to enlisting on administrative duties related to the war effort. Evidently, he carried out these early wartime duties with distinction. A testimonial signed by the chairman of the Easter Ross District Committee, which was in charge of these activities, reads:

> We have pleasure in testifying that we have known Mr Alex. Runciman, factor, for the last seven years. During all that time he has been resident in this district, and in full charge of the extensive Cadboll Estates. In that capacity he has had to carry through many important negotiations (particularly in connection with the recent development of Invergordon into a Naval Base), and we have been impressed with his excellent method of managing men and carrying on work without friction.
>
> Mr Runciman is within military age, and we understand he is about to join the colours. In view of his training and experience he would be admirably adapted for supervising road construction work etc., if his service could be utilized in that direction.[13]

Alexander, therefore, did not depart for France until 1916 and, except for leaves, was then absent from the Runciman household until 1919.

Mac's recollections of the First World War are understandably dim, but he felt the absence of his father, later remarking how "in my very young formative years he wasn't home."

While Mac does not recall the war in detail, his experiences of the events were not without an element of trauma. Some of his recollections can make us laugh from an adult perspective, but it is not likely they were laughing matters to a boy under five.

> A World War I incident which shows how the stresses of wartime can affect even very young children occurred during a visit to my grandparents at 9 St. Fillans Terrace in Edinburgh. The exact date of this occurrence is unknown but we stayed with Granny and Grandfather for different short periods as we came and went from one place of residence to another. Whatever the exact time frame, we were living with them when I suddenly developed an absolute refusal to go to the bathroom for any purpose. After much puzzlement for my elders, and prolonged questioning of me, it was finally established that the reason for my attitude was that I had heard that the German Navy was in the Black Sea. Apparently in my mind the Black Sea and WC had enough in common to make me decide that I wasn't about to risk going there, no matter how pressing the need, if it involved even the slightest risk of encountering the German Navy.[14]

Immediately after the war, when personnel were hard to find, particularly for agricultural work, young Mac was pressed into service to take beer out to the fields for the workers. "I can remember," he told me, "starting out to the harvest field one day with quart bottles of beer and I guess it was a warm day and with the jiggling of the beer in this basket I was carrying it in, the corks started popping and I got panicky. Of course, I had come through a war and anything that went 'bang' was dangerous. I ran for home because the bottles were exploding and somebody had to go back and assure me that it was all right to take this hot beer to the drinkers in the field."

The family was not able to stay at Invergordon with Mac's father away, and so, after another brief stint in Edinburgh with his grandparents and shortly after the birth of his sister Joan in March 1917, he and his mother moved to the historic Border town of Melrose.

> We arrived in Melrose in 1917 and lived there until some time in 1919 as far as can be determined. Our residence there was a church manse, no doubt vacated by a minister called to the armed forces, as every able-bodied man was in those days. The grounds of the manse ran down to the river Tweed and I was warned repeatedly not to go near the river in case I fell in. In contrast to the case at Invergordon, I do have a few definite recollections of events in Melrose and family stories account for knowledge of other happenings in that period.

For example, I can recall quite clearly getting my thumb caught between the door and the frame of a kitchen cupboard and my mother and my 'Big Auntie Beatrice', her sister, having to call in a man with a kit of tools to remove a hinge and liberate me. I can also recall going to our garden gate and watching the children pass on their way to and from school.

My most vivid recollection of that period is of loud knocking at our back door in the small hours of the morning soon after we took up residence in Melrose. That was rather alarming to Mother but she went downstairs, taking me with her. When she opened the outer door of the back kitchen, which was floored with stone slabs, she was confronted by four men, one of whom said, in a broad local accent, "Here's your fush, woman", and handed her a large salmon so newly taken that it was still wriggling violently. Mother did not know what to make of the situation but she closed the door and laid the fish on the floor. The distinctive nature of the noise it made as it thrashed about and its tail slapped on the bare stone floor still echoes in my mind. Apparently the manse garden was the avenue of approach to the river for local poachers, who were paying their dues quite possibly without knowing that a new resident had taken over the premises.[15]

Sometimes, our response to circumstances in early life foreshadows the kind of person we are to become. Mac is no exception. One incident of his life at Melrose stuck with him, and is indicative of his sense of responsibility, which emerged so strongly throughout his life. Very shortly after the move, his mother fell seriously ill with the flu, so ill "that she could not attend to basic chores herself," and "being new to Melrose she had no friends or acquaintances on whom she could rely for assistance." Although Mac is not given to introspection, this incident did cause him to question whether our early behaviour reflects our inner nature or the values inculcated in us by others. "My sister was young," he remembered, "she was just an infant and I have faint recollections of stoking the fire and heating my sister's baby bottles and trying to make tea or soup for my mother and things like that, and this is when I'd be about – I'd say that was 1917 – I'd be three, three and a half. And again, whether that fitted in with my actual nature, or whether it was thrust upon me and made part of my nature, I never knew and never will know."

We now know, of course, that Mac's life was to be one of service to his community and industry, so it's not surprising to hear of his assuming, as a very young child, responsibilities somewhat beyond his years.

He and his mother lived at Melrose until his father returned from the war. His parents told him about his participation as a young, uninvited guest in the local celebrations marking the war's end.

Mother often told how I left our garden and marched behind a body of troops on their way to the Mercat Cross for ceremonies marking the Armistice that terminated the fighting of World War I. The story goes that, having reached the town centre, the idea of standing with the troops while various dignitaries made speeches and said prayers seemed not to have appealed to me. So I chose instead to sit behind the main speakers on one of the tiers of stone making up the base of the town cross, which stands in the same position to this day. Once Mother tracked me down, she stood amid the crowd making desperate signals for me to come to her, but apparently I was quite satisfied with my situation and did not stir until the ceremonies were over.[16]

The family had another brief stay with his grandparents in Edinburgh, during which his father secured another position as factor, this time at the estate of Sir George Baxter at Invereighty. Mac was now approaching five years old, and was almost ready to start school. But on the very eve of this event, he had his first experience at earning a living.

For some reason or other, I guess I must have been what you call a worry wart. Whatever was the task of the day, I seemed to want to help out with it, and there was so much concern about the lack of help and everything in the fall of 1919. With many men still in the army, and the men being demobilized all looking for jobs in the cities, who wanted to go back and farm, you see? And for the harvest of 1919, there was a desperate shortage of help. Well, it was the potato harvest, and they just didn't have help enough, so I volunteered. I guess they kind of joked about it, but they gave me a half-stint[17] and I was able to pick that half-stint. But when I think back to Graham, my grandson, at six years old – you know, I wonder, how on earth did I do it? But on the job, you had to pick your stint – whether it was a full stint, or a stint and a half, or a half-stint – every time the plough went past, because if you didn't, there was a strip of the field that got left behind with potatoes lying on it. The plough went by, uncovering the potatoes, and then the potatoes were picked into baskets. Then a horse and cart went up and down, and the baskets were dumped into the cart as it moved along, so everything had to move across the field in unison. Every time the plough went past, you had to be ready to pick again. So you had to keep up. And best of all, I got paid. The grieve[18] came along at night and paid me my money. And I started school the day I was five years old, so this happened before I was five years old.

But again – and I still have a little streak of this - I'm not aggressive in wanting to get things going; in fact, that is one of the weaknesses of my makeup as I see it. I am not aggressive in getting out and initiating things, but if somebody else will initiate something I think is worthwhile, I will sure help them with it. And that seems to be part of my makeup. I'm trying to be quite analytical about myself.

This was not a conscious sense of duty, because at five years old, do you have such an animal? But it was a job that needed to be done. And I guess everybody thought it was a big joke, but I did all right that first day. The next morning, the first thing I realized was that the cart with the workers was going past the house to the field. I jumped up and got dressed and ran down the road after the cart, because I wanted to be there when the work started. They did make me come back and have breakfast that morning, but from then on they realized it was for real. Now, I have no recollection of how much I made or how many days I did it for or anything else, but I know it was more than one day because as I say I ran after the cart the second morning and other mornings I rode the cart out to the field.

For Mac, the potato-picking experience foreshadowed his future: "I was paid cash on the barrelhead for picking potatoes in Scotland before I went to school, and I picked the half-stint for several days. So I was farming with my hands from the time I was a child, and never thought or wanted to do anything else."

He started school in October 1919, and he completed a grade or two while at Invereighty. However, he didn't continue, because his father, who by the early 1920s had worked in estate management for almost twenty years, longed for a place of his own. In January of 1921, he was able to rent a small property under a program for veterans of the war. It consisted of some fifty-two acres, with perhaps forty-six cultivated. The farm bore the address, "The Glen, Thornton, Innerwick, near Dunbar, East Lothian," and was located right on the east coast of Scotland. They raised cattle, milked cows, raised chickens and pigs: "large blacks, just as black as white pigs are white, and Dad had one of the best bloodlines in Scotland. And if you ever saw a little black pig, you would not forget it. They are as cute as a button."

Mac lived at "The Glen" during the latter part of his childhood, and it was here, too, that he met one of the most influential figures of his life. As one of Robertson Davies's characters observes, it is often "the fathers we choose" who are more influential in our lives than our natural fathers, and Mr. Downey seems to have been a role model for Mac.

A schoolmaster in Scotland, who was also leader of the local scout troop, taught me many valuable lessons in and out of school: athletics, hunting, fishing, boxing, camping, integrity, sportsmanship, as well as a wonderful range of information centred around the school curriculum. He was just a first-class teacher, a little too left wing for my dad, but an excellent individual.

I have to think of him as the source of so many pieces of general knowledge I have today. Frequently in my life, since then, when I have come up with an unusual piece of information, and people have asked, Where did you learn that? the answer has been, Mr. Downey taught it to me. He was such an excellent teacher that he made learning interesting - almost exciting. Here is a little example of what I mean. You may know that poem by Coleridge – I can't recite it all nowadays – but it starts out:

> In Xanadu did Kubla Khan
> A stately pleasure-dome decree
> Where Alph, the sacred river, ran
> Through caverns measureless to man
> Down to a sunless sea.
> So twice five miles of fertile ground
> With walls and towers were girdled round

At that point in a grade eight literature lesson, Mr. Downey raised the question of the size of the piece of land thus "girdled round", and so it triggered a general discussion on that point. And that is the way Mr. Downey was. You could start off with arithmetic and end up in geography. You could start off in literature and end up in mathematics. It followed a very interesting pattern. So he got the discussion going: "It says in Xanadu and so on, and it makes a reference to the size," and Mr. Downey got discussing it on the basis of what the difference would be in size if that was square miles or miles square. So he makes us figure that out: well, ten miles square would obviously be more than ten square miles. Well, then, how big would it be if it was ten square miles? How big is a square mile? How many acres in a square mile? Well, there are 640 acres in a square mile, so he would go on and on.

Well, about four years later, while going to a rural school in Saskatchewan, the teacher asked the class, "How many acres are there in a square mile?" Every one of those kids in school – and there were twenty-six of them – was living on a section of land, and they had been born and brought up on prairie farms, and not a one of them knew at all. But I knew, and I kept thinking, That can't be right. These kids are bound to know because they live on these sections, and so forth. So she finally turned to me and said, "Mac, do you know?" And I said, "Well, I think there are 640 acres in a square mile." And that is right. And how much in a quarter section? Well, 160 acres. So the kids said, How did he know that? Well, it was Mr. Downey back in Scotland who taught me that and that was a little example of how good he was in passing on general information.

It was Mr. Downey, more than his father, who helped Mac develop his athletic and outdoor skills. "Dad was no good at cooking, camping, outdoor work or any of those things," he said. "He just wasn't an outdoor man in the usual sense of the word." He wasn't - to use one of Mac's good Scottish words - "knacky" at certain outdoor work, which is to say he simply lacked "the knack" of doing certain things, including the physical part of farming. "He had a certain awkwardness. He wasn't afraid of work, and though he took good care of livestock, he wasn't a natural horseman. I'm not saying he couldn't handle horses, because he had worked with them in the army, but he wasn't at ease as a horseman. Well, he was just too old when he started doing the hands-on things to be a natural."

But if Mac did not learn physical skills from his father, the lessons of honesty and integrity imparted by his grandfather were reinforced in his own family life on the farm in Scotland.

> One little example stuck in my head. Dad owed some money to a potato merchant in the town and he gave me a letter one evening and he said, "Now, I want you to take this to Mr. Bowes before you go to school in the morning." And I said, "No. If I do that I will be late for school," because the train that I went into town on went through at a certain time and it gave you about fifteen minutes to walk down to the school, but to go down to Mr. Bowes's office and back would certainly make me late for school. He said, "Son, I don't care if you are late for school. That doesn't matter. I promised - I gave my word - to Mr. Bowes that he would have his money by nine o'clock tomorrow morning and he must get it. When you give your word to someone you must keep it." And that incident stuck in my mind quite strongly. So the family had again good principles.

Like all boys growing up, Mac had thoughts about what he would be; some of them, again like all growing boys, not terribly practical. He recalls wanting to be a sailor at one point, and later, perhaps under the influence of Mr. Downey, to be an Olympic athlete: "I had the world record for the hop, skip and jump and for high jump and all those events measured out in the yard and I would practise each one of them, you know, because someday I was going to be an Olympic athlete and I came about fifty feet short in the hop, skip and jump, but that didn't matter." More prophetically, from about age twelve, he also wanted to come to Canada - if only because it would involve a voyage on an ocean-going vessel.

The farm in Scotland was not financially successful. It was not for want of planning and management, because that was clearly where Alexander's skills and interest lay. The farm was simply too small and, as Mac pointed out, "with himself and a hired man - whom we had to have - it was financially just too much. It became obvious that the cash flow was insufficient to carry the small acreage, and we had to do something."

In 1926, Grandfather Runciman and Aunt Beatrice went to Canada to visit Mac's uncle James, or "Jimmy," as he was known to the family, who was then living in Regina. When they returned, they talked about the trip, according to Mac, "in such glowing terms" that it awakened Evelyn's own fond memories of her experiences in western Canada, and appealed to a broad streak of romanticism in the family. So they made the decision to emigrate, and in 1928 young Mac, his sister Joan, his brother Jim (who had come along in 1920), and his parents set sail on what was to be a new venture and a new chapter in the Runciman family's life.

As he set off for a new life in Canada, Mac was on the verge of adolescence, and had been raised in a strong and remarkable family. His parents were people who clearly marched to their own individual drums: his father, city-born and -bred, but nonetheless pursuing a career in agriculture, and, in mid-life, setting off for an entirely new life in Canada; his mother, a woman who made her own way in life and, in doing so, voyaged partway around the world at a time when women generally did not do such things.

His immediate ancestors on both sides of his family were people with more than their share of initiative and independence. Both father and grandfather were skilled administrators who built their professional lives on these talents. His mother's immediate forebears were entrepreneurs, while her own siblings, like herself, made their way in a wide range of ventures, dispersing themselves far and wide in the process.

I had the sense, as Mac and I talked about this period of his life, that he had been rather closer to, and more admiring of, his mother than his father. He spoke of her several times as "a truly remarkable woman," and indeed she was, on the evidence of her own travels and career prior to her marriage, if nothing else. But her remarkable nature also showed later, as a woman who, raised in comfortable surroundings in Edinburgh, endured the hardships of a prairie farm during the Great Depression.

His relationship with his father, on the other hand, was somewhat more distant, partly owing to his father's absence during the war, partly to the lack of leisure activities they might otherwise have shared - the fishing, hunting, and camping that Mac learned from his schoolmaster and Scout leader, rather than from his father - and partly due simply to the fact that Alexander was, in Mac's words, "a hands-off father."

Quite early, Mac had absorbed a strong set of values and principles from his family and from his mentor, Mr. Downey. Sportsmanship, fair play, honesty, prudence, integrity, independence, and a strong sense of duty to those around him – all these values were clearly inculcated in him from both sides of the family, and found fertile ground in his own character. It was these qualities that Mac displayed in later years, and which earned him the very great respect of many people.

Later in life, he assumed a mantle of leadership as naturally as if it were made for him. However, the leadership role was thrust upon him; he did not seek it out. In his stories of his childhood and upbringing, there is no particular evidence of that overweening ambition that so often characterizes the early years of people who go on to prominence. We do not hear of his being captain of the school team, or of having a driving need to excel or to stand out from his peers. In fact, if anything, the reverse is true. As he later pointed out, he was more inclined to help out in a good cause, than to initiate it himself.

But it will not do to paint too definitive a portrait. His life is better told on its own terms. The next chapter of his life took him from the east coast of Scotland to the centre of the Canadian prairie and through one of the worst economic depressions of modern society.

The Young Man: Saskatchewan, 1928 – 1939

2

On the 24th of March, 1928, the Runcimans left "The Glen, Thornton, Innerwick," for the voyage to Canada, and thus Mac got his wish, however briefly, to go to sea.

Jokingly, he feigned a certain reluctance to tell me that he arrived in Canada on April 1. In some lives, the opening of a new chapter on such a date might have been an omen of folly. It was not so in his, although, given the severity of the economic depression that followed eighteen months later, the family could have been forgiven if they thought so. Nevertheless, it was April 1, 1928, when the family disembarked from their transatlantic voyage in Saint John, New Brunswick. Here began the second major phase of Mac's life: coming to adulthood in Canada, on a prairie farm.

Their original intention was to settle in the Peace River District and to start farming in a newly opening area. This goal itself tells a good deal about the kind of people the Runcimans were. The Peace River country, in 1928, had an aura of frontier pioneering that, said Mac, "appealed to the romantic and venturesome side of their natures." However, it was not to be. In Saint John they were greeted with a telegram from Mac's uncle James, his father's younger brother, who advised against it.

"Uncle Jimmy," as he was known to Mac, had emigrated to Canada in 1912 and had experienced first-hand the uncertainties of a new world. Immediately upon graduating from law school, he had signed up to join a legal firm in Saskatoon.

"In those days," said Mac, "you didn't fly to Saskatoon overnight. It was a week on a boat, and five days on a train – that sort of thing." When James got to Saskatoon, he found that his contact in the firm – a man called Shannon – had gone to Regina to take a position as assistant legislative counsel and law clerk. "Jimmy felt Shannon had a bit of an obligation to him, so he went down to Regina and made this point to him," a point Shannon evidently accepted, for Jimmy was taken on to work in the law library. Jimmy thereafter followed in Shannon's footsteps, being appointed assistant when Shannon was promoted to legislative counsel and law clerk, and later succeeding him in that post, as well.

By 1928, Jimmy had been sixteen years in Regina, less the time he served in the First World War, and his advice, wired to Alexander on his arrival in Saint John, was to forego the Peace River and to "look at settling in a more developed area." With this advice in hand, the Runcimans travelled by rail to Winnipeg, where they were met by Jimmy. A family conference ensued. Jimmy must have had some appreciation of where his brother's skills lay - and where they did not. As Mac himself said, his father was not "knacky" in certain areas, and "that is what his brother told him when we met in Winnipeg that day. Moreover, he added, 'The Peace is a young man's country. You're forty-six and not as young as you used to be.'" And so the plans were altered, and the Runcimans' journey came to an end in Saskatchewan.

Mac now suspects that his uncle had done some preparation for their arrival, and had anticipated winning Alex to the idea of staying put in Saskatchewan. It seems that arrangements had already been made for the family to occupy an abandoned farmstead about eight miles northwest of the town of Balcarres, and contacts had already been made regarding employment.

Mac attended school in April and May of that year, and then both he and his father "worked out" as hired hands over the summer months. Alex started with a man called Ernie McKay, who later became a good friend of Mac's, and Mac, after school let out, worked for Ernie's brother, Wes. Unfortunately Ernie McKay had "pretty high-strung horses," and, with Alex not being a natural horseman, Ernie was reluctant to leave them entirely in his care. "Dad came home one weekend really down in the dumps," Mac recalled, "because Ernie had told him, 'Alex, I don't think you should be handling these horses this summer.' So then he went down into the Qu'Appelle Valley to work for a fellow called Billy Olive at Ellisborough and he started there, I would guess, the first of June or something like that, and he worked right through to the end of harvest. He pitched sheaves, and stooked, and did all types of farm work."

Alexander found the rigours of farm work particularly hard, but he persevered through that first year. Curiously, he got a brief chance to exercise his natural talents and interests in a local school building project. Mac described how he "helped a contractor who was building a new school with a problem of moving material, dirt or sand or something, and it was bothering him because it was going to cost him so much to do it. And Dad said to him, 'Well, did you ever think of doing it this way?' and he showed him what he had in mind. And the contractor said, 'By God, no.' When he put a pencil to it, he said, 'Say, you know, that would work!' So Dad was in his own element talking to this contractor."

This first summer, then, was spent earning a living and learning about their new surroundings, which "gave us an opportunity to become familiar with farming methods – and not only farming methods. I remember yet the first day I walked into Wes McKay's barn and saw a team of horses fully harnessed with breechings[1] on them. And I looked and there were straps here, and straps there, and straps the other place, and I thought, Well, this is a hopeless proposition. I'll never learn all those fancy things. So we had to learn a lot about the details of farming in western Canada."

Early the next year the opportunity came to buy the half section on which they had been living. The property had been abandoned by its previous occupant, a First World War soldier who had acquired it as a returning veteran. The Runcimans agreed to purchase the property for the sum of $5280, and became full-fledged Saskatchewan farmers in the spring of 1929.

In retrospect, of course, 1929 was not the time to buy farmland. In October, stock markets crashed and soon carried the entire economy of the western world down with them. As Mac put it later, "We never paid for the farm, and I doubt if we made any payments during the '30s, although we did pay the municipal taxes each year."

So the Runcimans' career in prairie farming, after the initial year's working experience, started under the worst possible conditions. And it was under these conditions, and in the social and economic turmoil that followed, that Mac came to his age of majority, learned the craft of farming, and began to develop the political and economic views he carried with him through the rest of his life.

The farm was a mixed one, and they were fortunate not to suffer from the soil-drifting that so devastated other areas of Saskatchewan. They grew grain, and had both dairy cows and sheep. Later in the 1930s, as Mac slowly assumed more responsibility for the family farm, he and Ernie McKay bought a flock of purebred Hampshire sheep.

Sheep worked out very well for the Runcimans because, with Mac, his brother and his father, they had extra hands when needed. They kept cows, which meant milking, and that made for extra work, but sheep were particularly demanding, especially if lambing was late and came along at the same time as seeding. "Many people, on a farm alone," Mac said, "just couldn't look at sheep. But they worked in very, very well for us. And you got the wool clip in June, which was a bit of a 'harvest.' Raw wool went for ten cents a pound, and a ewe would yield ten pounds. We had 100 ewes, so it brought in about $100 cash, which was important."

The 1930s, of course, were a time of terrible devastation for many people. The Runcimans did not escape hardship, and Mac recalled:

> I felt terribly sorry for my dad and mother – for my mother particularly because of the comfortable way she had been brought up, and what she had to go through in the '30s. For Dad, because of the frustration of it.

> So much of his farming in Britain had been the indoor kind: the management, the bookwork and the planning. But when you have only fifty-two acres, as he had in Scotland, these are not very big functions, and when you have no money on a half section in western Canada, they are not very big functions, either. Dad would sit for hours, planning crop rotations we never really implemented and all sorts of things like that. Very, very frustrating not to be able to put his skills and knowledge to work.

It was, he said, "a harrowing time" for his parents, but he also recalls that "for us kids, I don't know what particular harm it did." Only rarely did the ravages of that terrible time touch him in ways that he could remember, and, looking back, it is perhaps his own personality that led him to count himself well off in comparison to what others suffered.

> I remember one occasion: there was a hill out to the west of the barn and Dad was coming over the crest of the hill one evening just at sundown and I noticed he was limping. When he got down to the yard, I said, "Why are you limping, Dad? Do you have a sore foot or something?" He turned his foot up and there was a hole in the sole of his boot, and he said, "The cardboard that I put in this morning wore out."

> I guess that was the only time I really felt angry at conditions in the '30s – that somebody who worked as hard as he did couldn't have a decent pair of shoes to work in. That was the only time that I ever remember getting up-tight about it.

> I think we were streets and streets ahead of people in a similar position in the city who couldn't really do much to help themselves. We could have vegetables; we could have meat and potatoes; we had milk; we had eggs.

We produced the food ourselves, you see, and we always had work, whether it produced any return or not. We could ship the five-gallon can of cream – which meant milking eight or ten cows for five days or something like that – and we would get two dollars. Dad would shake his head and say, "This is terrible, boy. This is just buying money."

It took me a little while to get through my head what he meant by that, but you know, hours and hours of work, and then take it to town, and the two dollars was all that was left after shipping costs. And then you had to go to town to pick up the empty can. But those two dollars were very, very important.

The greatest harm that he recalls from the Depression – and it is debatable whether it was the Depression or merely the character of his parents - was that he never learned to use credit. He had to acquire those skills in the post-war period when he returned from overseas and started farming again. But his mother was a worrier, "not so much that she couldn't enjoy herself when everything was going well, but to the point that she would say, from time to time, 'You know, I'm worried because things are going so well, I'm afraid something is going to go wrong.'" And one of the things Evelyn worried about was debt.

She hated the thought of owing money to anybody, and we never owed anybody any longer than we could help. I forget the exact year – probably in the spring of 1932 - we got some seed oats through the municipality, which distributed seed because there wasn't any seed from the year before. Mother just never slept properly that summer until we threshed grain in the fall and paid for our seed oats. In 1938, [federal agriculture minister] Jimmy Gardiner cancelled the payment of the 1932 seed oats advance, and I think we were probably one of two people in Saskatchewan who ever paid for 1932 seed oats. But Mother was just so strict in her thinking. "Never get into debt," and credit to her would mean debt, and I guess she drilled that into me. Dad was very much the same, but not nearly so much as Mother.

During some of the many evenings that Mac and I sat and talked, by far the most interesting moments occurred when he began, as he put it, "to ramble." I would then get the most vivid impressions of his life, as, for example, when he talked about working with horses: "Right up to the time of the war, we farmed with horses. In the working season, when you're farming with horses, you got up at ten to five in the morning so they were fed by five o'clock. You started pulling them out of the barn about quarter to seven, and, if you were lucky and you didn't have grain to pickle[2] or something like that in the evening, you were ready to get to bed by eight-thirty or nine o'clock."

When Mac became president of United Grain Growers (UGG), and people would speak of the elevator system being designed for horses and wagons, he knew from personal experience what they were talking about.

I used to try to haul two wagonloads a day in the fall, and I would be loaded up in the evening, and get going by seven o'clock the next morning. It was quarter after nine by the time you got into town and got your load off if there wasn't a line-up of wagons waiting, and you'd jog the team a bit on the way home, which took an hour and a half, maybe. You were likely late for dinner – the noon meal – by the time you got your wagon loaded again, so you were lucky if you were on the road by one or one-thirty. You took a different team of horses – the same man, but different horses. And then you'd have to get home and load up the night before. So you were hitting the road at seven o'clock in the morning, and it was probably seven o'clock at night before you got your load on and ready for the next day to enable you to take two trips to town.

Well, for years, I hauled with a wagon box that held sixty-two or sixty-three bushels, and then I was able to buy one that held seventy-eight bushels to eighty bushels. Well, it gave me a twenty-five percent increase in volume. It made you work harder to get your load on twice a day, but with a twenty-five percent increase in volume, two trips a day with that, I was hauling 150 bushels to town instead of 120. And that was my first step, you might say, to modernization.

I had a little over eight miles to haul one way. Our trouble was that, from our house, you went down through a coulee and then up, and that brought you onto the highway, and then you had to go up a steep hill. Well, once I got the seventy-five-bushel box, that was a tough lug for a team to take up that hill and up onto the level. So we used to do what we called "put a snatch team on" ahead, and take it up the hill with four horses, and then take the snatch team off and head for town with the two horses.

Some people in our area had longer hauls than we did. From Balcarres to Ituna is thirty miles. So people at the halfway mark had fifteen miles to haul to market, and the people who were off to the side had maybe another five or six miles.

Hauling a load of grain fifteen miles is pushing five hours on the road with a team. So it would take a full day to haul one wagonload to market for those people.

One evening, he told me about the difficult year the family had in 1931, when they experienced three fires and a tornado between the spring and the early winter. He told the stories out of chronological order, starting with the fire in early November.

Around a farm in those days, in the fall, you would thresh a great big oat-straw stack behind the barn for winter feed and bedding. You'd stack all your sheaves for feed for the next summer, and with the hay there and everything else, fire was a real hazard.

In November 1931, if there hadn't been a road construction crew camped nearby, we would have lost everything: barn, feed, straw, everything. A neighbour came to the door, Orm Earl – you remember Bill Earl, who used to work for the company [UGG]; Orm was Bill's father – well, Orm came to the door, and I was still in bed. It was about twenty to five in the morning. Dad was a timekeeper on the highway construction crew, and he wanted to be at work by six o'clock, and Mother and he were having breakfast. I was still in bed and I heard Orm come and bang on the door and shout, "Your sheaf stack's on fire! Your sheaf stack's on fire!"

I got up out of bed and I looked out the east window of the house, and as I looked across I could see these flames and I thought the flames were coming out of the loft we just filled with sheaves a few days before. I ran down - I thought of the horses, you see - and I ran downstairs. I was halfway across the yard when I suddenly realized I had nothing on except my undershirt. There was white frost on the ground because it was the morning after the 11th of November.

On the 11th of November there was always a big celebration in town and a dance, and there was some drinking and so forth. So whether there was a drunk on the way home from the party the night before, we never knew. But when I saw it wasn't the barn, but it was the sheaf stack beyond there, I ran back into the house and got my clothes on. By that time the people from the highway construction camp had come down and we got the horses out. We took cables and we put them around the sheaf stack that was burning and had the horses drag it out that way, and keep dragging it away from the rest of the buildings and feed stacks. With a combined effort, we saved it.

Well, if I wasn't fire-conscious before, I sure as heck was fire-conscious after that.

This story triggered his recollections of other near-catastrophes that had happened earlier that year, including the fire that occurred on the "hot, dry, windy 5th of April."

Our house was banked with sawdust, which we used for insulation, and we had a little back porch and we kept the milk out there. My brother, sister, and I drank nothing but milk, and at that time of year you kept it nice and cool out there. My sister went out to get some more milk, then she came back in, put the jug on the table and sat down, and she said, "You know, that's funny, I thought I smelled smoke out there."

"Oh," we said, "it couldn't be any smoke."

"Well, I thought I smelled smoke," she repeated.

She went back out and opened the back door, and all of this sawdust was on fire and the flames were going up the side of the house with this strong wind that was blowing.

Well, we were on "fast time" in the summertime. In that particular part of the country, some people went an hour fast in the summer, some a half-hour, and some stayed on slow time. We were an hour fast, but our neighbours were half an hour fast. So while we were eating dinner they were just going home for dinner and the two of them had outfits of horses. They tied the horses to the fence, and they came running over and started to carry pails of water from the well. Between shovelling the sawdust away from the house and then throwing water on, they helped us save the house.

I had a sliver in my hand that day, and when we were through fighting the fire, the sliver had been burned out of my hand, because the handle of the fork I had been using had been sitting at the back of the house in the flames. I dashed out and I grabbed it, and I started throwing the sawdust away from the house. I didn't feel the heat. You are impervious to sensation under these conditions.

So that was the 5th of April, 1931. In June the stovepipes in the house caught fire. Mother was home alone and the stovepipes fell down, and the flames got onto the curtains and started to go up. Mr. Miles, a neighbour –

"a cool hand Luke" if there ever was one – came along in time to put the curtains out and help Mother. She was just in an hysterical condition, almost, by that time.

Well then, in July a cyclone went through the yard. It almost wrecked the house; it took the roof off a barn that had just been built in 1928; it took every granary that we had and blew them away. The eye of it must have gone right through the yard, because we had an outdoor toilet - you know, the old two-holer - and the wreckage of it went southeast and the wreckage of the barn went northwest, so the eye of that cyclone must have gone right through the yard. The house was trembling and the front door started to bend, and hailstones were coming in at the top and my dad took the kitchen table and put it from another doorway across to the corner of the door, and he lay on top of it and he put his hands on the door to try to keep that door – and it was a strong door - from bending and letting these hailstones come in. So it was one hell of a storm and that was July. In November we had the sheaves-stack incident.

Early in 1933, Mac's grandfather Runciman bought a quarter section of land adjacent to the family's original half. He purchased it for his seven grandchildren (Alex's children, Mac, Joan, and Jim, and their four cousins, children of Jimmy's). The land was to be held in trust for the grandchildren on the condition that Mac would farm it and, on his twenty-first birthday, would take ownership of it. Thereafter, he was required to pay the other grandchildren interest on their shares. He was permitted to buy out their shares, and they were obliged to sell their shares to no one but Mac.

The quarter had been operated by a veteran of the First World War, who left to become a firefighter in Regina in 1929, so the land had lain idle for a number of years and had been taken over by couch grass. On this quarter section, Mac started farming independently of his family.

That was my first start at working a piece of land on my own. I got it in the summer of '33. We had sheep and we grazed the sheep on it, and that grazed the grass down, and then about the middle of July I put six horses on a two-furrow plough, and I ploughed up about thirty-five acres. It was so bloody dry and that grass had been down for quite a while, it all turned over like sod, and there wasn't a green leaf anywhere. I got a total kill of that couch grass on that thirty-five acres.

I worked it in the fall, and worked it again in the spring, and that was my first crop that summer of 1934. But when I seeded it that spring, there were so many of these couch grass roots on the surface that the seed drill couldn't get into the ground properly. It would run up over lumps and twists of this grass, and I thought, My God, I'm going to have trouble with germination. So I harrowed it once more, and we got an inch of rain that night, and everything just came up roses. So I really got lucky on that. And the rest of the land wasn't so bad with couch grass, so the next summer I got some more of it killed, and I had it all under control.

I experienced the total loss of a wheat crop in 1935, one of the most beautiful crops of wheat you could ever wish to grow, Marquis wheat standing about waist-high, but wheat stem rust just wiped it out. I cut it all with a binder, we threshed it all, even though my friend Ernie McKay had told me, "Leave it alone and throw a match in it." This was in July after we knew the rust was there, and I said, "But Ernie, look at it, the kernels are there, they are practically filled, they are bound to make something." And he said, "Well, if you want to take my advice, forget about it and burn it."

And again, this is how you ignore the advice of experienced people when you are a greenhorn. Ernie had come from Manitoba, and Manitoba had more experiences with rusted wheat than Saskatchewan did up until that time. He knew that it would amount to nothing. But I persisted, and he said, "If you want to make some "by cash" for the boys, I'll thresh it for you."

"By cash for the boys" was an expression we used with the teamsters. In those days they would get two and a half dollars a day, and on Saturday night they would come and ask for a couple of dollars, advance on their wages to go to town, and their pay slip would be marked, "by cash, two dollars." So he said, "If you want to give the boys some "by cash," I'll thresh it for you."

I went through the process of cutting it and it used twine like you wouldn't believe, because it was a heavy, heavy crop, and he threshed it for me. I ended up with around a bin and a half of feed wheat, which weighed about thirty-eight pounds to the bushel. It was so light, and by the time I paid for the twine and the threshing, there was nothing left. But that was a lesson I learned the hard way.

In 1938, Mac's father took up another career as municipal secretary, which turned out to be much more to his liking than farming. Mac recalls, "He really found his niche, and he did a lot of good community work. I think he was really happy the last twenty years of his life, doing municipal accounting, and meeting people, and chatting, and doing the clerical stuff that was the family background. [Federal agriculture minister] Jimmy Gardiner used to drop into the office in Abernethy on his way through, and sometimes he would make Dad so mad that Dad would blurt out all the things Jimmy wanted to know. The municipal office was a gathering place for local information."

His parents actually left the farm in 1938 when his father took up municipal work, and so Mac assumed the responsibility for the family farm as well as his own quarter section, working them as one with his brother and sister.

In the spring of 1938 Mac was first exposed to mechanized farming.

> Ernie McKay and a chap called Archie McClenaghan, who was his son-in-law, made a disk-seeder themselves. Ernie had a real good mechanical bent – he was very handy, mechanically. Archie ended up working with Minneapolis Moline after the war. He was also mechanically inclined, and the two of them put together, out of bits and pieces from the farm, a one-way disk-seeder, and it worked very, very well.

> I hired Ernie to put in a lot of the crop, and the basis of the hiring was to pay him two barrels of gas for each barrel of gas he burned. That's what it cost, which was awfully reasonable. I was doing road construction that spring to make some extra money, and I was making enough cash with a two-horse team to buy the gas and get the work done.

> It sold me on the concept: Yes, you can farm with a tractor.

By this time, the farm was starting to turn the corner financially and to show some profits. In 1938, Mac recalled, "I grew a crop of oats from registered seed, and they were perfectly clean. There wasn't a wild oat in them. I was getting fifty cents a bushel for them. I'd never seen money come as easy as that. I'd sell fifty bushels and get twenty-five dollars, I'd sell a hundred bushels and get fifty bucks. It was the most cash flow I'd ever had.

"It was 1938 when I bought the new wagon box, a new binder and a new cultivator, and could put an eight-horse team in the field if needed. I had a good crop there in 1938, and '39 was my last crop before the war."

Mac's formal education is, of course, an important part of his story. It was not extensive, which makes all the more remarkable his subsequent achievements, including the receipt of two honorary doctorates. Had fate and fortune given him the opportunity for higher education, indications are he would have done well. His report cards from his first year of secondary school in Scotland were more than commendable: ninety-six percent in arithmetic; 100 percent in algebra; ninety-four percent in geometry; eighty-one percent in French. He did rather less well in art (fifty-five percent) and music (forty-eight percent). Since Scottish schools of the time evidently wished to produce the well-rounded "Renaissance man," a student's results in music and arithmetic, and in art and algebra, were combined for the purposes of awarding academic prizes. Those art and music marks put him out of the running in both combinations, but he did well enough to achieve an overall average of sevent-seven percent, which placed him seventh out of twenty-six in his class.

As the family moved around Scotland, he was tested at each move to select the grade into which he would be placed. More than once he was moved up a grade, with the result that he had completed primary school at the age of ten. The rules required a student to be eleven before starting secondary school, so it was actually 1926, when he was going on twelve, that he started high school. By the time he left Scotland at thirteen, he was working at a level equivalent to grade ten in Saskatchewan.[3]

However, age, rather than accomplishment, ruled in the local school division, and the evidence of the East Lothian report cards and the level he had achieved in Scotland was set aside. The local school board placed him in grade seven, specifically because of a lack of knowledge of Canadian history.

When his father acquired the farm, he needed Mac's help, and in the spring of 1929, Alex approached the local school board to ask that Mac be released from full-time attendance. He got no sympathy. Mac recalled how "the chairman of the school board, when Dad went and asked for me to get off school in 1929 to help put the crop in, said, 'I can't have a free hired man, and I'm damn sure you're not going to get one.' So the school board voted against me getting off school."

However, it was apparent to Alex that his son was taking material he had already studied, and so he persisted, taking the matter up with the Department of Education in Regina. "Half the civil service was old Scots," recalled Mac, among them Uncle Jimmy, who knew the registrar of education, John Blacklock, who was another Edinburgh Scot. "So Dad told Jimmy what was happening, and Jim went to see Blacklock, and they sent him my Scottish report card." In due course, a letter came from the registrar's office to the school board, approving Mac's release from school.

This did not quite end his formal education. Four years later, he decided to finish high school, and the first thing he did was to re-establish the credentials he had acquired in Scotland.

> So in 1932, I took grade ten – which I had been taking in Scotland – by correspondence, and I was absolutely amazed. If you sat down to duplicate the curriculum I had in Scotland in 1928, you couldn't have done it more precisely. Right down to the literature: *Julius Caesar*. When I sat down to write the exam, the first question was memory work – twenty-five marks out of 100 - and it was twenty-five lines from *Julius Caesar* – "Friends, Romans, countrymen" – that I had learned five years before in Scotland.
>
> Algebra, geometry, history, science, you name it: identical! That was in 1932, and I wrote the exam in 1933. Then I went until 1937, and in '37 and '38, I took my grade eleven by correspondence. I wrote the exams in 1938 and would have passed with honours, but you needed over sixty-five percent in every subject, and I only got sixty-one in French, whereas I got over seventy in every other subject.

These marks were achieved in some difficult conditions. He took the course-work during the year ("it gave me something to do during the winter months"), but he had little time for studying in the spring, because this was the year he was working on road construction, while Ernie McKay was putting in his crop with his home-built disk-seeder and tractor.

Mac left home on the 12th of April, "to work on a highway construction crew, and worked on the construction crew until the Saturday night before exams started. They started on Monday morning, and the only studying I had done during the spring was when I could stay awake at nights on the weekends. Once the exams started, I used to get up at five o'clock in the morning, I would study for the exams for that day from five to eight, then I'd shave and go to school and write the exams. So I got my grade eleven certificate and that was the end of my formal education. It never went beyond that."

At the time, he entertained an ambition to go to university in Guelph, to become a veterinarian. "I didn't want to practise as a veterinarian. I wanted the skills because I'd seen too many animals suffer during the '30s when the price of a visit by a vet was more than the value of the animal. I did quite a bit of amateur veterinary work myself, but I was always concerned: Am I doing it right? You know, castrating calves, docking the tails on lambs, and helping an animal that was having difficulty foaling or calving. I had a certain sympathy

for them, and I wanted to be adequately able to care for them professionally. I suppose I would have done some work for people around, but I
didn't want to set up a business as a vet. I still wanted to farm."

In any event, attending Guelph was not to be, because in 1939 the war
intervened and all thoughts of formal education were abandoned.

However, his informal education is a good deal more interesting. In his
case, as with us all, it started at home. His parents were both well educated,
and their home showed it.

> Our house was full of books at home in Scotland. Basically they were
> pretty heavy - too heavy. There were the classics; there was a whole set of
> Sir Walter Scott; a set of books entitled *Classic Myth and Legend*, and an-
> other, *Celtic Myth and Legend*; Thackery; all of Dickens. All the classics
> were on the shelves there all the time, and I guess at one time or another
> I read most of them.

> We continued to do an awful lot of reading during the '30s. Dad was
> secretary of the school district, and the school used to have travelling
> libraries. The travelling library was a box with over 200 books and usually
> it was kept at the school. After people had read most of them, you rotated
> libraries and got another box, maybe every year or something like that.

> In the '30s, in our school district, they shut down before Christmas and
> didn't go back till the beginning of February, and there were very few
> houses near the school. Most of the people in the area who were readers
> were close neighbours of ours, but on the periphery of the school area
> itself, so they could get the books more conveniently from our house. So
> we would bring the school box of books to our house for the January
> break and some time before it went back to the school at the beginning
> of February, we had read most of the books. For example, I read every bit
> of *The Count of Monte Cristo* - 2000 and some pages in the unabridged
> version. I read every word of it.

> We just read whatever happened to be at hand, and I'm still very much
> that way. I just read what comes down the pike, not pursuing a particular
> study or science or anything else, but if I am sitting around doing noth-
> ing, I'm "itchy" without something in my hands to read and it doesn't
> matter if it is garbage, as long as I'm reading.

> As a matter of fact, every once in a while Mother would read the riot act
> and say, "Now, this family is going to stop reading at the table at meals and
> engage in some conversation." Because we would arrive at the table with

whatever we were reading, and sit and continue. There would be two or three of us sitting around the table reading and eating. We were a very poor conversational family; we just never got into extended discussions of affairs of the day or anything else. We listened to CBC farm broadcasts and kept current with what was on the radio, but to get into philosophical debates or anything, there was none of that in our family as we grew up. Dad had his views, they were pretty right wing.

So the Runciman home was a place where learning was respected and books were appreciated, but was not a forum for political or philosophical discussion.

Not that there was a lack of things to discuss. The Runcimans arrived at a time of intense debate about farm policy, and emotions were running high. The grain marketing and handling system had come through something of a revolution in the four years prior to their arrival in Saskatchewan. By the early 1920s, the central marketing agencies, which had been set up to handle wheat marketing in wartime, had been disbanded, and this had been followed by a short but severe depression. The grain industry at the time was largely owned and controlled by private enterprises, and by 1923 grain was again being traded through the Winnipeg Grain Exchange. None of this was to the liking of a significant number of farmers. Between 1923 and 1928, when the Runcimans arrived, the Wheat Pools came into existence, signed up some fifty percent of western grain production to be marketed through them under price-pooling contracts, and built or bought chains of country elevators to source the wheat for their marketing organization, the Central Selling Agency (CSA).

Neither the Pools nor the CSA used the facilities of the Winnipeg Grain Exchange to market their wheat, largely for ideological reasons. Private marketers and, of course, the Pools' great rival for the allegiance of farmers, United Grain Growers, hedged their wheat purchases on the Exchange, and thus were protected against price fluctuations. Because the Pools did not use the Exchange, when the downhill price slide commenced in 1929, they had left themselves largely unprotected. While they had deducted "commercial reserves" from the sales of wheat, these reserves were insufficient to cover their financial liabilities against so large a price drop, and by 1930 they were bankrupt. Only provincial government loans, together with the revenues they received as country elevator operators, saved them from disappearing altogether.

The Pools' financial difficulties did not cause support for centralized marketing and price pooling to disappear, and over the first seven years of

Mac's sojourn in Canada, the debate on the virtues of a wheat board was in full swing. "When we came to the country until 1928," Mac said, "they were doing things like discussing compulsory pools. And oh, there used to be violent arguments out in the country."

Mac's father was drawn into these discussions, but he never really became deeply involved, partly because of his own political philosophy, and partly because he was disappointed in the level of discussion.

> Ernie McKay and a fellow called Archie Reid used to come and pick Dad up and they would take him to meetings on farm issues. I can remember Dad going to a couple of these meetings, and I can recall Dad tended to be a conservative in the Old Country, and he was pretty turned off by the left-wing nature of them.

> But you know, as I grew up as a child, people in Britain, right down to the worker on the farm, were much more politically conscious and informed than Canadians. When we first came to this country, they didn't seem to reason their way through situations at all. You were either black or you were white, you were Liberal or you were Conservative, and there was really no point in debating it. But Dad could never buy into this extreme left-wing stuff.

Mac spoke of his father's feeling it was a waste of time to debate such issues when the political dialogue was so unsophisticated and so lacking in depth.

Mac himself, of course, was barely into his teens when they first arrived, and initially he did not comprehend much of the debate. "Most of what happened," he said, "I read about in the newspaper, and that would be a weekly paper. After 1933, when we got our first radio, I would hear radio reports, but the people involved were just names. I can remember the Stamp Commission, for example, on the Grain Exchange, being discussed. But those were the sorts of things that went right over my head. There was the Rowell-Sirois Commission, too. I would read reports of that, and it was just as though you landed on Mars and it was populated, and you didn't know what had happened in the last thousand years. I had no background on the subjects."

Still, not everything went over his head. After 1930, when he turned sixteen, he was at the age when a young person comes to some understanding of the world into which he is growing up. He listened attentively to what was going on around him.

> One of the greatest locations in the world at one time was the office at

the livery barn in town in the wintertime. The farmers came in from the country with their big fur coats and gauntlet mitts on, and they hung them up in the office there, and they would sit down and warm up a little bit, or they would go and buy some groceries and come back and put them in the cutter, and then they would drop into the office.

And you talk about b.s.! Some of the stuff that went on in that office! But that was where the real "coffee row" arguments in those days took place. And I often sat in the corner and just listened, you know. Some of the stuff, you knew it was garbage. It just didn't hold together, even to a kid with my knowledge of the world, but it was the opinion of those people, very strongly held in some areas, too.

He soon began to form his own opinions on what he heard, and he recalled that he "didn't like the battling that went on for a compulsory pool. They had a heck of a time getting up to fifty percent in the first place, and then the tactics that they began to use for a compulsory pool, I didn't particularly enjoy. I never got involved in the battle, for or against, or anything else. I sort of casually reacted to what the influences were. I guess it was the inner me coming out, because I never gave it conscious thought as to what I should be doing or wasn't doing, and I suppose I have never been ultra-conservative. I've certainly never been extreme left wing. I guess I've always been pretty middle of the road."

Whether his views had matured sufficiently by the early 1930s to be classified then as "middle of the road" may be debatable. However, he did not judge what he heard on ideological grounds, and as he listened, he recognized some validity to the arguments on both sides of the debate. One of the strongest opponents of pooling and centralized marketing was an old-timer called Abe Newstead, the father-in-law of Wes McKay, for whom Mac worked that first summer in Saskatchewan. Abe was "determined that no s.o.b. was going to sell his crop for him; he was definitely on the 'No' side." On the other side, however, was his friend Ernie McKay.

Ernie just resented the grinding down of the common man by conditions; not necessarily by the government or by rich people or anything. For example, one thing that I can remember Ernie being so annoyed about was the scale of wages brought out for the use of horses on highway construction one summer in the '30s. It was twenty-five cents an hour for a team of horses and twenty cents an hour for the man, which meant forty-five cents a hour, so you could earn four and a half dollars a day with a team of horses and man. But Ernie was vehement that the day a team of horses is worth more money than a man, is the day he didn't want to see. And you know, without being an extreme left-winger, you can see some of his logic in that.

But it was the sort of viewpoint he had, and he practised some of what he preached. He wasn't the world's most energetic man, and especially when the weather was cold in the winter, he wasn't too fussy about going outside, but his horses were always fat, his cattle were always fat, his stock was always good quality. He really looked after stock. But he had at least one, if not two, hired men around there in the wintertime and they probably worked for five bucks a month and their board, or something like that. They did the chores and all the rest of it, but he could have got along with one, or he could have got along without any, but those guys would have had a hell of an existence during the winter if he hadn't given them a place where they could live and work. So he was a very humane sort of person and the type of a left-winger that I can accommodate, not a left-winger because he wanted to run the world and make people do what he thought should be right.

Mac also came to have considerable empathy for the people whose lives had been devastated by the Depression years. More than once he told me of his "sympathy with the underdog," and part of that sympathy came from what he heard and saw as he was growing up.

The people really had to struggle to survive. They came out of that period with the opinion that there's got to be some better way. And the only alternative being offered was a socialist government. But anybody south of the mainline of the CPR, and a heck of a lot of them north of that mainline of the CPR, had every right to come out of the '30s with a feeling that this is an absolutely impossible type of society in which to live. Well, they couldn't live; they could only barely exist.

Nobody, in a wealthy society, should have to be subjected to the hardships that people were subjected to in Saskatchewan in the '30s, it's as simple as that. And those harsh experiences of the '30s were the foundation of a great deal of the left-wing thinking which eventually led to the CCF and the NDP.

Nevertheless, as Mac developed his views, he came to lean away from compulsion, from intervention, from centralization, and generally from solutions which we associate with the left wing in economic and political thought. And it was, he said, not "long dissertations" that directed his thinking along these lines, but rather "just little milestones and sign posts."

I told you the story about the fellow whom we bought our first horses from when we came to Canada. He had a payment coming due on a new 1928 Chevy car and a new threshing machine and tractor that he bought in the fall of '28. He sold these horses because he wasn't going to need them, because he had the tractor.

We bought those horses from him, and we took delivery around the 17th of March. His payments weren't due until the end of May, and he had this lump sum of money and he put it in the Grain Exchange. As a result of that, when 1929 prices were on their way down, he lost his car, he lost his threshing machine, he lost his tractor, and as long as he lived, he blamed the Winnipeg Grain Exchange because he lost them.

They stole the money from him, you see. That was the prevailing attitude in so many farm homes. Grandpa was rooked by the Winnipeg Grain Exchange. Grandpa speculated and lost; he gambled, in other words, and lost, and you weren't going to blame Grandpa, and Grandpa certainly never blamed himself. It was just like "Damn the CPR," exactly the same mentality. So I was never overwhelmed by that sort of thing.

To me, the Exchange was there for people who used it for business purposes. It fills a business need, and if other people want to use it for other purposes, that is their business. And if they get stung, it is still their business; I am not going to weep for them. But there was such a feeling: if wheat was worth sixty cents a bushel, they set the price at forty-five and put the fifteen cents in their pocket.

Increasingly, therefore, he came to be critical of the belief that centralized marketing could achieve its goals in relation to grain prices.

There were a lot of people who signed up for fifty percent, but didn't want to go for 100 percent, and that began to make an impression on me. A lot of people who became significant Pool people, who were just totally committed to 100 percent pooling, to a Central Selling Agency, to single Board marketing, and all these things we've heard about since, and I guess - even as a kid - I just couldn't believe that you could, in isolation, in the middle of the continent of North America, set up a system where the buyers of the world were going to accept your price, because you've got to meet your customer on common ground somewhere. But the Pools and the CSA visualized this as a method to hold them up and make them pay more money.

And I think it was an ignorance of, or a failure to accept, the real economic facts of life that led to Saskatchewan being the first home of the CCF. They held out these glorious theories and people would think, It's a hell of a lot better than what we've got, so let's vote for it. The fact that they are economically impossible just didn't bother them at all.

So Mac's objections to the left-wing position tended to be based on pragmatic grounds: the Exchange served a purpose for business, and at least some of the animosity to it arose because farmers misused it; a centralized selling agent quite clearly could not dictate price in a large world market. He began to question the support for a compulsory Board, and the alleged evils of the Grain Exchange.

I asked him whether there were not two themes emerging in his own thinking at the time: one, that he did not like the compulsory aspect of central marketing; and two, that he could not accept the concept that Canada could dictate price. But he said he was not comprehending matters in those terms. In fact, he is not, in general, of a particularly analytical turn of mind, and he has always tended to form his views intuitively:

> I just followed my instincts. You know - left wing, right wing - it took me a long time to know what these expressions meant, and I just went by my basic feeling of what I liked and what I didn't like.

In any event, not all the dialogue about marketing policy was conducted at an intellectual level, and not all was acrimonious. Even then, despite the strong feelings, some people kept such matters in reasonable perspective. Mac's friend Ernie McKay was one of them.

> There is another little anecdote of how it went at the local level. I would sit without knowing the background, without having a history of association with this side or the other, and we used to meet and have card parties and dances at a little local school which was halfway between our place and this little hamlet of Patrick. I used to haul grain to the elevators at Patrick where Bill Whittingham bought grain for the Pool, and Frank Henley, a Yorkshire man, bought for Reliance. The Henleys and Bill Whittingham - who was single at that time - got along very well together and one night at a dance, Bill was dancing with Mrs. Henley. They knew each other really well, and they were dancing in quite a cosy sort of a way, and Ernie McKay, who became a great friend of mine, in a quiet moment, says, "You know, I can't see any reason why a compulsory pool wouldn't go over pretty good at Patrick." Here is the elevator manager from the Pool with the other manager's wife in his arms. So these were the sort of expressions of local attitudes you got on occasion.

Mac's education in farm politics, agricultural policy, and farm management and practice all came to an end in 1939 with the onset of the Second World War. He, like most men of his age, felt impelled to enlist, and so began the third phase of his life: his wartime career.

Mac's wartime experience is the subject of the next chapter, and it begins with the story of his enlisting in Regina in the winter of 1939 to 1940. But the story of the farm of Alexander Runciman came to an end when Mac, on a short leave just prior to his departure for overseas, went back to the farm to close things up.

I signed my papers on the 5th of January and we went overseas on the 24th and here we had a farm out there with horses, cattle, sheep, pigs, chickens, you name it. My sister was home alone in January and the weather turned really vicious. They were so short of training time, they decided there would be no embarkation leave. I went and applied for leave and they said, "No, there is no embarkation leave. You can't have one."

And I said, "Look, I have a farm out there and my sister is living alone on it." Bill Earl was doing the chores. He was a neighbour, and he was coming across the field every day and doing all those chores in that bitter cold weather.

So I said, "I've got to get rid of that farm. You either give me a pass or I'm going A.W.O.L., there is no question about it."

I got off on a Thursday evening, I had to be back on Sunday evening. I had left the car on the street in Balcarres when I left for Regina to join up, and it was still sitting there. But while he was in town, David Hyndman, who later married my sister, had taken the battery out of it and had taken it inside to warm it up. He met me at the bus and I went out to the farm. He had organized things for me and by the next morning at eight o'clock the yard was full of teams and sleighs and neighbours and trucks and cars. They just stripped that farm right down. I couldn't believe it. I went back that night to make sure that the buildings were properly closed up. My neighbours had even pulled the tacks out of the linoleum on the kitchen floor and rolled it up. It was a very traumatic day.

We sold off the grain and I went into town in the afternoon to cash the grain tickets and go downtown and pay off any bills that I happened to have, which were very few, and then I drove out to the farm to make sure the doors were shut and everything was all right. As I left, the road turned and went up a hill, and I remember stopping and looking back at the house and buildings and thinking, What kind of a damn fool have you been? You've worked for twelve years to get as far as you got and here you are walking away. And my first fear was the war would be over too soon and I wouldn't have enough cash accumulated to get started when it was over.

The original half section, on which Alexander had staked his hopes of becoming a farmer in a new land, was given up during the war. The quarter that had been bought by Mac's grandfather was owned free and clear, and it remained, for the time being, in the family. Mac's brother went into the army at the same time he did, and his sister went to live with his parents, who by then were living in Abernethy, where his father was pursuing his new career in municipal work. Mac headed overseas, closing one chapter in his life, and opening a new one.

The Soldier: England, Sicily, Italy, 1940 – 1945

3

"All I can tell you," an old acquaintance once said to me, "is that there are times in your life when you live much more intensely than you normally do." My friend was trying to convey the impact of a particularly moving experience, and while it is easy to grasp, in a general sense, what he meant, his words do little more than underscore just how ineffable the effect of such "intense" periods can be on our lives.

The war, for Mac, was just such a time of "intense living," and for this reason I approached the writing of this chapter with more trepidation than any other. Over the course of our many interviews, he told me a good deal about his wartime experience, and more than once mused on how seemingly small incidents in that period played such a pivotal role in determining the course of his life. The animation with which he spoke of those times made me appreciate just how intense they were for him, and raised great doubts in my mind as to whether, between us, we could convey the meaning those years had for him.

However, if I cannot be sure of what the war years meant to him personally, I think I know what they meant professionally. He enlisted as a private and by the end of the war had risen to the highest non-commissioned officer rank.[1] At the beginning of 1944, he was selected for (but, because of a twist of fate, did not take) officer training. As he was steadily promoted, he had increasing numbers of men under him, and during these years his inherent leadership abilities came to the fore.

When I came to write this chapter and to review it with him, I related the words of my former acquaintance about intense living. They immediately struck a responsive chord. "You know, Paul," he said, "this whole exercise with you has made me realize he is exactly right, because there are whole stretches that I remember nothing about. And there are stretches when I can see it happening."

Certainly, his enlistment was one event he could still "see happening." He told me this story twice throughout our interviews, and when we began to draft this chapter, he wrote about his enlistment in the same elegant style with which he related his birth and childhood in Scotland.

> "Canada declared war on Germany this morning." My brother's words brought the fateful tidings to the crew assembled on the morning of September 10 to thresh my 1939 crop. He joined us immediately after the daily 8:00 a.m. news broadcast on CBC radio, which was our pipeline in those days to information from the world beyond our neighbourhood. So we learned that the die had been cast in the global conflict that was to have major effects on the lives of all of us.
>
> The fact that a threshing crew was sitting around idly chatting at 8:15 on that morning of warm harvest sunshine was in itself unusual. Normally, by that hour, it would have been hard at work to satisfy the threshing machine's seemingly insatiable appetite for sheaves. But it happened that fog and heavy dew overnight had dampened the straw and made it "tough,"[2] and it was ten o'clock before the warm fall sunshine evaporated the moisture on the stooks and rendered them "dry" and fit to be threshed.
>
> The next hour and a half was passed in excited speculation about what the news meant to each of us and what our attitudes would be to joining Canada's armed forces. Of the ten of us present that morning, it was unanimous, with one exception, that we would seek to enlist. The single exception was the owner and operator of the threshing outfit, who was a generation older than the rest of us.[3]

The resolve to enlist was not a passing enthusiasm for the men in the threshing crew. Eight of the ten followed through, but for Mac, it was not done quickly. To begin with, arrangements had to be made before he could leave the farm. Moreover, enlistment was brisk at the start of the war and it was not long before the immediate personnel requirements of the forces were met. His brother Jim, six years his junior and known as "Pim" to the family, tried to join up immediately after harvest, but was turned away. He first tried the air force, but was rejected because he had only grade nine education, and in 1939, the air force would accept only university graduates. "A year later," Mac said, "they were begging people to join, but that was their attitude. It was a very 'la de da' outfit in those days." Jim then turned to the army, but all he was able to secure was a spot on the waiting list for an army ordnance unit.

"Joining the armed forces in 1939 was not easy," Mac recalled, and the surfeit of volunteers left him free to "mull over" the question of his enlisting for some months. "Then," he wrote, "the answer came with dramatic suddenness in late December. My brother received instructions to report to his unit in Regina on December 30th. It only seemed logical to postpone that action until after the first of the new year. My brother, sister, and I went to Abernethy on New Year's Day to have dinner with Dad and Mother, and of course everyone was excited about my brother's impending departure. That afternoon I felt that the time of decision had arrived, and I asked as calmly as I could, 'If Pim is going, how would it be if I went, too?' The idea was not too seriously considered at first, but the point had been made and January 2 saw me on the bus to Regina."[4]

He knew, from the experiences of Jim and others, that, wherever he might try, the units would likely be full. Since Jim had finally found a spot on the waiting list of the Canadian Ordnance Field Parks, he tried there first. But he had even less luck than Jim. No, they said, they were just full up. They only needed 150 men, and already had 500 on their list, and it would not be fair to take him before the others. He was resolved to try elsewhere despite Jim's experience, but as it transpired, that was not necessary.

> Fate took over. As I thanked them for their attention, and started for the door, I stopped and said, "The reason I knew you were recruiting is that my brother is on your list and received his call to report." Oh! was the reply, and what is his name? I told them, and they looked it up, and asked when he was coming in. I told them he would probably be in the next day.

> They conferred a moment, and then said, "Well, if you can come in when he does, perhaps we can make a mistake and put you both through on his application."

> And that is how I ended up in the army. And it just shows you how a person's fate can be determined by a chance remark made on the spur of the moment.[5]

So on January 5, he became a full-fledged Canadian soldier, and after the forty-eight-hour embarkation leave to wind up the farm, he found himself enroute to Britain.

Why did he enlist? When we discussed this question during our interviews, he spoke of his "sympathy for the underdog, and the absolute injustice of what

Hitler was doing to Poland and all the various countries in Europe." He picked these themes up again as he prepared his written account.

> I knew as clearly as I had ever known anything that I must be involved. Just why? To this day I am still not sure. It was only twenty years between the First World War and the Second, and as a kid I was quite conscious of the first war. Dad had been in the army and Uncle Jimmy had been in the army, so it was "in the family," as you might say. Beyond that, was my resentment of the injustice done to Poland and other early victims of Hitler's so strong that it dictated the pattern of my thinking? Was I looking, as so many young Canadians were, for some relief of the monotony and grinding hardship of the 1930s? I shall never be sure but I knew I must go.[6]

We can make too much of his retrospective attempt at analysis. Months before this was written, he had told me, "it wasn't a matter I agonized over or anything else. It just seemed as natural as getting up in the morning and putting on my pants. So it really wasn't a 'deep thinking' thing. So much of my life has been that way. Things just seem to happen; there is no game plan."

The concept of life "just happening" is one that recurred often through our interviews, and is an important key to both Mac's life and character. Doors opened and he went through, and so much of what he experienced came to him, rather than his seeking it out.

Once he had enlisted, he received only a few days of orientation, and on January 24, after an emotional farewell between the new soldiers and their friends and family, he left Regina by train.

> At Halifax we boarded that pride of the Canadian Pacific Line, the *Empress of Britain*, for a very stormy crossing to the Clyde in Scotland and then by train to that much-storied base of British soldiery, Aldershot. There we were quartered in one of the ancient three-storeyed barracks named after the battles of the Peninsular War: Corruna, Badajos, Salamanca, and so on. There in wintry discomfort, with poor messing broken only by the thrill of five-day "landing leaves" (which my brother and I spent visiting relatives in Scotland), we underwent some of the basic training of which we had had so little before leaving Regina.

> Relief from the stereotypical military life of Aldershot came in the form of a move to the Midlands city of Nottingham, where we would be near the great central Ordnance Depots of the British army, and could learn the basics of the ordnance work we were recruited to perform. If Alder-

shot could be classified as a soldiers' hell, Nottingham had to rate as a soldiers' paradise. The civilian population in general was very good to us and to that could be added that we were billeted, to begin with, in a centrally heated building just down the street from a first-class ice rink, which eventually produced the ice dancing stars, Torval and Deane. But the crowning touch was that this city of light industries – Player's Ciga-rettes, Boots the Chemist, the Raleigh Cycle Works and an extensive textiles industry – had a female-to-male ratio of six to one in its working population, with Nottingham girls having a countrywide reputation for being the best dressed in England. Need more be said! In that environ-ment we had a number of casualties but a lot of pleasure. Once we were settled, a routine of regimental and ordnance training was established in very comfortable circumstances.[7]

Nottingham provided the first opportunity "to do something directly connected to the war," and another experience which Mac is still able "to see happening." In June of 1940, the historic Dunkerque evacuation took place, and many of the evacuees were brought to Nottingham for rest and recovery, and to identify which units they were from, before being sent home to recuperate from their ordeal. Mac vividly recalled the day of the evacuation:

We didn't know, when we were called on parade that evening, that the Dunkerque evacuation was taking place. We knew that the British army was in retreat in Europe, and the Germans were running roughshod over the French, but we knew nothing about Dunkirk, so this was the first news of it that we got.

Then they told us what we were going to be doing - meeting some of the evacuees off trains, and giving them food and beds and blankets - and by the time the explanations were over, and our orders issued, we were all strung up. So when the commanding officer barked, "Ordnance Field Parks: Attention!" every left foot on the parade just came down simulta-neously with a sound like a cannon shot. We were on a wooden floor on about the third storey of the building, and that is why the noise was so noticeable, but if I live to be a hundred I'll remember that sound, because every man was on his toes to do what he could that evening. Well, that is living intensely.

In Nottingham, the army first noticed Mac's leadership potential, and in July of 1940, he got his "first hook" (which is army slang for the V-shaped stripe a lance corporal wears on his sleeve). This gave him his first taste of command, "doing regimental things like mounting guards and pickets and so forth."

He had been classified as a driver-mechanic and in September he received the first assignment that allowed him to practise his trade, in the headquarters of the Canadian Ordnance Field Parks. He and his unit were then moved to Epsom, in the south of England, and he was one of five men who served as staff to the commanding officer, Colonel Bailey. As driver-mechanic, he had to take a quick course in how to ride a motorcycle, which he did in a rather dramatic way.

> I nearly killed myself! The Trent River runs through the city of Nottingham, and there is a Trent Bridge. For defence purposes, three huge concrete blocks had been placed laterally across the bridge. The blocks had holes in them, and iron bars could be threaded through these holes to block the bridge entirely to armoured vehicles. The blocks were spaced so that one lane of traffic went through one gap, and the oncoming traffic came through the other.
>
> I was riding through the downtown area, and getting pretty bold with my motorcycle, and I thought I'd go over the Trent Bridge. And I'm going along, following a bus, and I thought, Well, there's no point in my slowing down for him. I'll just pass him and go through the gap for the oncoming traffic.
>
> But because of the concrete blocks, I couldn't see what was coming. So I got to about halfway past the bus, and I thought, This is kind of stupid because there might be something coming the other way. I'll go through on my own side. Well, I didn't realize the bus had speeded up, and I got through, between the front of that bus and that concrete block, by the bloody skin of my teeth.
>
> I gunned it when I saw what was happening, I went right over to the other side of the lane, and I hit the curb, and I laid the motorcycle over on its side. If the wheel hadn't been caught by the curb, the motorcycle would have skidded out from under me, and the bus would not likely have been able to stop. But the curb caught me and straightened me out.

When Mac pulled off the road a minute later, he was shaking with the adrenalin rush. "If I had been killed," he said with his typical dry wit, "it would have changed my whole life." It certainly would have, but it seems that fate had other plans, and was not going to allow him to do away with himself inadvertently, however hard he might have tried.

Being driver-mechanic for the CO of the Ordnance Field Parks was, Mac recalled, "an idyllic sort of life." About twice every three weeks he would be required to drive the colonel up to the Nottingham area depots, where they would spend two or three days. "I had a 'living out' allowance; I used to go to a bed and breakfast place; it was just an unbelievably acceptable job."

The trips to Nottingham were slow – often taking six or eight hours for the 200-mile trip – because the traffic on the road moved in a single lane. There were even steam trucks whose top speed was only twenty miles per hour. So the trips provided ample opportunity for conversation, and he found the commanding officer an affable person with whom to talk. "We spent hours, and we would yak away," Mac recalled, and as they "yakked," the CO came to recognize his driver as a person whose discretion and advice was to be trusted. One time, he mused about a personnel problem he was having with one of his officers.

> "I just don't know what to do about that man," he said. "He is just not measuring up. He's got me into trouble a couple of times already. I'm going to get him moved, but I don't know who to put in his place."

> So I said to him, "Well, Lieutenant Elwood seems to have a lot of common sense about him."

> "Oh God," he said. "He's pretty green. He hasn't had much experience."

> I never thought any more about it. But he got in the car one morning and he said, "Well, you're in trouble now. I'm going to appoint Elwood as commanding officer of the Corps Field Park, and if he doesn't work out, you're in trouble." As it happened, Elwood ended up as a brigadier general, with a fine record of performance.

Elwood never knew the favour Mac did him in his military career, but years later, he very inadvertently tried to repay the favour by enticing Mac to go with the Ford Motor Company. Fortunately for the western Canadian grain industry, Elwood's blandishments failed.

The commanding officer moved on to other duties early in 1941, and his replacement proved to be a difficult man for whom to work. Mac recalled one night, in the blackout with headlights painted over, driving him and some friends to a dance in a brand-new car whose brakes had been improperly installed. Neither he nor his CO knew exactly how to get to their destination, and so they had to follow another car. Suddenly, he found that the brakes were failing altogether, forcing him to slow down. The CO was not happy. " 'Step on it, Runciman, step on it,' he said. 'You're falling behind, and going to get lost.'

"And I said to him a couple of times, 'Sir, I haven't got any brakes.'

" 'Oh, don't be so damn silly.' he said, 'It's a brand-new car. It's got brakes.'

"Well, we came to a T intersection, and just as I came to the corner, here's a man on a bicycle. Right in front of me! And to this day I don't know how the hell I avoided running that man down."

Somehow or other, he got his passengers to the destination without disaster, and managed, while they were enjoying themselves, to get and install new brake parts. "We were in a total wartime blackout," Mac recalled, "and I had to take the brakes apart and install the new parts completely by feel. There was no light at all. I didn't know how much brake fluid I'd lost, but I topped up the brake fluid with water, and by God, it worked, and that is the way that car ran for as long as I drove it, and I only drove it for a month or two after that. I got a real sense of satisfaction out of being able to do that little job under those circumstances.

"But that's the kind of a guy he was, and I think it was the man on the bike who changed it for me. I just wasn't able to play his game."

So Mac became convinced that the time had come for him to move on. He wrote, of this decision, "I found it increasingly difficult to satisfy the demands of my new commanding officer. My duties became less and less satisfying as my best efforts apparently failed to meet his requirements. The resulting situation bothered me and I began to consider ways out of it. I had always got along very well with the sergeant major of the headquarters unit, and told him that I no longer felt I was doing a satisfactory job and would like to get into ordnance work. He was fully aware of my problem and its causes, and had the courage to speak to the commanding officer about it and my transfer was arranged."[8]

And so about the first of July 1941, he was transferred to the Corps Field Park. It was then located at a nearby estate of Lord Roseberry called The Durdans, which included a horse-training establishment. There, a huge training stable for racehorses had been requisitioned for housing most of the unit's vehicles and stores. The horse stalls had been converted to offices, and Mac served here until about the end of the year.

The stock records in the Field Park were not in very good shape, and he recalled that he "went through every piece of paper in the stock records, and I found stores that had been lost track of."

After his first few months at The Durdans, he applied for a secretarial course. However, by the time he was accepted for the course, the army had discovered that a secretarial course was not the best use of his time and talents. How he came to apply for the course, and what happened when he was accepted, is an interesting story.

While acting as driver-mechanic, he and three others on the headquarters staff had been attached to the Corps Field Park for rations and accommodation. Their presence was not appreciated by the sergeant major of that unit, who had no authority over the headquarters staff. As Mac put it later, "It just used to burn his ass that he couldn't assign us to regimental duties." But once transferred to The Durdans, he came under the authority of this sergeant major, who decided to make up for lost time.

> He'd been in the First World War, and that's why he was made a sergeant major. He seemed to enjoy having me under his thumb and so of course I really didn't feel appreciated, and I really wanted to get away from him. So I thought that secretarial course in London sounded pretty attractive, and I applied for it. But by the time my name came up for the course, I'd established myself well enough that they had made an acting corporal out of me. And I can remember the adjutant called me in one day and he said, "Runciman, I've got an order here for you to report in London to a clerical course."
>
> "Oh," I said, "that came through. Good."
>
> "Well," he said, "what the hell do you want that for? You've got a good future here. Stay here and work it out."
>
> I said, "Look, they didn't seem to want me around here very badly when I applied for it, and I applied because I wanted it, and I'd like to take it."
>
> So he said, "Well, it's your decision. The order's here. You can go if you like."

So Mac took the secretarial course, and he can still touch-type. But by this time, as the conversation with the adjutant had shown, the army had again recognized his leadership abilities, and were prepared to use them. They were, as he put it, "waiting for me when I came back," and he very quickly rose in rank. He was confirmed as Corporal in April 1942, immediately on his return, and in July was promoted to Acting Sergeant.

"When I was made Sergeant," Mac said, "I was transferred to a larger unit of about 200 men, and they were basically an Ottawa unit with some pretty high political influence. I was dumped in there as a sergeant over all sorts of Ontario corporals who didn't particularly like it. But they were new to the game, and I had enough experience that I had them on-side before long. In fact, I developed some very close friends among those fellows."

Mac was confirmed as Sergeant in October 1942, and promoted to Warrant Officer II (or Company Sergeant Major) rank in November. Normally, it is a three-month wait between an "acting" appointment and confirmation, but in this case, confirmation came a month later, on December 17, 1942. The reason for the haste was an assignment in North Africa to train with British ordnance. He was among a group of about 150 commissioned and non-commissioned officers who were selected from units throughout the Canadian army in Britain to gain field experience in Algeria, in an actual theatre of war, with the British army. The group landed in Algiers just at the New Year, and spent the following four months with various British army units. The experience got off to a tough start.

> We were not toughened soldiers, we were ordnance personnel who had been working at office jobs in Britain. There were four ordnance men out of a group of 150 Canadians, and we went over there together and were attached to the British First Army. Because it was winter, we left England with longjohn underwear and all the rest of it – full kit and kit bag, overcoats, scarves. When we landed on the dock in Algiers, the temperature seemed like eighty degrees Fahrenheit, and we were marched twenty-one miles out to Jean-Bart with all this winter gear. When we got there – and this was the first hitch we ran into – we made contact with the British army, and they weren't expecting us, and it was pouring rain by this time.

> So they issued us with pup tents, and turned us loose on a hillside that was too rocky to put a tent peg into the ground. So we got together in twos and we laid our tents on the ground like sleeping bags. We dug a little trench around the sides, and water coming down the hill came down to this trench and ran around the tents.

> The main difficulty we had was when we wakened up in the morning. With our feet having been so hot and tired from the day before, they had swollen up overnight, and our socks were wet and our boots were wet and we had trouble getting our feet into our boots.

At the time Mac and I were reviewing this experience, there was a news story about a young recruit in Borden, Ontario, who had passed out because of the arduous nature of the training. Recalling his own introduction to North Africa, Mac was not impressed. "These guys are awfully soft who can't take the start of army training," he said. Despite the tough start, the rest of his North African sojourn turned out well.

He recalls they "had a letter of introduction to all the British First Army Ordnance units, and we were given a station wagon and a driver. Over the following months, we travelled an inland route to Tunisia, and eventually returned via a coast road to Algiers. The trip provided a marvellous experience. The Brits were good to us, and we went out and saw them in their actual wartime field conditions. This experience was just invaluable to us later in Italy."

North Africa was an active theatre of war, and it was here that he first came under fire – usually from the enemy, but not always. Mac recounted one occasion where "we stood and watched these planes coming over – American Flying Fortresses – and someone remarked, 'Somebody's going to catch hell today,' because they were coming from the west, heading east, and we assumed they were going to the front line, and the Germans were in retreat to Tunis by that time. And all of a sudden these funny little black things started falling out of the planes. They bombed us instead of their target! There were some terrible mistakes made of that nature."

One of the most dangerous places in the North African theatre was a twenty-one-kilometre-long, dead straight, stretch of highway in Algeria, about fifty miles from the coast. It was known to the Allies as "Messerschmidt Alley." In his history of the Canadian army, war correspondent Ross Munro recalled that the number of times they "hit the ditch" while travelling Algerian roads was too high to count. They dubbed the reaction "the Tunis twitch," and Mac's recollections show how apt the term was.

> The German planes could come up valleys from the Mediterranean at low level, escape detection, hit Messerschmidt Alley, zoom right down there and gun anything that was on it, and then duck out to the sea. Organized convoys weren't allowed to move on it in daytime because of this vulnerability. You were warned that only single vehicles were to proceed in the daytime, and if you saw a plane coming, "hit the dirt."

> One day we were driving along, minding our own business, when all of sudden someone shouted, "There's a plane." So we pulled over into the ditch and we jumped out, and we scattered and lay flat on the ground. We couldn't hear any noise, so we looked up and just about that time, the

stork flapped its wings. From our perspective, it had looked just like a plane coming down that road. So we sure felt sheepish. Here we were all lying in different places beside the road and the vehicle down in the ditch.

Mac spent about four months in North Africa, until almost the end of the African campaign, and in April 1943, he returned to England. By May, North Africa was in allied hands.

When he landed in England, he went to what was known as the Canadian Ordnance Reinforcement Unit at Camp Borden, where men awaited posting to units in the field. The practice was to have these men go on morning parade, and those who were getting a new posting would be detained and remain after the others had been dismissed, to await transportation to their new duties. There were also periodic muster parades, where every man's name was called out and everyone accounted for. At this particular unit, the muster parades were huge – up to 4000 men – and you had to know where to go and where your name was going to be called out.

However, for some reason, Mac was not properly "taken on strength" at the Reinforcement Unit, and he was never told just where he was to go. So he watched the muster parade without taking part. He knew that there had been a miscommunication somewhere, and was rather amusedly wondering how it was going to be sorted out. The resolution of the matter happened a bit more dramatically than he had foreseen.

> The next thing I knew, a runner came to my hut, telling me to report to the sergeant major. He told me I was on charge for not being on muster parade. "But I'm not on strength here," I told him. "Well," he said," go and see the sergeant major."

> Well, I knew that the officer in charge of the Reinforcement Unit was Colonel Bailey, and, of course, I had been his driver back in 1940 when I was in England. So I went to see the sergeant major, but as soon as he started to speak, I said, "Is Colonel Bailey around?" So he said, "Yes. He's in the office. Why, do you know him?" So I said, "Yes I do, and I'd like to see him." When Bailey came out himself, he said, "Runciman! Good God, where have you been? They've been phoning for the last three or four days. They want you at the unit right away." And to make a long story short, he laid on his car and driver to deliver me to my unit.

> So somehow or other I had fallen between the cracks. I think that they hadn't put me through the regular process. They were trying to short-circuit me back to my unit, and by trying to short-circuit me they lost

contact. Anyway, I got out to the unit and things were starting to shape up to get ready to go to Sicily and Italy.

On the 2nd of May, 1943, he was made Acting Company Sergeant Major, a promotion that preceded a special assignment to take six men to Scotland to re-equip the First Canadian Division for its part in the invasion of Sicily. Mac remembers, "We took in 3000 and some used vehicles and issued out 3000 and some new vehicles, and a whole lot of spare parts and other ordnance supplies that were necessary."

After that, he and his six companions rejoined their unit and began equipping it for the Italian campaign. It was here that he found the North African experience absolutely invaluable.

> When that was done, the boys and I went back to our own unit, which by that time had moved up from the south of England to a place near Hawick in the Borders, to a camp that was the home base of the King's Own Scottish Borderers, Stobbs Camp – in those days it was a famous Scottish regiment's home camp – where they were billeted. I rejoined them there.

> It was there that we started to get our unit ready to go, and that I was able to tell them, "Look, forget about axle assemblies for Jeeps, or four-wheel-drive axles for three ton trucks." In action, you cannibalize disabled vehicles for things like that, but you can't cannibalize vulnerable things like radiators and so forth.

> We knew the vulnerable parts from North Africa, and we threw out a lot of "bumf" – like the axle assemblies and so on that they never used in the field – and put in stuff we knew was going to be needed, and that's where the experience in North Africa helped.

The Canadian force designated to serve in Italy then set sail from Britain. They joined the Allied flotilla assembled off the southern coast of Sicily in preparation for the invasion that started on the 10th of July, 1943.

"That's where one of the tragedies happened," Mac said. "We disembarked at Syracuse on July 17th, and the German bombers were raiding us pretty heavy at night, and they sank the ship with our Jeep spare parts on it. I had the centre aisle of the truck filled with all the Jeep radiators we could get, and we lost them all, and we suffered and suffered and suffered for the lack of Jeep parts."

Unloading the equipment was a harrowing experience, and he recalls seeing some landing craft blown up when they were disembarking, and bodies of soldiers being thrown through the air.

During his time in Italy, he fully mastered the work of the Ordnance Corps, and, as he told me, "even if I say so myself, I got pretty good at reconnoitering camp sites." A person had to have a good feel for terrain and an eye for the way that vehicles and equipment could access the area to select a good ordnance supply location, and his skill at finding suitable sites came to be recognized by his superiors.

> We often used to be between the field artillery, who would be firing from just ahead of us, and the medium artillery, who would fire from just behind us. What we tried to do was to get behind a rocky ridge where enemy shells either hit the front of the ridge, or went over our heads. When you went to pick a new campsite, you had to find a spot that was sheltered by a hill, had room for dispersing equipment and vehicles, provided access for personnel picking up stores, and was both flat enough and spacious enough for trucks to manoeuvre.

> One advantage the Germans had in Italy was that they knew intimately all the country they withdrew from. And if they knew there was a road running around the shoulder of a hill, they would suddenly open up and shell the area where they knew you couldn't be protected, and that could get quite interesting.

> We had a new officer come in one time, and he thought he should be doing the reconnoitering. He really screwed things up a couple of times, and it was laid on from then on, "Runciman's going to do this." I just seemed to be lucky to have an eye for a place that would work.

His memories of his time in Italy are a mixture of the good, the bad, and the unnerving. Good food, wonderful people, and beautiful scenery stick in his mind, along with the minor miracles that make things bearable when you are surrounded by the hazards of war. Christmas of 1944 was one such occasion. "We had scrounged tables somewhere," he remembered, "and when I walked into that tent for Christmas dinner, I just gasped. There was a bottle of beer for every man, and the Christmas dinner was turkey and plum pudding and all the rest of it. It really was a fantastic effort for the conditions that the cooks had to put up with. I sure used to admire those army cooks."

One memorable experience for Mac – if, in retrospect, a trifle unnerving – occurred when he, with half a dozen trucks and fourteen men, nearly stumbled into being taken prisoner. A movement order had been received by his unit, but because a detail of its drivers was down at Bari, picking up replacement vehicles, the unit would not be able to move all its equipment at the appointed time. So they decided to take half a dozen trucks up to the new area the day before, and bring the drivers back for the official move the next morning. He was put in charge of this project, and given verbal orders and a map marked with the location at which the vehicles were to be dispersed. A few miles short of the designated area, the convoy came to a crossroads where a military policeman, or provost, waved them to turn either left or right. But Mac's instructions and his map showed that he had to go straight ahead.

> Finally convinced of my intentions, he waved me forward, but stopped me long enough to say, "I don't know where the hell you're going, but go ahead." That should have alerted me to a problem of some sort, but didn't.

> So I went ahead to the crossroads marked on my map and looked the area over with an eye to a suitable location for our new camp. To my left, a steep rocky ridge looked just right for protection from enemy shelling, but the area protected by it was not accessible from the road we were on, so I proceeded to the crossroads ahead and turned left. To my pleasant surprise, a short distance down that road, there was a narrow gap through the ridge, quite passable for truck traffic. This led into a large, flat area just ideal for our purpose: lots of room for dispersal of our numerous vehicles; easy access for unit representatives coming to pick up stores; well protected from shellfire by the rocky ridge; altogether an excellent campsite.

> I got the trucks moved in and, while spotting them, was surprised to see an artillery battery arrive in the general area and start setting up gun positions. To make a long story short, at first light the next morning, the artillery started firing and our infantry went in to capture the town of Vinchiatura, which was about a mile and a half further along the road. That explained why the provost was so diligently diverting vehicles at his crossroads the day before. Actually, we were right up with our infantry and within a mile and a half of the German line. In fact, they had advance units even closer to us than Vinchiatura. If the good campsite we found hadn't been where it was, we would probably have driven on for another mile or so to take a look, and landed among the German forces.

> As it was we left a senior non-commissioned officer, who had been with us all through our time in Sicily and Italy, and six non-driver reinforcements, newly arrived at our unit from Canada just a day or two before, in care of the six trucks we had brought to this new location. The rest of us

returned to our original camp in readiness for the scheduled move the following day. When the action started the next morning, the old-timer enjoyed telling his awed group of newcomers that what they were experiencing was nothing unusual; in fact, it could be considered a relatively quiet morning. Little did they know that all the time the old rascal was wondering what he had got himself into, because he himself had never been exposed to anything like it.

When we got back to camp, I went about finding out just what was going on. I then discovered that the dispersal area marked on my map was not the one in the movement order. It was several miles back down the road and we should never have been anywhere near Vinchiatura. I retained a map of the area and the original movement order because I wanted supporting evidence if ever I was accused of having pulled a real boner, which could have placed our vehicles and the future of twelve or fourteen men in jeopardy.

The next day we moved to the correct location, and picked up our six trucks and men from their overnight bivouac. Life returned to normal but it would have been a notable achievement if I had led six trucks and our men right into the German front line.[9]

As might be imagined, not all the memories from Italy were pleasant. Mac described to me "those black bags they brought down from the trenches and out of the hills. We had six young recruits who had just joined us, and a couple of days later there were about eight men killed up in the hills just above us. The newcomers saw these black bags lying beside the road. They were what were called 'body bags' and they were just like sleeping bags with a zipper on them. And they said, 'What are all those funny bags lying there?' And when you told them those were dead soldiers it kind of shook them."

Although, as I noted earlier, Mac told me about his war experience with an animation that showed how vividly these memories remained with him, he is not a man who readily reveals his emotions. The one and only time I can really recall him losing his composure was when he related this story. "They would bury the body bags," he said, "in shallow graves until the Grave Registration Unit could come along and disinter them and move them to permanent graveyards. In the meantime, they would stick their rifle in the ground and hang their tin hat on it, and put up a temporary marker with the man's name on it. And I recall a young soldier coming along and finding two of his brothers in this kind of grave. You had to feel for people faced with something like that."

Towards the end of 1943, Mac was sent, with about 100 other senior NCOs, to be interviewed as a candidate for officer training. However the journey was not uneventful.

> The CO gave me a Jeep and driver and headed me off to Naples. We got to the Sangro River, and the engineers had put a Bailey bridge a quarter of a mile long across the Sangro, and the water was running two feet deep over the top of that bridge, so you know how much water was coming out of the hills.

> Because of the flooding, the provost at the end says, "No traffic across the bridge." So we sat there all the rest of that day and we sat there overnight. The next morning there was no policeman on the bridge, so I said to the driver, "Do you want to take a whack at it?" And he said, "Sure, let's go. I don't want to sit around here with all this rain." And we went through there with the water almost up to the top of the Jeep wheels, but we had no problem.

He was selected, and arrangements were made for him to travel to England by about the middle of 1944. However, his journey was delayed because his unit was moved and his newly appointed commanding officer wanted him to stay on for a few days until the move was completed. Finally, he was able to leave for Britain, but the trip was not uneventful and it ended unexpectedly. "When we arrived, we camped outside Naples for the night and I got into the city about ten or quarter after eight in the morning, and found the ship I was supposed to take had sailed at eight o'clock."

So Mac quite literally missed the boat, by minutes, and thus missed his chance to become an officer. "But as it turned out, it was better that it happened that way. That was one of the real changes in my life, because goodness knows what would have happened if I had got back to England. The war was going to be getting pretty close to over before I would have qualified as an officer, because I think those training courses take several months." Mac said, "I never had any great regrets that I didn't have it because I was happy with what I was doing."

The Italian campaign was the last and the longest posting Mac had, and he was in Sicily and Italy from July 1943 until February 1945, when he was given thirty days of home leave.

Earlier I suggested that, during the war, his leadership abilities were discovered and developed, as was shown in part by his steady stream of promotions, his increasing responsibilities, and his selection for officer training.

But the real essence of his leadership is better demonstrated by two incidents that reveal just how well he exercised the fine art of command while earning the respect of those under him.

The first incident occurred while he was stationed in Nottingham, just after he was first promoted to Lance Corporal. He related the story to describe the pompous attitude of a particular officer, but to me, the story revealed at least as much about Mac himself.

One of his early – and none too agreeable – jobs was to take a couple of men and clean the toilets in their barracks in Nottingham, in preparation for a special inspection.

> We worked on the toilets until I felt they were clean, but this officer came in, and there still was a brown stain around the water mark, and he raised Cain about it. It had to be taken off because we had this inspection coming. Well, the guys tried scrubbing it and everything else, and we ended up with razor blades, scraping it off, and he came along, and he said, "What are you doing, Runciman?" And I said, "Well, I'm trying to get this stain off there."

> And he says, "You should be put on charge. You're the corporal. You're in charge of this party. These men should be doing this."

> I said to him, "Sir, I will never ask a man to do anything I wouldn't do myself, and I am just finding out whether I can do this myself."

> And he hummed and hawed and went away.

This reply was probably a mixture of indignation and quick thinking, but the story illustrates two significant facts about Mac's character. First, he never considered any job that needed to be done to be beneath his dignity. Second, he would indeed not ask anyone else to do a job he would not do himself, even where it involved burying his head in a toilet bowl. The men under his command recognized that and, as he himself said, "The guys liked it, too."

The second incident took place in Italy several years later, and illustrates the degree to which he was able to earn the respect of his men.

> I remember one night an officer from the 30th British Corps drove in, highly agitated. He had to have a truck to go down to Bari for some-

thing; it was an absolute, immediate urgency. I don't know what it was, the booze shipment must have been late at corps headquarters or something, and he said, "I need a three-ton truck and a driver." And I said, "Okay, sir, I will get you one." This is about two-thirty in the morning.

We had a young fellow, Cooper, who was a driver, and I knew his truck was empty, so I went to him. We just slept around anywhere out in the bush with our mosquito nets tied to a truck or a tree or whatever – beautiful summer camping weather, you know – and I went over and shook Cooper's foot. He wakened and I said, "Cooper, Cooper." He said, "Yes sir!" and he came to attention, still lying down! And this English officer is there, and I said, "This officer needs a truck to go down to Bari, and I'd like you to go." So Cooper got up and got dressed and had the truck on the road in no time at all.

I heard afterwards that the English major had said before he left that he thought it was amazing there was that kind of relationship, where you could wake a man up at three o'clock in the morning and he would call you sir and come to attention while lying in his sleeping bag. I thought that this, coming from an English officer, was one of the nicest compliments I had ever had.

Mac told me this story when we were talking about his years as president of United Grain Growers. He referred back to the war, what he had learned then about human relationships, and how he had applied things from his army background. "As a sergeant major," he said, "you were used to standing up in front of a body of men and expecting them to do what you wanted them to do. You had the authority to order them to do it and you could make them do it if they didn't like it or didn't want to, but you would get far better results if you could ask them to do it and they did it because they wanted to. I think there is an element of that in my conduct of meetings and things like that. As long as you are going in the proper direction and getting the right things done, why make it an ordeal for people?"

Why indeed? Perhaps this is the kind of thing he meant when he told me he "got more education out of the army than I ever got out of schools."

Mac left Italy for home leave in February 1945 and returned to Canada. He had every expectation of going back to Europe, and had actually returned to duty in Regina at the end of his leave. However, the war in Europe ended in May. Shortly thereafter, he applied for demobilization. Thus, on the 5th of July, 1945, his wartime career ended, and he was faced with returning to civilian life. And for Mac, that meant returning to farming.

Mac's grandparents, Alexander McInnes Senior and Jemima, "a rather typical middle-class late-Victorian couple."

Mac as a boy, about five years old. The building to the left is a chicken coop, which Mac had been given the job of cleaning out. However, he closed the door on the coop, and when the chickens returned in the evening, they went under the coop where some of them suffocated.

Left; Mac as a Boy Scout. His Scout leader, Mr. Downey (who was also his teacher), was an influential figure in young Mac's life in Scotland.

Above; Mac and his sister Joan at about nine and seven years of age.

"The Glen," the farm acquired by Mac's father in Scotland after the First World War. The farm proved uneconomic, which led to their emigration to Canada.

Mac's mother, Evelyn, standing in front of the house on the family farm in Saskatchewan. This farm was given up during the war.

Mac's father, Alexander, in 1936. He was working as a time-keeper on a highway construction project at the time, and at the left is the company's tent, which served as his office and living quarters.

Mac, his parents, and brother and sister at the time of their emigration from Scotland. The picture was taken for purposes of immigration to Canada.

Mac, about 1934 or 1935, standing in a field of oat stooks.

Mac's brother, Jim (known to the family as "Pim"), with the dog, Peter, hauling firewood by sleigh. The horses are Pat (on the left) and Prince.

Mac on a binder cutting oats in the 1930s.

In 1934, Mac harvested the first crop he had raised on his own, from this quarter section of land. It was purchased by his grandfather, Alexander McInnes Runciman senior, for Mac, his brother and sister, and his four cousins (Uncle Jimmy's children) on the condition that Mac farm the land.

Mac overseas, with Morris Miles, a neighbour from Saskatchewan. It was Miles's father, "a cool-hand Luke if ever there was one" according to Mac, who helped extinguish a stovepipe fire in the Runciman's house before the war.

Mac and his brother "Pim," in uniform with their parents and sister Joan, standing in front of Uncle Jimmy's house at 2900 Hill Ave. in Regina, just before shipping overseas.

Mac visited his mother's sister, Elizabeth (Aunt Cissie), several times on trips to Scotland during the war. She died of cancer before the war's end. She knew about her condition the last time Mac saw her, but she said nothing about it.

In 1940, while serving in Britain, Mac narrowly escaped a very serious accident while learning to ride a motorcycle.

Mac's grandfather's house in Scotland. As a boy, Mac helped lay a few of the bricks for this house when it was built in about 1926. Later in life, in a talk given in Winnipeg to a church group, Mac mused that perhaps he should have been a bricklayer.

Mac was selected for officer training in 1944. He is pictured here (second from the left) at a sanatorium in Italy, which was under construction, and served as a temporary billet for this group while they were awaiting formal interviews for selection.

Mac's unit on parade after about a year in Italy. He was Sergeant Major Runciman by this time and he is particularly proud of the precision with which these men are marching, where every man's hand lines up with that of the man behind and in front.

Mac sporting a very dashing moustache during the Italian campaign. At one point he had grown the moustache to a length of nine inches from end to end.

Mac and Marj's home on the Saskatchewan farm after the war. The house was built to their own design and was wired by Mac for a thirty-two-volt farm system. Rural electrification brought power to the farm in 1952, before the farm system was installed.

Mac and his wife, Marjorie (nee Dick), on their honeymoon in 1949.

The Farmer: Saskatchewan, 1945 – 1961

4

When Mac and I began to prepare this chapter, he once again assembled some autobiographical notes to describe how he re-established himself in farming when he returned to civilian life. "So!" he began, "There I was on the street in Regina on July 6, 1945, faced with making a living after five and a half years of being fed, housed, clothed, and otherwise cared for by the Canadian army. If asked while they were in uniform, most long-term service people would say that to get back home and on to 'civvy street' was at the top of their wish list. It was, however, a sobering thought to realize it had happened to me and that at long last I was free to do whatever I wanted - maybe. Settling into civilian life was probably easier for me than for many ex-service people because it had always been, whenever the thought came to mind, my intention and desire to return to farming."[1]

The element of doubt – the "maybe" – he felt about resuming farming sprang from his assessment of the hurdles to be overcome. With both sons in the army, the family had been unable to continue operating their half section, and it had been given up. So Mac was obliged to start afresh. Fortunately, he did not have to do it entirely on his own. Help was available for returning veterans under the Veterans Land Act (VLA). Once a suitable property was found, it was the job of the Department of Veterans Affairs (which administered the VLA) to purchase it for the applicant and then, if necessary, to assist in obtaining machinery, livestock, and whatever else might be needed for the farm to become fully operational. The veteran would then purchase the land and chattels from Veterans Affairs.

However, the onus was initially on the veteran to locate a suitable piece of property, which he could do either from an inventory of such properties which Veterans Affairs had identified, or completely on his own. During the war, Mac's sister had married and she and her husband David were working his family's farm not far from the Runcimans' former property, and so he began looking in the same area.

> A mile and a half from the quarter section which my grandfather had purchased for us, and less than a mile from the farm of my sister and her husband, was a half section which, with the exception of a very sandy two- or three-acre triangle at the extreme southeast corner, consisted of some of the best land in the district. It had a complete set of buildings, including a house, new in 1937, a good well, and established shelter belts. It was a perfect set-up for a person like me seeking a place to start farming, and what made it more attractive was that I knew the place well, having worked on it when the former tenant threshed our crop for a number of years and we exchanged labour with him. I had even helped build the house. To me the place seemed heaven-sent, especially as the price being asked by its long-retired owner, who had deliberately saved it for an ex-service person, was only $5000.[2]

Mac made application under the VLA to acquire the half section, but, of course, this took some time. While he was waiting, he set about finding something else to do.

> During the months when I was being qualified under the VLA to purchase the property, I was fortunate enough to be able to find full employment, first, from late July through into October, by helping my sister's husband harvest their considerable acreage of grain crops. He was a good farmer and was glad of my help because manpower was still at a premium on prairie farms. Although this period let me get up to date on the changes the war years had brought to farming, it also encompassed a great tragedy when the twenty-month-old only child of this couple, a bright, active boy, died following an operation to relieve a sudden and totally unexpected bowel stoppage. This sad event devastated the young couple, who were quiet, unassuming people whose whole life centred on their farming operation and the son they lost.

> When harvest was finished I went to live with my parents in the village of Abernethy, where Dad was the secretary of the rural municipality of the same name. Again, I was fortunate. Directly across the street from their home, a large - by Abernethy standards - building was being erected. During the summer the contractor had employed two university students who had to leave him when classes resumed in the fall, and I was hired to replace them.[3]

The building was originally designed for a typical kind of small-town enterprise on the prairies at the time. Mac described it as "basically for farm implement and automobile sales, tractor, implement and vehicle repairs and so on. They had three mechanics on the job in the back shop. It was also a service station, selling gas and oil and doing auto servicing, and I'm sure they sold things like twine and weed spray, as well. It was a typical small-town service operation. This one, Bates, was in Abernethy, Greenfields was in Balcarres, and somebody else would have been in Lemberg, and so on down the line. Today, this kind of business is a dead issue. Now you'd go to Melville or Yorkton to buy your machinery rather than to a small town."

While Mac worked as a carpenter's helper, Veterans Affairs forged ahead with his application. However, they committed a major blunder, which was to shape his life significantly. When the VLA assessor went out to appraise the property, he examined only the sandy southeast corner, and on the basis of his inspection of these few acres, declared it totally unsuitable for settlement. "But," Mac wrote, "before I could take action to remedy this obvious error on someone's part, the owner, disgusted by the Veterans Land Act assessment of the property, sold it to a local resident for the $5000 he had been asking. The new owner on being approached certainly had no interest in reselling it. At that stage I really felt that my luck was out but had I settled on that farm my whole future would surely have unfolded in a vastly different way. The assessor's decision was a poor piece of work for which, as things have turned out, perhaps I should be grateful.[4]

Had the assessor examined any other part of the property, most probably Mac would have acquired the land and begun farming. Would he then have become involved subsequently with United Grain Growers? It is unlikely because there was no nearby UGG elevator to which he would have hauled his grain, and he would not have met W.R. Motherwell's granddaughter, Dolly, whose stories about the early UGG pioneers had a significant influence on his thinking. The assessor's error, therefore, was one of those fateful occurances Mac later realized had so markedly shaped his life. Losing out on this parcel, he was obliged to search further, and "after looking at two or three other farms that were on the market, it came to my attention that one and a quarter sections of good land, about five or six miles south west of Abernethy and about the same distance south of Balcarres, was on the market with the owner anxious that it be sold to returning servicemen."[5]

This time, there were no slips. The property was purchased under the VLA, and a deal was concluded for Mac to acquire a half section, with the other three-quarters being taken by two other returned men. Over the winter of 1945 to 1946, purchase of the property was completed, although he had some difficulty initially getting possession because there was a tenant on the land who did not want to move out. These difficulties were resolved before it was time to start seeding. Because of wartime shortage, some of the machinery he had acquired prior to the war had been used by his neighbours, but it was now returned to him. He obtained the rest of what he needed under the VLA.

The purchasing and equipping of the Abernethy farm was financed in several ways. First, he had the money he had earned in the army, which amounted to about $2000. Second, there was the quarter section Mac's grandfather had bought prior to the war. Although the family no longer had any interest in his father's half section, this quarter was owned free and clear. The original purchase price had been $900, giving each of Alexander McInnes senior's grandchildren a share worth about $128. The trust agreement provided that, should any of the other grandchildren sell out to Mac, he was to pay them the original value of their share plus accumulated interest to the time of the sale. It was agreed among the seven that the quarter should be disposed of, with Mac buying out the others' shares, but in recognition of the disruption caused by the war, they agreed to waive the interest charges that would have accrued during the war years. The land was sold for a total of $2000. Mac paid the others out and the rest of the proceeds went towards financing the new farm.

As it turned out, the amount that Veterans Affairs was willing to pay for the parcel of land under the VLA was less than what the owner wanted, so a side deal was unobtrusively concluded to top up the VLA payment with some of the funds from these two sources.

Even these sums were not sufficient to pay for the property and equipment, and so, despite the aversion to debt inculcated by his parents, he was required to borrow. Mac approached the manager of the Balcarres branch of the Royal Bank. "He was a fellow called Stan Shaw," Mac recalled, "a First World War veteran. He asked me how much I wanted and I said, 'Well, I thought maybe a thousand dollars,' even though I was thinking I would need something more than that. 'Could you use two?' he asked me, and so he loaned me two thousand, probably as much as anything on the strength of Dad's reputation, because I had no previous credit rating with the bank at all."

Accordingly, by spring 1946, after a busy winter, he was ready to start farming once more. However, farming after the war turned out to be somewhat different from what it had been before. The post-war years were a time of exceptional technological change in farming, with increased mechanization being one of the major developments.

The outstanding difference was farming with a tractor as compared with the use of horses, which was what I had known until the end of the prewar years. The John Deere tractor that I purchased was tiny in both power and price by modern standards – about twenty-five horsepower or so – and it cost me $1326. They wouldn't use it for a garden tractor nowadays, but it opened up a whole new pattern of work on the farm, and I used it for years. Instead of a normal nine and a half hours in the field each day with horses and another three or four hours feeding, harnessing, watering, and cleaning them and the stable, field work could be done with that little tractor for twenty-four hours a day with only occasional short stops for fuel and maintenance. What a delight to be able to go and go without all that time-consuming work on the side![6]

His search for precisely the right combine for his operation took some years.

For my first crop after the war, I got custom combiners to come in and do it. But they made two rounds on the last forty acres and it was too green. I had to stop them. And a couple of days later came a whale of a snowstorm. We got about a foot of heavy wet snow and it just laid that crop down flat. So my neighbour, Harold Gibbens, loaned me his outfit, which was a Massey tractor with a pull-type combine.

With the crop lying flat on the ground, the combine had to pick it all up and put every bit of straw through instead of cutting the heads off and threshing them.

The wind had blown diagonally across the field, and Mac had to pull the combine against the direction in which the wheat was lying. At the corners of the field, he would make a short cut, and then have to circle back to make the next one. Across the centre of the field, he would have a long run across the diagonal of the field, then have to retrace his steps back to the far corner to make his next long cut. After he got past the centre, the cuts got shorter again, but at the end of every cut, an empty return trip was always necessary before he could make the next one. It was slow work, Mac said. "I started at one corner, and picked up a short cut, and then went back and did another, and I did that whole forty acres, one way, picking up every inch of straw, with Harold's pull-type combine - and that tractor had steel wheels, so you really felt the bumps! And I finished on the 3rd of November in beautiful warm sunshine. But the wheat was all damp or tough."

The second year Mac purchased his own combine, but it was not what was needed:

I made the stupid mistake, based on advice from the University of Saskatchewan, of buying a small pull-type combine that my tractor could handle. It had a sixty-inch-cut - five feet - and you went round and round and round. It was made by Allis Chalmers - brand new, it cost me $1039 - and it did a beautiful job of threshing. But it was so slow.

Anyway, Harold Gibbens came along after a while, and made the suggestion that we go partners. Harold still had the pull-type outfit that I had borrowed in 1946, and he made the suggestion that we buy a self-propelled combine, so we did that. I traded in the little Allis Chalmers and he traded in his old Massey.

He was farming 560 acres, or three and a half quarters, and I was farming 320, which was two quarters. So he owned seven-elevenths of the machine and I owned four-elevenths.

It was sometime after going into the partnership deal that Mac's aversion to debt caught up with him. Harold decided to retire, and his machinery, including the combine, was sold.

Combines were very hard to come by at that time - the post-war shortage was still in effect - and they were selling very high at auction sales. And it went for a very good price. But I was an idiot not to have gone to the bank and tried to arrange the financing of it, because I already owned four-elevenths of it, and even though the price went very high, it still would have been less than a new combine. I should have gone to the bank and said, "Look, I want to buy Harold's share of that combine." And it was only to stay out of debt that I didn't borrow the money and buy it outright. So what did I do? I bought a second-hand one, and I suffered agonies for the next several years with it.

Then, after that, I went in partnership on a real good combine: a John Deere with lots of capacity. It was kind of funny: my partner, Bob Rickard, was so reluctant to admit that this John Deere would be any good. He had had a Cockshutt for years, and he grew a lot of durum wheat, and it grows long straw. Well, he would creep along and crawl along with that bloody Cockshutt, and we used to wonder how he had the patience to do it. But we got the John Deere and we pulled in there the first day, we took off fifty acres that went fifty bushels to the acre, and we had 2500 bushels in the bin. It would have taken him a week with the old combine. Yet, he was still kind of convinced there must be something wrong. Finally he became a fan of John Deere.

That partnership stood up until I came to Winnipeg. In fact, my renter, Garry, and he harvested together for a year or two after that.

The other major technological changes in farming in the post-war years were the vastly increased development and use of pesticides and non-organic fertilizers.

Another new experience for me in 1946 was my first use of a chemical weed killer. The heavy soil south of Balcarres where I had located had long been plagued with wild mustard, which was virtually uncontrollable. In that part of the province, grain fields used to be seas of yellow when the weed blossomed. In its day this was an even more dominant feature of the summer landscape than the blossoms of today's canola. Not only were grain yields reduced as the mustard used valuable moisture and plant food, but, until we had harvester combines, large amounts of additional binder twine were taken up in tying into sheaves its stalks which were cut along with the straw of the crops. The chemical 2-4-D, simple to apply and relatively inexpensive, was just coming into general use at that time. In proving to be dramatically effective, it was a godsend in completely controlling this particular pest as well as some of the others preventing optimum yields.[7]

For more than a decade following the war, most of Mac's energies went into building a farm and a life in rural Saskatchewan. While this was a period of great satisfaction, his sense of achievement was diminished by the disappointments of poor returns.

In large measure, the poor financial returns realized by prairie farmers in the immediate post-war years arose from some contentious marketing policies. In those years, the British Wheat Agreement was one of the most resented of farm policy initiatives taken by the federal government. Under this deal, Canada had agreed to supply wheat to Britain at certain specified prices. Unfortunately, world wheat prices rose, and the Agreement cost Canadian farmers dearly. "I recall Mr. Brownlee saying that farmers lost $600 million through that deal," said Mac. There was a lot of bitter coffee-shop talk about the resulting injustice. Resentment lives on even today over the deliberate suppression of wheat prices at that time.

One of the more contentious policies of the post-war period, and even up to the 1970s, grew out of ideas that had gained a great deal of currency in the 1920s and 1930s.

During that time, when wheat marketing policy was so intensely debated, and when the Wheat Pools, and ultimately The Canadian Wheat Board (CWB), were formed, the notion of withholding product from the market in order to sustain and stabilize prices gained a considerable number of converts. In order to influence the prices they received, growers had to organize into a cartel and pool their product under a central marketing agency. Where these concepts were implemented, growers turned their product over to the central agency, which then distributed the proceeds from sales pro rata on the basis of farmers' deliveries.

The concept achieved some success with fruit growers in California from 1910 to 1920, and the experience gave rise to pooling movements all across North America. Growers everywhere, of all kinds of products, were optimistic that they could replicate the experience of the California fruit producers. Western Canadian farm organizations dispatched emissaries to visit California, and the return visits of lawyer and agricultural co-op organizer Aaron Sapiro are legendary, although somewhat overrated, in their importance as an influence on farmers in the Canadian west.

What gave the policy its success in California were the nature of the product, and the technology of transportation and storage. Unsold fruit soon spoiled, eliminating any surplus that might overhang and depress the market. At the same time, since long-distance transportation for perishable products was not then possible, neither alternate sources of supply, nor substitute products, were available and the market was relatively localized. Accordingly, the potential market power of an organized body of growers who undertook to control the flow of product to market was substantial.

Wheat, however, is not fruit. Wheat can be stored and what is not sold in one year acts to depress future prices. It can be transported readily and easily from surplus areas to deficit areas. And buyers have choices. Some can switch to lower qualities of wheat, and some can switch to alternate grains or foodstuffs. The market, therefore, was (and is) worldwide, and since Canada produces only about five percent of the world wheat crop (and an infinitesimal proportion of all grains and comparable foodstuffs), the market power of western farmers - whether organized into a cartel or not - was (and is) virtually zero.

The practice of centralized marketing and price pooling tended to solve another problem that plagued growers: short-term price instability. Agricultural products are the textbook case of goods with "inelastic demand," which means that price does not, in the short run, tend to have a large influence on consumption. When the creation of the Wheat Board was being debated, many growers believed that demand was almost totally inelastic. They argued that, while the world needs wheat to live, it still consumes only so much. The market will not take significantly more because it is cheap, nor significantly less because it is costly.

In the debate of the 1920s and 1930s, experienced grain traders argued against this view, pointing out that wheats could be substituted for each other, for some feed grains, and for other foodstuffs. Demand, they pointed out, was a good deal more elastic than farmers thought. If the price of high-grade wheat dropped, it would displace lower quality wheats, which in turn would displace feed grains, which in turn would displace silage and forage crops. Supply and demand would come into balance without disastrous impact on price. Of course, these advocates of laissez faire were as unrealistically optimistic about market behaviour (believing that prices would take care of themselves) as the farmers were negative (believing that one bushel too many would send prices plummeting).

Arguing that "the world only takes so much wheat," many farm leaders believed that fluctuations in supply because of poor or abundant crops led only to unstable prices whose fluctuations harmed, respectively, either the consumer or the producer. One remedy envisaged for this kind of violent instability was for buyers and sellers to work together to set a "fair" price, unaffected by the vagaries of weather and crops, or by the whims of the market.

These ideas found avid acceptance in the dominant farm organizations in western Canada. Many of the farm leaders in Canada also harboured a fundamental hostility to free market economics. They believed the grain market was manipulated by speculators, and wanted pricing decisions taken out of the open market altogether. Pooling, price stabilization, withholding grain from the market, and direct negotiations between primary producers and ultimate consumers were all attractive ideas to these critics of laissez faire, and came to be grouped under the ambiguous phrase of "orderly marketing." The term was used in both the US and Canada, but its most enthusiastic proponents were in the Canadian prairies, where it became the slogan under which the Wheat Pools were formed in the 1920s, and The Canadian Wheat Board was created in 1935. In fact, the Wheat Board Act to this day defines the objective of the Board as marketing grain "in an orderly manner."

The goal of removing wheat from open market pricing was realized in 1943. By that time, wartime conditions had interrupted the world's grain trade, and so wheat trading on the Winnipeg Grain Exchange was terminated and the Wheat Board was given monopoly control over marketing. Wartime also saw the advent of a quota system for farmer deliveries to ration access to markets. Quotas were set on a "bushels per acre" basis, thus giving farmers delivery rights that were approximately proportional to the number of acres they had under cultivation.

Grain policy makers in the United States did not embrace either the rhetoric or concepts of orderly marketing as completely as they did in Canada. However, both countries sought to stabilize and strengthen price through storing grain and holding it off the market, and through an International Wheat Agreement (IWA), which was modelled in part on the earlier British Wheat Agreement. Wheat storage and the IWA were principal elements of grain marketing policy in both countries in the post-war years.

In the early 1950s, a series of exceptionally good crops worldwide caused a build-up of stocks. The situation was alleviated to some extent in the United States by food aid programs under which the American government disposed of a significant proportion of their surplus. The American action was seen by Canadians as an indirect way of satisfying certain markets and depressing prices, and thereby worsening the Canadian situation. It was a subject of some dispute between the two countries. However, large carry-overs accumulated in both the US and Canada, and The Canadian Wheat Board, the federal government, and the government of the United States all shared the belief that dropping price to clear stocks would be detrimental to the goal of stable prices. Such actions, it was held, would lead to a bidding war that would only drive prices down, to the benefit of buyers, without adding to total world demand.

The policies associated with holding high stocks caused a great deal of grief, and were the source of much bitter debate in the early 1970s. The underlying theories have largely been discredited since the mid-1970s when the CWB changed its practice and, as far as possible, began disposing of each year's production before a new crop was harvested. While moving supplies to market as quickly as possible may cause lower prices in the short run, it has been amply demonstrated that by clearing stocks, farmers are provided with needed cash flow, the value of stored stocks is not consumed by storage and interest charges, and stored grain does not then overhang the market to depress prices in subsequent years. However, in the 1950s and 1960s, policy makers were much influenced by the beliefs of the 1920s and 1930s, and the impact of these errors was disastrous, not only for farmers, but for Canada's grain handling and transportation system, as well.

So while Mac's farm gained from the efficiencies of mechanization and from advances in pest control and chemical fertilizer, these advantages were offset by the restrictions on moving wheat to market.

The economics of agriculture had not benefitted by comparable improvements. The greater cash inputs necessitated by the changes in farm practice posed a financial problem often difficult to cope with as low prices and limited delivery quotas severely restricted cash flows. In comparison with the farm costs of the late 1990s, costs in the decade starting in 1946 appear trifling, but even so there were grave problems in meeting them. The economic pressures that were to lead to expanding farm size and depleted rural population over the next fifty years were firmly in place and the inevitability of their effects could be discerned but not easily accepted by those affected.

Figures from my income tax returns for that period demonstrate indisputably the pressing necessity for change in the number and size of prairie farms. Yes, I joined the ranks of income taxpayers in 1946 to the tune of $16.17, and was taxable in five years of the decade, but never in an amount as high as $50.00. Only in one year of its last six was our operation taxable, even though sales of a few cattle were by then added to our sources of farm income. The notorious cost-price squeeze of those years was increasing in intensity as delivery quotas in a low price era fell to disastrous levels. The following figures from my tax returns for the years 1946 to 1955 support the point about the need for dramatic change if the farms of western Canada were to become viable units.[8]

Year	Total Farm Receipts	Total Farm Expenses	Net Farm Income	Off-Farm Income	Taxable Income	Income Tax Paid
1946	2537.44	2106.88	430.56	374.80	805.36	16.17
1947	2512.70	1572.10	940.60	60.00	1000.60	42.12
1948	3854.19	3027.36	826.83	392.74	467.57	21.90
1949	4968.88	3349.03	1619.85	543.13	162.98	24.45
1950	5474.81	3576.05	1898.76	60.00	(46.24)	0.00
1951	4732.24	2665.98	2066.26	60.00	0.00	0.00
1952	5824.86	3813.29	2011.57	0.00	85.57	15.83
1953	5052.77	2752.02	2300.75	0.00	(37.18)	0.00
1954	4308.28	2162.31	2145.97	0.00	(44.05)	0.00
1955	3915.13	2894.70	1020.43	392.00	(903.10)	0.00

When I looked at the tax return figures, I was curious as to the source of the significant piece of off-farm income in 1948 and 1949. As it turns out, it came from a little-known part of Mac's professional experience – a job that winter as a "floorwalker" in the Simpson's department store in Regina. One of Mac's recreational activities was curling, and he had a yen to curl on artificial ice. This led to a sojourn in Regina (one of the few locales at that time where artificial ice was to be found) and while he was there, he thought he might as well earn some money. So he worked for about six months in the retail business, up to Christmas in the toy department, and thereafter in hardware.

The large carry-overs, and the Wheat Board's practice of spreading market opportunity equally among farmers, required a very tight control on delivery quotas, with severe restrictions on the amount of grain each farmer could deliver. The quota policy gave every farmer an "initial quota," an opportunity for every farm, regardless of its size, to sell a fixed quantity of grain: 300 bushels of wheat, 500 bushels of barley, or 800 bushels of oats. After farmers delivered their initial quotas, delivery opportunity was offered on a bushel per acre basis, and each farmer's subsequent delivery quota varied in proportion to farm size.

Over the course of our interviews, Mac and I discussed the impact of the CWB's restrictive quotas several times, and he referred to one particular year in the 1950s when he was unable to sell any grain from the beginning of the crop year on August 1, until the middle of January.

> We went from August to December without delivering a bushel of grain. I had grain running out of my ears! I had bought a big barn and moved it onto the farm, but I still had the smaller old barn and it was full of grain, and every bin I had was full of grain. There was even grain sitting in piles on the ground, and I couldn't sell enough to pay my taxes or pay the fuel bill.
>
> The elevators were plugged to the doors, there were no rail cars coming in, and it was a desperate situation, really. We finally got a dispensation of cars down that line because some people with political influence went to [agriculture minister] Jimmy Gardiner, and Jimmy managed to squeeze somebody into putting some cars on that line.
>
> But to show how bad it was: the initial quota was 300 bushels for wheat. A third of the farmers would have plugged the elevators again once the cars were shipped, so the only way to make it go around for everybody was if you got to deliver 100 bushels instead of 300. And as I say, I'm talking the 14th of January. So it was a desperate, desperate time.

These experiences made a profound impression on Mac, and were to influence the positions he took on marketing policies after he assumed the presidency of UGG. He wrote later:

It was a period when officialdom failed to realize that grain income is derived from price times volume. The prevailing philosophy seemed to be that grain could be withheld from the market when prices were low, and farmers would enjoy a bonanza when prices improved and large volume sales were made. That didn't pay the bills in the meantime and led to much financial stress across the prairies. It was years before the message got through to Ottawa and they had the Board experiment with barley. This had dramatic results from one year to the next as far as volume of sales and farmers' incomes were concerned, and not since has the same callous disregard of the need of farmers for regular cash flows been so blatantly exhibited.[9]

Although times were not affluent, farming remained Mac's ambition and dream, and he was not at all prepared to give it up, even when an opportunity to do so presented itself. In the immediate post-war period, former Lieutenant Elwood, the man whose army career Mac had incidentally aided by a rather casual conversation with his commanding officer, came to visit him. "He had been with the Ford Motor company before the war," Mac said, "and after I moved to the farm in Abernethy, he came out three times to see me. I can remember him saying to me one time, 'Runciman, what in hell do you want to bury yourself here on a half section of land for when you could be with the Ford Motor company and have a real position?' " But Mac was not interested. "I told him, 'Look, I want to be a farmer, not a Ford Motor company man.' If I had left and gone somewhere else, it would have been the Ford Motor company. But I have no regrets that I didn't."

However, farming did not consume all Mac's time. He had played British rugby before the war, and one of his former rugby teammates, Elton Dick, became a curling companion afterward. It was at the local rink that Mac met his friend's sister, Marjorie. He had met her once before the war, as a very unhappy eleven-year-old on her way home from the dentist in her brother's car, having just had an abscessed tooth treated. By 1945, Marj was attending business college in Regina, and she and Mac began to see a good deal of each other. The relationship deepened, and soon they contemplated marriage.

At this point, an unfortunate family illness occurred. Mac's brother Pim had followed in their father's footsteps and had become a municipal secretary. When Runciman senior retired from his position in Abernethy in 1948, Pim had been the successful candidate to replace him. But he had not been in the job more than a few months when both he and his wife were diagnosed with tuberculosis. They spent several years in sanatoriums, first in Fort Qu'Appelle and later in Saskatoon.

Pim and his wife Ann had been living in a comfortable suite of rooms above the municipal office. This building had originally been a bank and the suite had been the manager's residence. While the illness was an unhappy development for the Runcimans, the vacated residence above the office provided a first home for Mac and Marj when they were married in 1949. Although living in town away from the farm was not to their taste, they continued to live in the Abernethy municipal office building until they built a place of their own on the farm.

> I was not going to be a suitcase farmer and live in town and go out and work the land. So in 1950 we built a good house on the farm to a plan we designed entirely by ourselves to suit our anticipated needs. The house is still known as one of the warmest homes in the district. Where the funds came from to build it is now a bit of a mystery to us, especially in light of our meagre income, but build it we did and what a sense of pride and accomplishment that gave us.

> In retrospect, it is hard to account for the progress that was made with our slender resources. But I can say with certainty that those years of establishing the farm were the most satisfying and fulfilling of my life. While the disappointments were sometimes hard to take, the satisfaction and sense of accomplishment from our gradual progress in developing a viable and effective enterprise were reward enough to keep us keen and interested and pressing towards our goal.[10]

The house was finished in 1950, but other family matters required that they continue living in town for one more winter. So it was not until 1951 that they left Abernethy and took up residence in their new house on the farm.

It is a little sobering to realize that in 1950, when the Runcimans built their house, rural electrical service was not available. Mac wired the house for a thirty-two-volt generating system, but the rest of the system was expensive and beyond their immediate financial reach. For a while, therefore, they used oil lamps for light, and the furnace was operated with a manual control. As things turned out, completing the farm generating system was never required. Rural electrification brought power to their house about eighteen months later. The transition was another of those post-war changes that revolutionized rural living. "Before the rural electrification came," Mac recalled, "when it got dark at night, I'm telling you, it got dark.

And all of a sudden, all across the country there were lights. In every farm-yard there was a yard light, you see, and it just changed the whole feel of living in the country. And then of course it brought TV and all sorts of other things that were possible, too."

Mac's plans for the farm included livestock, and they developed a herd of unregistered Aberdeen Angus. His first priority was to build up the breeding stock and in one memorable year, all the new calves were female. By this time, the Runcimans had two daughters (Dorothy, born in 1955, and Cathy, in 1959). This put him in a peculiar position on the farm: "The total population of the farm that year was a bitch dog, thirteen cows with their female calves, Marj, our two daughters, the bull and me. Thus, on the farm my only male companionship was the bull, and although he was a good-natured, friendly type he wasn't a really great conversationalist. Even so, we found much solace in each other's company."[11]

The acquisition of livestock was not only part of Mac's vision for the farm. It was also a way of diversifying production and getting another source of income. He had produced only wheat for the first few years, largely to simplify grain storage, but later added barley as well, first for feed and then for malt. A farmer does not grow "malting barley"; he grows a variety suitable for malting (which frequently does not yield as well as feed varie-ties), harvests it carefully to avoid cracking or peeling the kernels, and then hopes that a malting company will select his barley as suitable for malt production. If it is selected, the farmer could deliver a whole carlot of barley over and above regular quotas. At that time, this would amount to about 2000 bushels, which could represent the production from as much as forty acres. "In those days of limited delivery opportunities," Mac said, "the proceeds from the sale of a carlot of malting barley could spell the differ-ence between a good year or a bad year financially on the farm."[12]

By the early fifties, with the farm becoming established, Mac took his first steps towards participation in public life.

The municipalities took no responsibility for snow removal, and so we organized a Snow Plough Club south of Balcarres, and they insisted I be the president of it. I'm not sure exactly why this happened, but you know, it's hard to describe the relationships that developed between older fami-lies in a rural district like this at that time, because their lives were so intertwined.

There was a school not too far away - Saltoun School - and it was away out in the middle of a section because the Rickards had wanted it in one place, and the Gibbens had wanted it somewhere else, and the Stephens had wanted it yet some other place. And they actually put it out in the middle of a section because of these conflicts.

They were loyal to each other, and if there was a problem in the district they'd all pitch in and help, but there was always this background sort of tug and pull. And I think it was that that led them to say, Look, here's a new guy. And he didn't try to stop me from having the school at my place, and he didn't try to do this or that, you see. So I was the only one who was sort of neutral.

A more significant involvement for him – and the first step on the road towards the presidency of United Grain Growers – came with the arrival of UGG in Abernethy.

Prior to the war, as a teenager and young man in his early twenties, Mac had been only marginally aware of United Grain Growers and of the UGG pioneers of the farm movement, knowing them only as names. But when he returned from overseas and was living with his parents, a granddaughter of W.R. Motherwell – the first president of the Territorial Grain Growers Association, and eventually both provincial and federal minister of agriculture – was working as a secretary with Mac's father in the Abernethy Municipal Office.

Dolly was very aware and proud of her grandfather's activity in forming the Territorial Grain Growers Association, and very conscious of the work the old-timers had done. There were others from the Abernethy district who had worked with W.R. on it. I developed enough interest in that, and got to thinking about what it was they had in mind and what it was they were trying to do.

Marj's father was a pioneer, and I knew some of the other old-timers. So it grew bigger in my mind that those old chaps had done a pretty darn fine job in getting themselves organized and trying to control their own destiny a bit. And I thought how difficult it must have been for them in those days, and what a great thing it would be to be able to get involved in that sort of thing.

Mac delivered his grain to Abernethy after the war when there were four elevators operating in the market: Saskatchewan Wheat Pool, Federal Grain, Reliance Grain Company, and Western Grain. The Reliance elevator had been built in 1904 by a company called Northern Grain, and had been bought by Reliance in 1939.

In 1948, United Grain Growers bought Reliance Grain, and with his heightened awareness of the history of the farm movement and of UGG, Mac became a customer. He explained that "some of my grain had gone to the Pool and some had gone to Reliance, but when the Grain Growers came on the market, that suited me just fine and I was a solid Grain Grower customer from then on. There was no two ways about it. But I never dreamt that I would ever have any other involvement with the company than as a customer."

However, a far broader involvement than he could ever have imagined was about to begin.

The basis for UGG's governance structure was (and to a lesser extent still is) a system of "locals," which coincide approximately with the network of country elevators, and which give customers of each elevator a way of helping to shape the company's policies. Each of these locals elects a delegate to go to the annual meeting, and the delegates elect the company directors.[13]

The purchase of Reliance required the creation of new locals where the company was not previously located, to give the new customers an opportunity to participate. This was not done too hastily, because it was recognized that the Reliance purchase would likely result in some elevator closures and consolidation. "There wasn't much point in setting up a local one year, and then dissolving it the next. That kind of thing tends to rankle people," Mac remarked. The first step was taken with the formation of a new local at Lemberg, about eleven miles to the east of Abernethy, to represent customers and members not only at Lemberg, but also at Neudorf, Grayson, Killaly, and Abernethy. Each local also elected a local board to represent members to the company and to advise on local conditions. Mac became a member of the Lemberg Local Board in 1952, and was selected as delegate to the annual meeting for the same year.

The annual meeting was to take place in Calgary, and the company sent the delegates a package of material to allow them to make their travel and accommodation arrangements.

"It was held," Mac remembers, "at a place called The Paget Hall. Marj and I had never been to Calgary and we didn't know where we would stay. When they sent the material out for the annual meeting, they sent a list of hotels and their prices. So I added up the prices of all the hotels and divided by the number of hotels and came up with an average and we went to the hotel that was the average price. It turned out to be the St. Regis. I had no idea whatsoever where the St. Regis was. It might have been two miles from The Paget Hall for all I knew, but it was only about two doors away."

Mac was much impressed with the meeting itself. "It was a real eye-opener for me," he said. "I surprised myself because [company president Mr. John] Brownlee raised a question about something or other and I had the answer and the exact numbers I had read in the paper about two days before. I don't recall the issue, but it was something to do with wheat bonuses or wheat payments. It was my only speech at that meeting. So that was my first direct contact and involvement and I thought it was great. It was a marvellous experience for me to see a meeting of that sort which I had never experienced before."

A second step in the structuring of new locals, following the Reliance purchase, took place in 1953 when the Abernethy-Balcarres Local was formed. Mac was unable to attend the founding meeting of this local, but was subsequently told he had been elected *in absentia* as secretary. It was in this role, as secretary to the new Abernethy-Balcarres Local Board, that he began the career that led him to the president's chair.[14]

Early in 1955, it became known that Stan Loptson, one of the Saskatchewan directors, was to be appointed to the Board of Grain Commissioners (now known as the Canadian Grain Commission). The appointment would require him to resign from the board, and so a search began immediately for a replacement.

"I knew," Mac said, "Stan's departure would create a vacancy on the board, but I had no thought of filling it. I didn't know then that the company's charter says that in the event of a vacancy the board shall appoint – it's not 'may,' it's 'shall' – a replacement."

Neither did Mac know that Loptson's pending resignation sparked at least two vigorous lobbying campaigns by aspirants to the vacant post. The first of these was Jim Snedker, an active Liberal who later became an MLA and Speaker of the Saskatchewan Legislature; the second was Tom Neal, a quieter and less aggressive man, but an active Conservative.

It was part of the job of both company directors and the employees then known as "fieldmen" to be on the lookout for capable young farmers who might one day serve on the board of directors. It was also unbeknownst to Mac that he had been identified as just such a person. In February 1955, Brownlee had written to Fred Dickinson, Superintendent of Field Service, apprising him that a Saskatchewan vacancy was possible and asking him to identify some potential candidates. On March 4, Dickinson replied with a list of five names, Mac's being one.

Dickinson had included a map with his list, indicating that the southwest corner of the province was under-represented on the board, and suggesting that a man called Mr. Ortel Hoffas from Assiniboia be considered.

"While it is true," he wrote, "that our Board of Directors has in the past been Anglo-Saxon in personnel, I believe this man is suitable in every way." He went on to note that "jealousy would occur if either Mr. T. Neal or Mr. Jas. Snedker were appointed."[15]

The board of directors subsequently arranged a trip to Saskatchewan. Whether they looked at any of the other potential candidates Dickinson had recommended is not known, but they did visit Mac. "I think they had a board meeting in Regina," he said, "and they came out and visited at the Abernethy elevator and one or two other points up the line. The way they buzzed around and talked to me and so forth, you wondered if there was something in the air."

However, Mac was not one to draw any inferences about such things. He was not aggressive for honours and position, nor would he have encouraged, in his own mind, much speculation that the Abernethy visit portended an invitation to replace Loptson. Nevertheless, that this was precisely what was "in the air" became apparent a few weeks later during a visit by Joe Busch, the local travelling superintendent for UGG. "Travellers," as they were commonly called, were the first line of management above the elevator managers.

> The first time I got any inkling there was anything in the wind at all was when Joe Busch arrived at the farm one day, and started to talk about a big celebration that was to be held at Indian Head. It was one of numerous events that were held during the fiftieth anniversary of the founding of Saskatchewan as a province, and they were going to have a great big gathering, with people like Mr. Brownlee and [Saskatchewan Wheat Pool president] Jack Wesson, and Tommy Douglas, and you name them. The man who became the Chief Justice of Saskatchewan, Ted Culliton, was the chairman of the provincial anniversary celebration committee, and he was going to chair the Indian Head meeting too.
>
> The event was planned to unveil a cairn commemorating the establishment of the Territorial Grain Growers Association in 1901, so Marj's father, Jimmy Dick, was interested in going over to it, because he hauled grain to Indian Head in the early years, across the valley. He was a neighbour and personal associate of W.R. Motherwell and he thought that he would like to go.
>
> And then Joe Busch came along, and asked if I was going and I said that I wasn't sure and that I'd think about it, etc. But Joe kept pressing for an answer as to whether we would go and he finally broke down and he said

as he was getting into the car to go away, "Well, are you coming to Indian Head or aren't you?"

And I said, "Well Joe, I'm not sure yet."

And he said, "Well, if you're not smart enough to know that you're supposed to come, you're not smart enough to be a director of United Grain Growers anyway."

It is clear that Joe had been deputized to make sure that Mac showed up in Indian Head, because Mr. Brownlee was to be present and wanted to use the occasion to invite him to be on the board.

They drew over 2000 people on a very hot August day, as I remember correctly. A big gathering of dignitaries, as well, and they set up a platform of lumber that they borrowed from the lumber yard. It was all white and shiny and the sun was beating down on it and reflecting up and I guess the platform party that day just baked up there.

There was a family of Blairs at Indian Head and for the occasion they fired up an old steam engine, which was a real hobby of theirs, and it was sitting over to the side. I don't know if you know what it means when a steam engine "pops off." There is a safety pressure valve on it, and when the pressure builds up to a certain level, this valve lets go and the result is a great loud noise with the steam going out. So one or two people had spoken, and Tommy Douglas was up and just nicely started when the safety valve went and the engine "popped off." Well, it took a while for the noise to stop, and when it stopped he turned around and said, "Liberal sabotage."

Well, at that time, there hadn't been a Conservative member in the Saskatchewan legislature for twenty years, but the Blairs, who owned the steam engine, were Conservatives, and when Tommy Douglas said "Liberal sabotage," Harold Blair reached over and gave just one little pull on the whistle. Tommy never hesitated. He turned around and he said, "Who let that Conservative in here?" He just had the crowd in stitches even before he got started. It was just a prime example of Tommy Douglas's quick-wittedness. On his feet on the platform, he was a formidable opponent and things like that stick in people's minds.

So that was one of the little side-lights, and I don't remember much about the speeches or anything else, but I do remember that the platform party had a terrible time. Mr. Brownlee came down off the platform and he said, "Well, after that session, I have no fear what it is going to be like in Hades."

Anyway, it was at Indian Head very definitely that Mr. Brownlee spoke to me and asked me if I would be interested in joining the board.

Mac surmises that he was chosen for the vacant post against the two other contenders because of their strong political connections: "They were afraid to appoint either one of those because they were such high profile – Tom, being Conservative, you see, and Jim, Liberal – and Saskatchewan being a very intense community for politics. So really why I ended up being on the board, I'm just as sure as could be, is that they were going to put so many noses out of joint by taking either of these that I went up the middle."

Mac, as usual, is too modest. Snedker and Neal were not the only other possibilities, as Dickinson's note to Brownlee proves. Mac was selected, not only over these two, but over Hoffas, whom Dickinson favoured.

After the meeting in Indian Head, he was busy with harvest, and "we almost got to believing that the whole thing must have been a flight of our imagination." But it was not, and in due course a letter from the corporate secretary informed him of a board meeting on September 23 in Winnipeg. A room had been reserved for him at the Marlborough Hotel, which was to cost the princely sum of $3.50 per night.

His initial appointment lasted only until the company's annual meeting in November 1955. At that point, he would be required to stand for election by the delegate body. This was done, and Mac was elected for his first three-year term.

His first official function as an elected director proved to be the denouement of the Neal and Snedker story. It was UGG's practice at the time (and continues so today) to hold delegate report meetings, at which each delegate provides the local board and other members in the area with a report on what had occurred at the annual meeting. Sitting directors attended as many of these meetings as they could, and, not long after his election, Mac was invited to go to the delegate report meeting at Clonmel. One of his rivals, Neal, was from the Clonmel area, and Snedker was not too far away – from near Bredenbury. He thought it was going to be the worst meeting he would ever attend, but his fears proved unfounded.

It was the first meeting that I ever went to following an annual meeting. There was a school and an elevator and the elevator manager's house and that was all there was at this siding. I walked into the school and I couldn't believe my eyes. The building was packed to the walls with people! They couldn't have gotten another five people in there with a shoehorn!

And there were these two opposing sides, those who supported Neal, and those who supported Snedker, out to see what this wonder child was who had received the nomination. It could have been a hostile arena. But it turned out that Neal supported me, and Jim Snedker was always a strong supporter for me. Right from the beginning, that night at that meeting, it seems that people were kind to me.

Mac's first few board meetings were, as he put it, "pretty frightening," as he was slowly introduced into a new and different world. He confessed that at first he felt, "That guy is a director of United Grain Growers. I thought of him 'up there' and me 'down here.'" This feeling did not last long, however, and "after a few months, the strangeness wore off, and I soon established some friendships."

One such friendship was with Don Trapp, a man about Mac's own age who had been elected as a director not long before him. There was a certain kinship between them, because they had both served in the war. "Don was an average fellow of his generation," Mac said. "He was better educated than some, and he used to instruct at the University of Saskatchewan in the winter months. But he was very good in introducing me to the company. At my first board meeting, he invited a bunch of the senior staff people to come over to the hotel in the evening and have a drink and meet the new director. I got along fine with the senior staff people and I was very comfortable within a meeting or two. Everybody was very good to me."

Gradually, Mac got to know the other directors, and he learned about their strengths and weaknesses. They were colourful characters, cast in a somewhat different mould from directors of larger companies in the corporate world.

J.D. McFarlane was a bit pompous, a bit of an egotistical sort of fellow, but very practical in a way too. He was the manager of the W.R. Motherwell farm near Abernethy when W.R. was in the provincial legislature. Then he took up holdings at Aylsham, Saskatchewan, and became very successful up there. He did a four-year hitch in the Saskatchewan Legislature as a Liberal, but oddly, he was also a real crony of John Diefenbaker's.

He used to sidle up to me and he would say, "Maybe you should do so and so or maybe you shouldn't do this or that," and I can remember the advice he gave me, just after I was elected as president, was, "Well, you are going to do all right, son," he says, "but watch the booze. Too many good men have gone down on the booze when they get into a position like yours, they get carried away, they need to be pepped up and going."

I had a great respect for Bob Brown, although he could be annoying at times. He was always taking a pill for this or a pill for that. Bob could very well have been the president of United Grain Growers if certain things had been a bit different, but he never, never acted miffed or anything else. I think he was a director for about forty-two years, and there was so much he could help me with and he was a very good speaker. He had won oratory contests at the university, and in some ways, he rivalled Mr. Brownlee. His arguments weren't as soundly based, but as far as presentation of an argument was concerned, he was better.

Snow Sears, you took him as you found him. Snow would get on a hobby horse and away he would go. He stood up before the annual meeting one time, and he had got onto protein grading, if you please – way back before I went on the board – and he'd read up on it. He went up on the platform with books about protein grading and talked about how we should have it. He was using long scientific words and it ended up with the delegate body booing him off the platform. He was mad as hell because they wouldn't listen to him. He spoke like a machine gun, and it was awfully hard to follow his lines of thought.

Harvey Lane? Harvey just wouldn't take any responsibility. He would not take any firm position at a farm organization meeting, and if he was going to go to a meeting, he would phone Mr. Brownlee and say, "Mr. Brownlee, what shall I say? They've asked me to go that meeting. What should I say?" So Harvey had no initiative on farm organization matters or anything else.

In Alberta, there was Hugh Allen, who had been in the Alberta cabinet with John Brownlee. I had a great respect for him, but I mentioned his deafness.

But characters though some of them were, Mac had great respect for them, and he wrote later that "they were all able men in their own right with backgrounds of success in various types of farming, ranging from straight grain operations through mixed operations to principally cattle ranching in the Alberta foothills. All of them deserved respect for their ability and their strong commitment to the company. Three of them had served in provincial legislatures, some as cabinet ministers, and they were all aware of sound business and public meeting procedures. For many moons

I was the neophyte among them, but they unselfishly shared their knowledge and experience, and I was eager to learn."[16]

They used to stay at different hotels in Winnipeg. Mac usually stayed at the Marlborough or the St. Regis. Harvey Lane, who was careful with money, stayed by himself at the Vendome, a small hotel just off Portage Avenue where the rooms were two dollars a night; Snow Sears and Hugh Allen stayed at the posh CP hotel, the Royal Alexandra. But despite this scattering about, Mac recalls that "there were no clear-cut groupings" and in the evenings they would generally eat supper together, now with one bunch and now with another.

The board was very much dominated by the president. John Brownlee is probably best known as a premier of Alberta, and a man who was involved in a scandal when he was accused of what would today be termed "sexual harassment." However, Brownlee was also an important figure in the cooperative movement in western Canada, and he acted as a legal advisor to the Alberta Wheat Pool when it was conceived and formed. He participated in a number of Pool meetings and conferences, and early group pictures of him as a young man at such gatherings show a seemingly humourless man, staring intensely at the camera.

Brownlee played an important role as a mentor in Mac's life. Brownlee's story has been told elsewhere, but Mac's recollections add a further perspective on the man, as well as telling us a great deal about how Mac developed from neophyte director to presidential successor. Mac saw Brownlee as "an awesome person. Nobody could jolly along with Mr. Brownlee. He inspired – I was going to say respect – but it was almost awe, just by his very presence. He was a tall, solidly built man, and by the manner in which he conducted himself, he just had an overwhelming presence. Very few people, especially in the company, ever thought to challenge Mr. Brownlee on any sort of a debating basis. Not only because of this awesome presence, but he had a tremendous mind, just an encyclopedic mind. And, of course, because of his many years in politics as premier of the province of Alberta, he knew how to handle people. And he was an orator."

Despite his oratorical abilities, Brownlee was often reluctant to speak in public, particularly at the country meetings so important to UGG's life and culture. Mac speculated he might have been fearful of the unfortunate events in his past being thrown back at him.

His reluctance to speak in the country was a source of frustration for many in the company. Bill Winslow, a senior grain man who eventually became general manager of the company, used to say, "If we could just get that man to go out to the country meetings and let the farmers meet him and see what he is like, it would be so good for the company's business." He was persuaded to do so only once, and in Mac's opinion, he more than met Winslow's expectations:

> It was really a remarkable two or three days. One day, they had a delegate report meeting in the elevator office at Wilkie in the afternoon and a public meeting at night. The hall wasn't all that big, but they filled the hall to the point where all the chairs were taken and they brought in five-gallon cans and put planks on them to make seats. You can well imagine, planks on five-gallon cans aren't the most comfortable seats that have ever been invented. Mr. Brownlee talked to them there for over an hour that night. At the end of it, one fellow said when he stood up, "You know, after he got started speaking I forgot how hard that seat was." And that is the sort of a speaker that Mr. Brownlee was. He could really hold an audience.

A second stop on the same trip provided an uncomfortable moment when Mr. Brownlee was not immediately recognized by his small audience.

> We pulled into an elevator point - I forget which – and the elevator manager was out in the driveway unloading a load of grain. We all walked up, and he said, "Oh, good morning, gentlemen. Go on in the office. I'll be in as soon as I finish with this load."

> So we went in, and there were seven or eight farmers sitting around there, and if you ever got into an icy sort of atmosphere, it was in that office. Bill Winslow was there and you know how Bill could get along with people. He tried to make conversation, but it just wasn't working. Then one fellow sitting back in the corner said, "Say, are you Mr. Brownlee?"

> And Mr. Brownlee turned around and said, "Yes, I'm John Brownlee."

> "Well," he said, "why the hell didn't you say so. Are you all from the Grain Growers?"

> "Sure we are," we said.

> "Oh, for Christ's sake," he said, and he sat back. "With the white shirts and jackets and suits and everything we thought you were from the income tax department."

And that is so basic rural western Canada, you know. And the atmosphere in that room just changed like that, we were friends all of a sudden.

Brownlee was both president and general manager, and he lived and breathed United Grain Growers. He spent hours reviewing handlings at every country point. He knew not only the business affairs at every country point, but something about the local culture and the kinds of people in the area, and he took a hand in selecting the elevator managers with an eye to these social factors.

Although Brownlee was reluctant to attend country meetings with farmers, he would take a major role at elevator manager meetings. Mac recalled how "he was very good at summing up the essence of things and conveying it to you. At elevator managers' meetings, he had a funny sort of way with him. He would sit there with his head down and you'd swear he was having a bit of a nap and maybe sometimes he did. But he'd listen for an hour, as different people spoke. And he would sort of shift his gaze and then he would say, 'Well men, it would seem to me then that our general feeling is thus and so.' And he would do a five-minute wrap-up, and if we had had tape recorders and had done a recording and had it transcribed, you wouldn't have had a better summation of the situation and the conclusions that were reached."

Brownlee's home was in Calgary, but of course he spent much of his time in Winnipeg and when he did so, he lived at the Royal Alex.

> There was a hotel employee – a bellhop or something – who used to say that he thought that old guy in 298 must be crazy, because he sits in the room at night and talks to himself. Mr. Brownlee, every night, answered every piece of mail that came to hand, even if it was a four-line acknowledgment of a note or something like that. He would drive down to the office in the morning with the old Dictaphone – the kind with the belt – and he'd have a package of these belts for Miss McFadyen to start typing.

> He ate well, and he loved to eat, but I don't think that he ever went to a movie or a theatre show or anything when he was in Winnipeg. United Grain Growers was his total life. Mrs. Brownlee would sit and knit. She often came down with him, they had a suite – 298 in the Royal Alex Hotel – and he would go on about his dictating and she would go on about her knitting. I don't think he played cards or chess or anything like that. It was just one hundred percent United Grain Growers.

Mac showed me lists that Brownlee had compiled, classifying elevator points into those to be kept, those to be closed, and those which were "doubtful." He did a lot of the research work and analysis himself. One day, the company's treasurer, Lou Driscoll, discovered him looking up numbers on handlings at individual elevators: "Lou told him he shouldn't be getting into those details and that there were people who could do that kind of work for him. They left it at that, but Lou got a hold of Jimmy Welsh, who was in charge of compiling statistics and so on, and had Jimmy and a bunch of them work half the night and he gave the results to Mr. Brownlee in the morning. He glanced through it and he said, 'Driscoll, I guess you think I'm a damn fool.' And Lou said, 'No, I wouldn't think so, Mr. Brownlee.'"

John Brownlee cast a long shadow, even after his death, and his reputation was one that Mac was in some ways called upon to live up to.

> I can remember a chap called Nat Kine, who was a real Texan type from western Saskatchewan. He wore a cowboy hat, and cowboy boots, and I met him in the elevator office there one day and he looked me up and down and he said, "Have you got big feet?"
>
> And I said, "Pardon?"
>
> And he said, "Have you got big feet?"
>
> So I said, "Yes, very good-sized feet."
>
> "Well, that is a good thing," he said. "If you are going to fill John Brownlee's shoes you better have big feet."

Mac had not been on the board long before he was thrust into the middle of a difficult and contentious piece of company business. The problem centred on the quality of construction in some of the elevator facilities built by a company called Harper Construction. His part in resolving it was an important step in his career. Some background is necessary to understand how the difficulties had arisen in the first place.

The 1920s were the greatest period of country elevator construction in the west. After a short but severe depression following the war, the period was one of prosperity and expansion, during which grain production rose, the Wheat Pools were formed and grew in importance, and each of them built their own line of elevators. After 1929, of course, development slowed down dramatically, but there was still some limited expansion, and the number of country elevators peaked in 1935. However, the Depression, the war, quickly improving road transportation, and the uncertainties in grain marketing as the Wheat Board slowly developed its post-war role largely ended any new building after that date. UGG had had a construction department during the heyday of the 1920s, but it had disappeared by the time Mac joined the board, and the limited elevator construction that took place in the post-war era was done by Harper.

Peter Watt, the assistant general manager, was a seasoned terminal elevator manager, but had had almost no experience in the country. He had a good relationship with the people at Harper, trusted them, and believed them to be doing a good job. The grain department, however, had a different view of matters, and there was considerable tension between head office and staff in the country over the issue.

Discussion of the construction issue had occurred at the board level, but few, if any, of the directors were aware of the depth of the problem. Without a doubt Mr. Brownlee knew, and it was a problem of some magnitude for him. Fred Dickinson, the superintendent of field service, also knew.

The field service staff were always in a peculiar spot. They held no operating responsibility, but they could exercise a great deal of influence through their role in the politics of the company. They organized country meetings, they had always to be on the lookout for farmers who might one day serve on the board of directors, and they often had a good relationship with board members. They also spent a lot of time with members of the local boards, and were expected to be a conduit of information back to the company on issues that were on the minds of members and customers. Between their contacts in the country and their contacts with directors, they were in a position to learn a good many things that were going on in the company, and they had a kind of power in the organization that had to be handled with great care and diplomacy.

The field service staff were therefore a rich source of information for Dickinson, and he knew just how serious the construction problems were. He also knew that the issue was unlikely to be resolved by management people. Mac believed it is most probable that Dickinson had discussed the matter with Brownlee, and that the two of them hatched the plan to bring the matter to a head. And, as Mac put it, "I was sort of the tool that did it."

The company's practice was for each local board to hold a local annual meeting, whose primary purpose was to select the delegate to go to the company's annual meeting. So Dickinson organized a tour of Saskatchewan for Mac, using the local annual meetings as the vehicle, but knowing full well that people would bring the construction deficiencies to the new director's attention at the local meeting. In fact, it is likely that Dickinson did a little quiet advance preparation to ensure they would.

Neither Brownlee nor Dickinson told Mac directly what was going on, nor suggested he should have an eye to the construction problems as he travelled around. Nevertheless, he saw a good deal, and after each meeting, he said, "Fred and I would have a little talk about it as we went on to the next point."

> I remember going into one annex[17] and the tunnel under the annex that accommodates the auger for pulling the grain into the elevator proper had collapsed. The elevator manager took us in there and showed us, and all that had been put in there to hold all that bulk of grain was 2 x 6s and those 2 x 6s had just gone. Well, you'd go into some of the other older annexes, and there would be 6 x 6s or even bigger timbers. To use 2 x 6s on two-foot centres to hold the whole weight of the grain in the annex above the tunnel was totally inadequate.

> Another one that had always stuck in my mind was a brand-new annex at Love – beautiful to look at on the outside – but while we were there, the elevator manager had to excuse himself and go up and shovel grain in the bin because the grain spout was not properly positioned.

After the trip, Brownlee wrote to Mac, asking for a report on what he had seen. Mac soon realized he had been put into a ticklish situation. "I remember writing back, trying to sidestep the issue to some extent. I didn't want to crucify people and I think I made the excuse that we were travelling hard and fast, meeting at night and travelling through the day. In fact, we had covered a lot of ground in Saskatchewan during two short trips, one about a week long in early August, and a shorter one a couple of weeks later. Fred would drive ninety miles an hour between points, and I said I did not make detailed notes (which was perfectly true) of the conditions at specific points. I ended up with a general impression of the sort of things that weren't being well done in a number of places."

One letter did not suffice for Brownlee's purpose, and he kept writing back, requesting more information. "In my letters to Mr. Brownlee," he recalled, "instead of saying that at point A I saw B and C, I said, 'My impression in a general way was of such and such failings.' I know I specifically mentioned both the situation at Love and the collapse of the tunnel."

The letters that he wrote to Mr. Brownlee have disappeared, but, remarkably, Mac still had the notes from which he composed them, written on small pieces of yellow paper. He read some of them to me: "The company must evolve a policy which, even if it reduces the rate of our greatly needed new construction program, will provide for proper maintenance of our present structures. As regards the defective new construction, I feel we must arrive at the solution to that problem before we can proceed with confidence to erect further new storage and handling facilities."[18] He concluded the letters diplomatically by expressing his gratitude for having had "the opportunity to become better acquainted with the above problem."

Mac's reports seem to have provided Mr. Brownlee with the information he needed to resolve the problem, but it was not done quickly, nor without a certain amount of confrontation, particularly between Fred Dickinson and Peter Watt, the assistant general manager. Before the dust settled, Dickinson had submitted a letter of resignation, which was refused. On November 12, 1956, he wrote to Mac that "the chief came to my room and tore up a letter," and giving Mac credit for his own role in bringing the matter to a successful conclusion.

"Personally," Dickinson wrote, "I am pleased that during all these difficult discussions only good has come out of them. You took a strong lead in a difficult task; it is better to keep quiet now and let others do the talking and acting."[19]

Dickinson's letter was the only overt recognition Mac ever received for what he had done. Brownlee never acknowledged his role or assistance in resolving the issue. But a few things happened subsequently that, in retrospect, were likely indicative of Brownlee's respect for Mac's abilities, and perhaps a recognition of his potential.

The most significant of these was an invitation to address the Vancouver Chapter of the Quarter Century Club, a club for employees who had served more than twenty-five years. The invitation came from Peter Watt, but it had been arranged through Mr. Brownlee, who usually reserved this task for himself. The speaking engagement was coupled with a very extensive tour of UGG's terminal facilities in Vancouver, and an opportunity to meet the terminal staff.

After the relatively dramatic Harper Construction affair, life on the UGG board became quieter, but no less intense. Mac wrote: "Having become a director of United Grain Growers, my way of life and interests began to take on new dimensions. Canadian agriculture and the western grain industry from farm to ship came into focus for me in a way not previously seen or understood. I began to get a grasp of the management structure of the company and its farm policy philosophy based on the views of farmer delegates, and the need for it to be practical in the overall Canadian and global farm commodity picture."[20]

United Grain Growers was a very active and vigorous voice in farm policy debates, with a very specific point of view. Although its founder, Ed Partridge, was something of a radical visionary, the company's policy position had soon moved towards what is sometimes referred to as the "pragmatic," as opposed to the "utopian," wing of the cooperative movement. It adapted itself to the use of the open grain market, and did not fully endorse or participate in the critique of laissez faire capitalism mounted by the Pools and other segments of the farm movement. While UGG was generally supportive of centralized selling and the creation of a Wheat Board, this support was not based on a moral condemnation of the open market, nor on the idealism that saw cooperativism ushering in a new and ideal social order.

In the post-war period, UGG was well equipped to address farm policy issues. Mr. Brownlee's political experience and his long and deep association with the farm movement were complemented by the skills and knowledge of Harry Griffin, who bore the simple title of Economist. Griffin was recognized as having one of the keenest minds in the agricultural policy field and he was extremely well connected. His telephone calls to virtually any senior bureaucrat or politician who was in any way involved in agriculture were generally returned. Moreover, he had a good relationship with the press and the academic world, and was responsible, among other things, for successfully inviting historian Donald Creighton to address the company's fiftieth anniversary annual meeting.

The extensive discussion of farm policy issues was new to Mac, and in this area he found himself apprenticed to Mr. Brownlee.

> I didn't even know what farm policy was, although we used to get the *Western Producer* on the farm; therefore, I was subjected to all pool positions in the 'nth' degree of detail.

> But at the Grain Growers' board table, there was extensive discussion of the farm policy questions of the day by both Harry Griffin and Mr. Brownlee, who would expound on them. They were examined in the most minute detail. One of the things they dealt with and defended most strongly was the Crow's Nest Pass Rates.

> For example, there was a long period in which "parity" was the goal: prices were going to have to be set by the government so that the farmer would get "parity" with every other earning group in the community. And it was on questions like that, that we had a lot of discussion.

So it was a good learning experience during those years, with a master instructor, because - and I never thought about this in this light before - but if I had been on a Pool board during that same period, I would have come away with a much different impression of how the world revolves than I did sitting at the Grain Growers' board table, because I would have been fed a heavy diet of Sask Pool propaganda. Well, United Grain Growers had a propaganda of its own, no doubt, but it covered matters from a much broader base. It wasn't the voicing of a left-wing philosophy; it was a philosophy that tried to encompass federal and provincial issues, farm policy needs, and the welfare of the business.

Of course, policy issues were not the sole focus of attention for the board of directors. Such issues tend to get public and academic attention because they are so intertwined with the politics of the day, but from the minutes of the board meetings, it is apparent that operational and business issues dominated the board's time. "We had very detailed reports of handlings," Mac recalled, "and always a full financial statement, with balance sheets and everything else. I never had any feeling that we weren't getting the facts. We met four times a year – five, including the board meeting before the annual meeting – and there was a full set of accounts every time. It was partly because Mr. Brownlee was president and general manager: he had all that stuff at his fingertips. I told you about the detailed reviews he did of every elevator point, and we all got copies of all his studies."

By the end of the 1950s, the company was facing a serious, developing problem with succession. Both Mr. Brownlee and several board members were well over seventy years of age, and a number of the senior staff was past normal retirement. "A whole group had grown old during the war," said Mac, "and they stayed on during the war because the younger men were away. Then the younger men came back and they still stayed there." What was going to happen "when Mr. Brownlee goes" was a matter of concern both in the country and in the offices in Winnipeg and Calgary.

That so many board members and staff had stayed so long is not, perhaps, as strange as it may seem. For one thing, Brownlee himself remained vigorous and effective right up until very near his death. Second, there was no age limit for directors, and the delegate body had continued to elect a number of older men. And finally, elderly board members were not likely to try to force older staff members, with whom they had worked for many years and some of whom had careers that went back to the founding of the company, to consider retiring.

It would be wrong to suggest that no attention had been paid to succession on the management side. Peter Watt, who was the most senior operating staff person, had written to Brownlee in 1955, referring to discussions between them about his successor and giving brief assessments of eleven other staff members, one of whom might be chosen to take over.[21] Brownlee himself had recognized the need for some younger staff with technical training to be brought into the company, and had hired a number of university graduates. This was itself something of a departure from accepted practice, which set great store by practical training, beginning at the lowest levels and working one's way up. Brownlee could see the changes that were coming in agriculture, and wisely sought to balance practical experience with formal training.

However, things eventually came to a head when John Brownlee fell seriously ill. He had undergone surgery for cancer in June 1957, but had recovered and returned to work. The disease remained in remission for over three years, but in January 1961, he was required to undergo surgery a second time. His recovery from this second treatment initially appeared to be progressing satisfactorily, but in March, he was forced to cut short a business trip to the west coast and return home to Calgary for medical attention for what he first thought was a bad cold. However, the seriousness of his condition was soon diagnosed, and it became clear that the cancer had recurred.[22]

Brownlee called the UGG board together for a special meeting in Calgary on June 6, 1961, where he told them that, "in view of his uncertain health condition," he had decided to assemble the board in order "to consider urgent problems."[23] First, he could not, because of his health problems, continue to carry the duties of both president and general manager. He told the board he had discussed reorganization of the company's management with First Vice-President Bob Brown, Treasurer Lou Driscoll, Assistant General Manager Peter Watt, and the company's economist, Harry Griffin. In these discussions, Watt had told Brownlee that, even though he was by this point over seventy, he would be willing to stay on for up to two more years if desired.[24]

The board minutes from the June 6th meeting indicate that there was a lengthy discussion on who was to be appointed as general manager, and the record is very complete regarding the outcome of these discussions. Mr. Brownlee recommended Lou Driscoll, and the board agreed. However, there was a problem. Driscoll had actually been approached by Brownlee on the preceding Friday, June 2, but had indicated that he would not accept the position. According to the minutes, the board was somewhat puzzled by this refusal, and appointed a committee to interview Driscoll to discover the source of his reluctance.

As to the presidency, other than the obvious implications of the reference to Mr. Brownlee's health, the minutes of the meeting are silent. Mac recalled that on June 6, in conversations outside the formal meeting, some board members had personally encouraged Brownlee to step down, but he would not. "All of us went up to his apartment and he was sitting there and he spoke to us absolutely coherently about his illness and about this, that and the other thing. But during the meeting he would slide between 'I've got to retire' and 'I've got to carry on' and it was really quite difficult."

No doubt, having dealt successfully with his illness before, he was hoping another round of treatment would enable him to return to work.

It would seem, therefore, that as the June 6th meeting concluded, there was a great deal of uncertainty about the future. Brownlee was unable to continue to carry the load of both president and GM, but the board's candidate for general manager was unwilling to take over these duties. Prudence might have suggested, in the light of Mr. Brownlee's health, that a search for a new president should have begun immediately, but the board would have been moving against his wishes to do so.

Mac and I spent quite a long time trying to reconstruct what happened after the June 6 meeting, and our efforts were not entirely successful. However, as we struggled to piece together the events of the following three and a half weeks, a fairly reasonable picture of what had transpired slowly emerged.

First, there was the matter of the general managership to settle. Evidently, the special committee met with Driscoll, and apprised him, as they were instructed to do, that he was the board's unanimous choice. Whatever the nature of the discussions, Driscoll was eventually persuaded, and his appointment was announced by Brownlee on June 19.[25]

Driscoll's appointment as GM caused quite a stir with Peter Watt, who, in his 1955 letter, had judged Driscoll to be "woefully lacking in knowledge of the operating end of our grain business." He felt that the appointment of Driscoll had somehow been done behind his back, and, according to a letter that he sent to Mac in December of 1961, he had been called to Calgary on June 13 and pressured by Mr. Brownlee to resign immediately in order "to make it easier for Mr. Driscoll."[26] Watt said he had already announced his intention to retire at the end of 1961, and Brownlee's request for his resignation made him feel as if he was "literally being tossed out on the street."[27] Watt's ruffled feelings were eventually assuaged when Mac replied to his letter the following August, explaining that the board had been unaware of the June 13th meeting with Brownlee and had not endorsed such actions. The board expressed great regret about what had happened.

There remained the issue of the presidency. Mac's best guess is that the next steps were taken on this matter by Driscoll and Griffin. This speculation is supported by a rather cryptic note in Watt's December letter saying that throughout late May and early June, "Frequent visits were made to him [Brownlee] in Calgary, more or less secretively, by one or two employees to whom he appeared to look for guidance."[28] Without question, Watt was referring to Driscoll and Griffin. Brownlee would certainly have had contact with Driscoll soon after June 6, first to convince him to take on the general managership, and then to discuss his new duties with him. At the same time, Mac pointed out, Griffin had a unique relationship with Brownlee. They had known each other a long time - had been classmates at university, in fact - and Griffin was one of the few people who would have been able to speak frankly to Brownlee about the matter of succession. When Watt visited Brownlee on the 13th, he described him as "dreadfully emaciated," and if the other two men were visiting Brownlee, they would have seen how rapidly his condition was deteriorating and would have appreciated the gravity of the situation.

Sometime after the June 6th meeting, Driscoll telephoned Mac more than once to discuss the matter of Mr. Brownlee's successor. Mac could not recall the precise dates or content of these calls, but he retains the impression of Driscoll's indicating that his name might be under consideration. However, since he had neither aspirations nor expectations in this direction, and since things were extraordinarily busy on the farm, he dismissed the significance of these calls at the time.

It is unlikely that precisely what happened after June 6, or the nature of the discussions between Brownlee, Driscoll, and Griffin, will ever be known. However, another meeting of the board was called, again in Calgary, for June 30th. While Mr. Brownlee still had not resigned, it had become clear that he could not carry on, and that the board was going to have to act.[29]

In the normal course of events, succession would have followed a clearly defined pattern: the presidency would have become vacant, either through death, retirement, or resignation, and the task of selecting a successor would have fallen to the board of directors. However, to the best of Mac's recollection, the board members arrived in Calgary without any clear idea as to how to proceed. A new president had to be selected, even though the incumbent still occupied the position.

By this time, it was apparent that Mr. Brownlee was, in Mac's words, "near the end of the trail and not consistently rational in his discussions." He was unable to attend the meeting itself, and the Chair was taken by Bob Brown. The executive committee undertook to liaise with Mr. Brownlee to determine his wishes, and, as Mac put it, there was "a lot of to-ing and fro-ing" between the board and the president to do so.

Although Mac was not privy to the committee's discussions, he was able to reconstruct some of the dynamics of the situation. First, the executive had to negotiate and receive an approval from Brownlee to proceed. Second, once such approval had been received, they had to consider the potential candidates for the job. "At the time," said Mac, "the logical thing to me was, if Brownlee goes, Bob Brown steps in." Brown, as first vice-president, might have seen himself as the logical successor, and Mac believes he would have taken the job if it had been offered. However, there were several factors against him.

"Bob Brown could speak well and he knew the business and the people and everything else," Mac said. "But his health was not good, and Brownlee knew from his own experience the pressures that the presidency and general managership put on you. He just didn't have the vigour and stamina to be a hard worker. He wasn't a hearty, strong man, and you need some of those qualities to stand the racket. So I think that Brownlee knew that, and I don't think Bob Brown's health would have let him last the first three months."

There were some personal conflicts, as well, that told against Brown. Mac recalled that when Bob Brown stood up at a farm meeting to comment on some matter, if Brownlee was present he would often enter the debate himself, and sometimes seemed to do it just to show he was a better debater than Brown. "Sometimes," Mac recalled, "it seemed as if Bob had been aspiring to be president, and had been trying to prove his skill and worth, and that set up a certain competitiveness between Bob Brown and Mr. Brownlee. I think Mr. Brownlee would have had no desire to hand the reins to Bob on that score alone. And he was aided and abetted by Snow Sears, because there was an antagonism between Bob Brown and Snow, which was fuelled by Snow, who tended to be disruptive."

Aside from Brown, the field was not wide, and as much as Mac respected his fellow directors, he had to admit that not all of them were presidential material. "The place," he said, "was not teeming with candidates."

The board also had to consider the feelings of senior management people. Mac speculated that Lou Driscoll's initial reluctance to become general manager may have arisen from the fact that Bob Brown was a leading candidate for president, and Driscoll may not have wanted to work with

Brown. Similarly, there was always tension between Harry Griffin and Brown. Griffin wrote in a somewhat academic style, which Brown, who was a pretty competent writer, as well, was always trying to edit. Mac speculated that, if Driscoll had had reservations about working with Brown, then Driscoll may well have received some assurance from Brownlee that he would not back Brown for president.

Brown's situation in these deliberations was a difficult one. As first vice-president, he assumed the Chair in Mr. Brownlee's absence. At the same time, as a potential candidate for president, with at least some aspirations, it would almost have been a conflict of interest for him to take the Chair when the issue of succession was being addressed. Accordingly, leadership had to come from elsewhere. "It is interesting," Mac mused, "how in crisis situations some people come to the surface, and the person who really became the go-between and messenger was Bob Wilson. He was from Gladstone, Manitoba – a very sensible, conscientious man; just one of nature's gentlemen, – and was the Manitoba member of the executive. He had been in the medical corps in the First World War, and had been awarded a medal for bravery. Bob could really keep his head in a crisis and he came to the surface as the leading figure on the board of directors during that difficult period."

It was Bob Wilson, therefore, who led the executive and the board through the options. Other than Bob Brown, most of the others were either too old, or were just not up to the responsibilities of the position. Don Trapp might have been a contender, "and might have had a justifiable right to think that he would be considered ahead of me, because he went on the board a couple of years before I did," Mac said. But Trapp simply had not garnered sufficient support from the other directors.

"So when you ran down the list, I guess they were scraping the bottom of the barrel," said Mac in his usual self-effacing way, and in the end, on the night of June 30th, the committee came to him and asked if he would be prepared to take on the presidency. He telephoned Marj to talk it over. "She said, 'Well, if we are ever to do anything other than farming, maybe this is the most attractive opportunity you'll ever get.' We were devoting our whole lives to becoming established on the farm, because all we wanted to do was farm. Had it not worked out, it was no skin off our nose at all. It wasn't the end of everything because we could go back and do what we wanted to do in the first place."

So he accepted, and on the 1st day of July 1961, on what was then called Dominion Day, Mac Runciman became the somewhat overwhelmed new president of United Grain Growers. "This is not false modesty or anything," Mac insisted, "but I had had absolutely no aspirations to be president of United Grain Growers. It was certainly never in my thoughts or mind that I wanted to be the president, or that I would be considered as a candidate for the presidency. And I think one of the reasons for that was that Bob Brown was a VP of many years' standing who, in the normal course of events, should have expected to move right up."

As we discussed the events leading up to his appointment, he stressed that not only had he not aspired to the presidency, but that, when he was asked to take it on, he could not quite understand what he had done to merit the board's confidence in him. "It was something that I really couldn't quite account for," he said. "I just couldn't believe it, and I often thought to myself, Now, what on earth did I do during those five years that made them decide that I could do it? I keep drawing a blank in trying to come up with reasons for their selecting me."

If Mac had been Mr. Brownlee's choice as successor, then the decision of his peers would be no mystery. This, however, is a matter which cannot be unequivocally determined. As we went over these events in our initial interviews, we discussed this question twice. The first time, I asked him point-blank whether he had been Brownlee's choice. "I don't know," he responded. "I just outright don't know. I suppose I could have asked the people on the committee, and maybe I knew more about it at the time and have forgotten."

We returned to the subject in a second interview, and he had evidently been thinking about it and discussing it with Marj. We skirted the issue several times as we reviewed yet again all the circumstances surrounding his selection: the qualifications of other directors, the appointment of Lou Driscoll, the Harper Construction story, and so on. Then, without my asking directly, he suddenly volunteered his answer as a very qualified "probably." "I have a feeling," he said, "that Mr. Brownlee may have urged on them that I was the man to take the job. In fact, if anybody said, 'What would be the deciding factor in you becoming president of United Grain Growers?' and I was pinned down for an answer (which, in effect, I am) I would have to guess that a major factor would have been the opinion that Mr. Brownlee had formulated that maybe I could do it, and I think that the help in cracking the construction nut may have been what gave Mr. Brownlee sufficient confidence in me to suggest to them that I was the logical successor."

Precisely how he gained sufficient confidence from his fellow directors to win the position will never be known in any detail. During the late 1990s, as this book was being written, only one of Mac's fellow directors from 1961 (Don Trapp) was still alive. In the course of writing this book, I was able to speak to one other (Lester Snyder, who subsequently passed away) and he was not able, when I met him, to cast much light on the question. However, we have seen how Mac's wartime experience revealed his leadership potential, and people who recall his career as UGG president will know the kind of leadership he displayed in the grain industry. So it is not surprising to anyone, except himself, that he did rise in esteem with the rest of the board between 1955 and 1961, nor inconceivable that Brownlee would have selected him. On the other hand, that it took the executive committee a full day of "to-ing and fro-ing" before they actually put the question to him suggests there was a good deal of discussion before a clear choice emerged. So either Mr. Brownlee was not forceful in voicing his opinion, or there were people on the board who had to be convinced.

Feeling as he did, and respecting Mr. Brownlee as he did, Mac's reaction upon entering the president's office comes as no surprise. He recalled: "I went down to the Calgary office from the Palliser Hotel the next morning, and Frank Allison met me and went with me up to Mr. Brownlee's office. I walked in the door and sat down in the first chair inside the door, and looked across at the big desk.

"Frank went and stood by the desk and said, 'No, not that chair. This chair around behind the desk.'

"I had a great sense of difficulty in making myself go and sit behind that desk and presume I could take Mr. Brownlee's place. I think that was as tough as anything I ever had to do."

Immediately after July 1, Mac started commuting to Winnipeg. He then settled affairs on the farm, and by Labour Day, in time for his older daughter to start school, he and his family had moved to Winnipeg.

Mr. Brownlee with UGG staff at an elevator-managers' meeting. Mr. Brownlee is the tall man with glasses just to the right of centre in the back row. The short man with glasses, two to the left of him, is Peter Watt, Assistant General Manager, and the person who felt slighted when Lou Driscoll was appointed General Manager (courtesy UGG).

The UGG Board of Directors when Mac joined the Board in 1955. Visible in the picture, from left to right are, R.M. ("Bob") Wilson, J.I. ("Johnny") Stevens, Lester Snyder, R.C. ("Bob") Brown, J.D. MacFarlane, Hugh Allen, John Brownlee, Mac, Harvey Lane, Don Trapp, the manager of the hotel where the picture was taken, and S.S. ("Snow") Sears. Harold Staples's forehead can just be seen between Sears's chin and the hotel manager's shoulder.

The UGG Board just after Mac was elected President. There are only eleven men in this picture, indicating that it must have been taken shortly after July 1961, after Mr. Brownlee's death, but before Allan Smith of Red Deer, Alberta, was appointed to fill the vacancy on the Board. Shown, from left to right, are: Lester Snyder, Harold Staples, S.S. ("Snow") Sears, Mac, Hugh Allen, J.I. ("Johnny") Stevens, R.C. ("Bob") Brown, Don Trapp, J.D. MacFarlane, Harvey Lane, and R.M. ("Bob") Wilson.

Among the many honours Mac received in his lifetime was his appointment as an honourary chief of the Blackfoot tribe. This picture was taken at a UGG Annual Meeting. The native leader is Ben Calf-Robe (courtesy UGG).

Mac with UGG senior management. "Herb" was Herb Stimson, UGG's traffic manager who evidently was ill and being sent Christmas greetings. Pictured from left to right are Jim Mants, John Wachal, Dave Miller, Eric ("Dusty") Titheridge, Lou Driscoll, Jimmy Welsh, Mac, John Clark, Joe Lazenby, Albert Cantin, Bert Berry, Art White and Keith Thompson. Driscoll (holding the sign with Mac) was then General Manager. Berry (third from the right) was Stimson's assistant. Clark (just to the right of Mac, peering over his shoulder) was in charge of UGG's public relations, and, under Mac's direction, wrote many of the speeches quoted in the text. Berry (third from the right) was Stimson's assistant (courtesy UGG).

Mac (on the right) demonstrates that he can still unload grain the old-fashioned way. This picture was taken at the opening of a new elevator in Morden, Manitoba, in April 1981. The first load of grain was delivered ceremoniously in bags in an old wagon, which is just visible behind Mac's head. The other person is Joe Lazenby, UGG's chief grain grader (courtesy Glenn Dickson, UGG).

Mac at one of many news conferences, of which he was a part. This one was likely on a Canada Grains Council issue. Identifiable in the picture to Mac's left are Gordon Harold, President of Alberta Pool, Bruce MacMillan, President of Pioneer Grain, Ted Turner, President of Saskatchewan Wheat Pool, and Jim Rae, CBC news reporter (courtesy UGG).

Honourary Doctorate degrees were conferred on Mac by the universities of Manitoba and Saskatchewan. Later, he chaired the Board of Governors at the University of Manitoba. Here, he is shown with the Honourable Otto Lang, who was receiving an honourary degree from University of Manitoba.

Mac delivering a speech at the opening of a new country elevator in Morden, Manitoba, in April 1981 (courtesy Glenn Dickson, UGG).

Hugh Horner (on the left) was deputy premier of Alberta and, later, coordinator of the Grain Transportation Authority. After he stepped down from the latter position he ran unsuccessfully for election to the UGG board of directors (courtesy UGG).

Mac and Marj on the occasion of his induction into the Canadian Agricultural Hall of Fame in 1982.

Mac and McCabe Grain president Charlie Kroft, in 1968, when UGG bought the company. "I remember a sense of satisfaction when I shook hands with Charlie Kroft over the acquisition of McCabe," said Mac about this occasion, "and Charlie was happy because it was going into what he thought were good hands."

Mac talking with Ted Allen (centre), who eventually became president of
United Grain Growers, and Allan Smith (right), who was vice-president for the
greater part of Mac's presidency.

The UGG board in the last year of Mac's presidency (1980–1981). Seated to the
left of Mac is Lorne Hehn, who succeeded Mac as president and later became
chief commissioner of the Canadian Wheat Board. Between them is Ted Allen,
the current (2000) UGG president, who succeeded Lorne. Shown, from left to
right, are: seated, Allen Smith (who took Mr. Brownlee's place on the board),
Bill Craddock, Mac, Ted Allen, Lorne Hehn, and Bud Morken; standing, Hugh
Dickson, Joe Omichinski, Walter Van der Walle, Sam Sych, Roy Piper and Roy
Cusitar. As of 2000, Roy Piper was the only person in this picture besides Ted
Allen who was still on the UGG board.

The UGG President: 1961 – 1970

5

As the newly elected president of United Grain Growers, Mac was about to embark on a new career, taking him from relative obscurity as a Saskatchewan farmer to prominence both in western Canadian agriculture and in Canadian life on a national scale. Coincidentally, he was now almost the same age his father had been when the Runciman family left Scotland for a new life in Canada. For Mac, the move to Winnipeg was no less dramatic a step, for he moved into his new role just as a number of policy and operational changes began that were to transform both UGG and the grain industry.

Mac's story – as well as the story of this transformation – is best told by concentrating on five major parts of his new career: the changes he wanted to make to UGG itself; his involvement in the world of national agricultural policy as a director of the Canadian Federation of Agriculture (CFA); his founding presidency of the Rapeseed Association of Canada; his founding chairmanship of the Canada Grains Council; and the leadership he and UGG showed in the grain handling and transportation debate that dominated the policy agenda during the 1970s. The latter four represented, respectively, his most frustrating, most rewarding, most disappointing, and most challenging undertakings during his years as president of UGG.

The events of these five parts of Mac's presidential career followed one another more or less sequentially, but there was a good deal of overlap in timing. Accordingly, the narrative in this and the succeeding chapters does not follow as precisely the chronological pattern that it has so far. In this chapter we will deal with only the first two items in the five: his agenda for UGG when he became president, and his experience with the CFA.

Mac had few strong ideas of what he wanted to accomplish when he assumed the presidency, and indeed, the reluctance he had felt about sitting in John Brownlee's chair in Calgary never completely left him.

I didn't come to Winnipeg with an extensive agenda, principally because
I was pretty well preoccupied with the farm in those days, but also because I had no prior expectation that I would ever need one. And it
happened so quickly, you see, between July and September. I left the farm
as a beginning young farmer – well, young? forty-six years old? – and
came home as president of United Grain Growers. It was a mighty quick
transition – and it came without five years as a vice-president, or three
years of knowing that I was the heir apparent. I guess I had shaped some
ideas about what we should be doing, but never along the lines of how I
would do them.

So I never had a sense that I should walk in the door and say, "I'm sure
going to make United Grain Growers hum and show the world how to
run a grain company." Never that at all. In fact, I always had a funny sort
of feeling that "This can't be me; I can't be doing this; I'm not really the
guy who is going to lead UGG on to great things. But while I'm around
and until we get somebody else, I'll do what I can." I always rather felt as
if I were a substitute - a custodian of the interests who was filling an
interregnum between Mr. Brownlee and whoever was going to come
along next.

There were always those sorts of feelings about it, and they lasted for
twenty years.

Few would accept his self-effacing assessment of himself as a custodial
president between more distinguished and deserving incumbents. His presidency of UGG, and the leadership he demonstrated in the western grain
industry, led to positions on the boards of directors of a number of large
Canadian companies (the Royal Bank and Canadian Pacific, to name but
two), and was to earn him sufficient respect in political circles to be invited
at one point to take the position of federal minister responsible for The
Canadian Wheat Board. He held directorships on the boards of a number
of agricultural industry organizations, received honourary doctorates from
the universities of Manitoba and Saskatchewan, was the founding chairman of the Canada Grains Council and founding president of the Rapeseed
Association of Canada (now the Canola Council), and was inducted into
the Canadian and Saskatchewan Agricultural Halls of Fame. His sense of
being a mere custodian stands in contrast to this record of achievement
and, more importantly, in contrast to the high regard he commanded in the
grain industry. There were many illustrations of this regard, but the one that

moved me most profoundly was a standing ovation he received from the delegates to a UGG annual meeting no less than a decade after he retired.

In fact, Mac had an early indication that his feelings were somewhat more self-deprecating than need be: "After his first meeting with me, Crerar wrote a letter – to Charlie Banks, father of Sam Banks who later came on our board – to say that he thought I might turn out to be one of the best presidents the company ever had – next to him, I suppose."

Crerar was, of course, Thomas Crerar, president of UGG from 1907 to 1930, former federal cabinet minister in several portfolios, and, at the time of the letter, a senator. Crerar's judgement, as it turned out, was accurate, but in 1961, broader accomplishment and recognition were all in the future. In the meantime, "doing what he could" entailed facing a number of internal challenges, of which the most immediate was conducting his first UGG annual meeting.

The structure and conduct of the company's annual meetings require the president to chair an assembly of delegates for a very full two days.[1] In 1961, the delegates numbered approximately 300, each of whom had been selected to represent the shareholders and members from one of the company's locals. The primary items on the agenda of the meeting were the presentation and adoption of the financial reports and the report of the board of directors, speeches by various invited organizations (the Wheat Board and Board of Grain Commissioners, for example), the consideration of resolutions brought forward by the delegates regarding both broad agricultural issues and the company's operations, and the nomination and election of directors (four every year, for three-year terms). At times, on controversial issues, annual meetings could (and still can) get tense. The Chair has to have a good command of parliamentary rules, and sometimes has to exercise fairly tight control.

Chairing an annual meeting, therefore, was not a trivial task, and for a person whose prior experience in this line was confined to the local snow-plough club, it was a bit daunting.

> I can well remember in the days leading up to that first annual meeting, I thought, My God, I've got to get up on that platform and do all the things that John Brownlee did after fifteen or twenty years in government, with his training as a lawyer, and his experience managing the company and everything. I'll be just so damn lucky if I don't get shot down in the first fifteen minutes.
>
> But the funny thing about it was – and this is what I've always appreciated – if I had got lockjaw that morning and been unable to speak, the

annual meeting would have gone off successfully, because I felt that every delegate came that year to make sure that the meeting went well and the new president made a go of it.

I think they saw me as a departure from Mr. Brownlee and Peter Watt and the old school. The common expression in the country for the head office in Winnipeg was "the ivory tower." It was always: "Those s.o.b.'s don't know what goes on." I had the advantage of coming right off the farm into that office and, boy, they were out there to see that I got along, and I just couldn't have asked for better support than that.

Mac believes the support he received arose in part from a strong feeling that the company's senior ranks had become too isolated from its customers and employees in the country, whereas he, as the new man "right off the farm," would be more in touch with local issues and conditions. This kind of isolation is, of course, almost inevitable in a large and geographically dispersed organization, but it had become particularly acute for UGG in 1961, and remedying it became Mac's first priority. As he put it: "We had to get closer to the people in the country. I felt there had to be a closer linkage. I was just determined when I became president that was one of the things that had to be done. We had to make our people realize that this was their company, and it was there trying to hit the ball for them."

This was easier said than done. With something like 300 local boards, visiting and meeting all of them every year would be a full-time job, and it was here - with the representatives of customers and shareholders - that the need was most acute. So after discussion with the board of directors, Mac instituted the practice of regional meetings, at which the members of a number of local boards, together with their elevator managers, could come together in one central location to meet with the president and some of the directors to express their concerns and get to know the people who had the ultimate responsibility for the direction of the "ivory tower."

He gradually developed a schedule, where, he said, "I tried to get around to all the locals once every three years. I wanted to be able to say that, once every three years, every member of every local board had had an opportunity to meet the president and the directors for that area to discuss the company with them. And I succeeded in that. By the end of twenty years, there wasn't a member of a local board in western Canada who could say that he hadn't had chances - not just one chance, but several - to come to meetings with the president and directors. It really brought them closer together and I believe it had a beneficial effect."

A second, and more modest, goal was to alter the way in which the company's board and executive meetings had been organized and scheduled by Mr. Brownlee.

> One thing that always bothered me - and I almost leaned over backwards to remedy it when I became president - was the annoying practice of holding an executive committee meeting the day before a board meeting, and then presenting the decisions reached the day before for ratification. It just irked the hell out of me. We would all be coming into Winnipeg anyway, so why shouldn't the whole board have discussed these matters?

> There were a lot of ruffled feelings over that among the board members who were not on the executive committee. Harold Staples was one who didn't like it, and I was another and I know Don Trapp didn't like it.

He quickly put an end to the practice of having an executive meeting precede each board meeting.

His third goal was to enforce normal retirement age for the staff. The age levels of senior management had had a negative effect on both the attitudes in the country among customers and shareholders, and on the company's reputation in the trade. Younger men in the company (and the management group was exclusively men at that time) were finding their career prospects cut off by a cadre of older employees who had stayed on well past normal retirement age. As Mac pointed out, "Mr. Brownlee was seventy-six; Peter Watt was seventy-two; we kept Harry Griffin until he was eighty-two; Gerry Bell was kept until he was sixty-nine. As a result, people like Don Frye never got a chance to move up to a senior management position, and Don was very highly regarded by the Grain Exchange community as a top-notch, dependable trader, and he had worked at Thunder Bay so he had a broad base of knowledge and experience that might have given him a chance for promotion, but he never got the chance."

No doubt, today's style would be to conduct a quick purge through buy-outs and enforced retirements, but things were done more deliberately then. Continuity was deemed important, and long service to the company valued. The senior people were consulted about succession, and Mac still has the letter referred to in the preceding chapter from the assistant general manager, Peter Watt, assessing the suitability of a number of other executives and middle managers for promotion. The foresight Mr. Brownlee had shown in hiring university graduates also paid off at this point, because by this time these younger men had experience in the company and the industry. A number of them received favourable assessments by Watt as being ready for promotion to more responsible positions.

It was several years before Mac's goal was accomplished, but once it was, he had brought in one of the most highly regarded management teams in the grain business of the time. On July 18, 1967 he was able to report to the board of directors: "Since June 1, 1961, retirements of senior staff members have created vacancies in virtually every senior position in the company. As a result, a completely different group of men now occupy these positions. It is a cause for satisfaction that [most of] the men who filled the vacancies were [from] our own organization. ...

"I believe we are fortunate in having at this time a dedicated, aggressive, imaginative group of men in our service, capable of ... holding their own with any management group in our industry."[2]

My own first exposure to UGG's management came about three years after he wrote this report, when I began working in Ottawa on grain transportation issues. As I travelled through western Canada, and met and talked with staff in all the grain companies, UGG's impressed me as among the most forward-thinking and imaginative, and this view was shared by a number of other industry people whom I came to know and respect. Although it was under Mac's leadership that this team was assembled, he was quick to give then-general manager Lou Driscoll a good deal of the credit, too.

> Lou had a very keen, perceptive mind, with a desire to be innovative. He had one handicap, in that he was totally a city boy, and he was so uncomfortable out in the country with farmers and country elevator managers. But this is really why he and I made a good partnership because I was strong where he was weak.

> But he was always looking for innovative sorts of ideas and directions. For example, he put the elevator managers' compensation on a completely new basis, grading the points according to the volume handled and the kind of plant they were operating. He had a very progressive attitude towards the benefits staff could have at reasonable cost to the company. He wanted fairness, and I believe it was Lou Driscoll's attitude to fringe benefits that kept the company without a union.

When he took the presidency, Mac insisted he would not assume the position of general manager as well, as Mr. Brownlee had done. These two positions had already been separated due to Mr. Brownlee's illness, and, as long as Mac was president, he was determined they would remain so. However, under the by-laws of the company, the president was still the chief executive officer, and that was an arrangement of which he approved.

> It was my strong feeling that the president should be the CEO, and I still think it has some good points. It kept the president's nose to the grindstone, for one thing. It also kept him fully knowledgeable about what was going on around him, because the general manager had to come and lay his business on my desk. And I would take it that when the general manager is the CEO, he doesn't have to lay his business on the president's desk. That's the point that I feel is significant.

> I felt very strongly that you shouldn't make the hired man the boss. I thought it was complementary to the philosophy of a farmer-owned company. I primarily saw myself as managing the business of United Grain Growers. And remember, I was out advocating that the farmer "mind his own business." So I could hardly come into Winnipeg and hire somebody to run their business for them. It would have been contradictory to my beliefs.

> Of course, I might have to change my position now that it's a public company. But then, I saw myself serving a cross section of farmers in western Canada. Now, as president you are serving a cross-section of shareholders across Canada, and some guy who owns 10,000 UGG shares in Toronto isn't going to be pleased with the same sort of decision as some guy who owns two shares in Rosetown, Saskatchewan.

Through the 1960s, Mac repeatedly used the phrase "mind your own business" in his speeches in a rhetorical way to tell farmers that "their business" went beyond the farm gate. He believed that the Wheat Board marketing system, which shielded farmers from the price fluctuations of the open market, had rendered them too complacent and uninformed about what happened to their grain after they delivered it to the local elevator, and it was time they understood grain marketing and transportation right through to the final customer.

The image of himself primarily as the manager of a business owned and controlled by farmer shareholders was intimately related to an underlying UGG philosophy that gave the company a unique position and role in both the grain industry and in western Canadian agriculture, in general. UGG was, of course, a cooperative – indeed, the oldest farm cooperative in the west – and had itself grown straight out of the "farm movement." But at the same time it never embraced what Ian MacPherson called the "utopian" strain of cooperativism, which strove for "a complete reformation of society." UGG supporters came from among MacPherson's "pragmatists,"[3] whose major goal was to allow farmers to control the organizations that provided service to them, and to have profits flow to them, rather than to corporate shareholders.

This pragmatic cooperativism was where the movement began in western Canada. In fact, probably the most important issue for farm organizations and the grain co-ops in the west was the question of who was to control the institutions that served farmers, and ultimately, who was to control farmers' livelihood. However, during the 1920s, many grain farmers adopted a much more radical stance and, as Vernon Fowke put it in his classic study, *National Policy and the Wheat Economy*, they came to hold "a belief – diametrically opposed to the free market tenets underlying the national policy – that the open market or competitive system, the system of freely moving prices, ought not to govern the marketing of western grain."[4] This view was predominant within the three provincial Wheat Pools when they came into existence in 1923 and 1924.

The distrust of the "competitive system" applied not only in grain marketing. The passionate attachment of prairie farmers to the Crow's Nest Pass Rates[5] grew not only out of a justifiable concern about railway market power, but also from a belief in regulatory, rather than market-driven, mechanisms for establishing prices.

This rejection of the marketplace was accompanied by an adoption of some of the more utopian and idealistic aspects of cooperative thought: that society could be freed from the base human qualities of greed and self-interest if only economic life were organized on a cooperative, rather than a competitive and individualistic, basis.

As the Pools and their supporters developed and refined their interventionist and anti-market views, this tended to institutionalize the philosophical split between the "right" and the "left"; between farmers who had no quarrel with the market, and those who favoured regulation and centralization as the appropriate ways to manage economic matters. The split was sharply defined by the Pools in the 1920s, and deepened and hardened further with the devastation of the 1930s. For the following thirty years or more, left-wing, interventionist philosophies ruled agricultural policy making in western Canada, but during Mac's presidency their hegemony began to break down, and the status quo began to be questioned.

UGG never subscribed to these radical views. Its philosophy continued to embrace a pragmatic view of cooperativism, and it did not endorse the view of grain marketing that saw the open market as essentially immoral and manipulative. This lack of ideological fervour caused the company to be drummed out of the Cooperative Union of Canada in the 1920s.

A large number of farmers did not subscribe to this radical critique, either. In the early 1930s, when the campaign to create a central marketing agency was in full swing, a number of farmers opposed the concept of "compulsory pooling." A substantial percentage of the individual farmers who appeared before the 1931 Stamp Royal Commission on futures trading disageed with the representatives of the Pools and the farm organizations, and voiced their support for the futures market. After the Wheat Board was formed in 1935, the voice of this component of farm opinion tended to be drowned out, and went largely unheard until the the 1970s, but it never disappeared. Farm opinion was (and remains) deeply divided over marketing and transportation issues.

Rightly understood, therefore, the debate during the 1920s and 1930s over grain marketing in western Canada, which culminated in the formation of the Wheat Pools and the Wheat Board, was more than just a disagreement over how the grain industry was to be owned and managed. Without an appreciation of these splits between pragmatic and idealistic cooperativism, and between pro- and anti-market beliefs, the emotional dimension of the subsequent policy debates cannot be fully understood.

UGG's philosophy gave it a unique position in western agriculture. On the one hand, support for the company tended to come from farmers who saw farming and agriculture primarily as a business, and who wanted economic, not social, goals to be the prime focus of agricultural policy. On the other hand, its status as a co-op and as a farm organization gave it an authoritative voice in policy debates. To some extent, it was the voice of the "right wing" component of farm opinion. But, at the same time, it was on "the left of the right" on many issues, and the company was often said to occupy a kind of middle ground in public debate between the Pools, with their centralist and interventionist economic philosophy, and the private grain trade, which represented a purely laissez faire, open market, view.

UGG's views tended to vary with time and in accordance with the particular issue under debate. When Mac assumed the presidency in 1961, UGG still unswervingly supported the Crow's Nest Pass Rates and, although somewhat less strongly and consistently, also supported the centralized selling methods of The Canadian Wheat Board. The unwavering support for the Crow was historically understandable. In the days prior to long-distance trucking, the railways held a monopoly over transportation of goods in the prairies, and control of monopoly power was and is always necessary. Moreover, railways had been seen by Canadians as instruments of public policy as well as private enterprises. Accordingly, both Crerar and Brownlee had defended the Crow Rates against any and all attacks.

The company's support for centralized selling and the Wheat Board was somewhat less constant. UGG president R.S. Law had opposed the compulsory nature of the legislation in 1935, and had not fully endorsed the Canadian Federation of Agriculture's pro-board position in the 1940s. Later, John Brownlee had given wholehearted support to the Wheat Board, and this undoubtedly reflected the views of UGG members at the time. The Board had been established in the depths of the Depression, when it truly seemed to many that capitalism was doomed. Mac's generation, having weathered the Dirty Thirties and the war, was more of a mind to rebuild their lives than to challenge a marketing system which, by and large, had worked up until the post-war years. However, as piles of unsold grain built up in the early 1950s, and a number of farmers, rightly or wrongly, began to question the wisdom of the anti-market philosophy that by then dominated grain policy, UGG's views began to swing again. Both Mac's and the company's sentiments on these issues underwent profound change over the course of the following two decades, as described in chapters 6 and 7.

As Mac pointed out, over his lifetime he developed a deeper understanding of the terms "left" and "right," and his sympathies leaned increasingly towards a more market-oriented, laissez faire, economic philosophy. At the same time, this inclination was significantly tempered by his compassion for those who had suffered real devastation in the Depression, and by his sympathies for cooperative efforts by farmers. UGG, therefore, provided a comfortable "home" for him and the many farmers who were sympathetic to market solutions to economic problems, but who also believed that farmers should own and control the enterprises that served their needs.

During the early years of Mac's association with the company as director and newly elected president, UGG's views led to accusations that it was "not a true co-op." This was an intensely debated issue in the late 1950s and early 1960s, but the accusations were patently untrue. The basic tenets of cooperativism are spelled out in what are known as the "Rochdale Principles,"[6] which were developed almost as soon as the movement began in 1844, and which were very much the principles on which the company was founded.

Mac said, "The cooperative aspect of UGG appealed to me, and the Rochdale Principles were very important. Really, the Act of Incorporation of United Grain Growers was absolutely based on the Rochdale Principles. They gave us a really good foundation to offset any of the accusations that we were not a real co-op. They couldn't deny that we were based on Rochdale, and often to a greater extent than they were."

A couple of years before he became president, Mac was challenged on this issue at a country meeting. UGG had just bought out another elevator company, Canadian Consolidated, and, as with the purchase of Reliance Grain in the early 1950s, reorganization of the local boards was required.

> I can remember in 1959 when we took over Canadian Consolidated in Balcarres I went there to attend a company meeting. Some farmers came in whom I had known for years, including a man called George Webster. He was the son of one of the pioneers of the district, and I thought, Oh, that is interesting to see George here.

> George was a real leader in the area, and a good talker, and he started in real rough. He said, "You come into this community masquerading as a cooperative, and you're not a cooperative. United Grain Growers is a joint stock company. It's got nothing to do with cooperatives."

> Until he took the floor and started to talk, it never entered my mind that George was there as an opponent. Well, fortunately by that time I was well acquainted with the company's charter, and I knew what was in it, and I could tell George what it said. Well, it really opened his eyes. He didn't know these things about UGG because his former source of information was Sask Pool, and it later dawned on me that Sask Pool may well have sent him out there to shoot me down. George changed his whole attitude towards United Grain Growers in Balcarres after that meeting.

Fighting this kind of innuendo was a constant battle, and a number of the speeches Mac delivered while he was president convey both his own and UGG's concepts of cooperative enterprise, and the rejection of the more idealistic elements which neither he nor the company accepted. In a talk to the eastern division of the company's construction department, Mac told the staff:

> As you know, a co-operative is a group of people working together for a common purpose. Our purpose ... is to enable our members to carry on various economic activities for their own mutual benefit. We consider it our duty to assist them in every way [we can].

> That is not the case with some co-operatives which set themselves broader goals to which we do not subscribe. For example, take Federated Co-operatives Limited [who say it is their fundamental objective] "to establish

> an economic and social order based on the principles and methods of
> true co-operation." ...
>
> I think that explains quite well why we don't share their objectives.[7]

He especially resented the implication that he himself did not understand or appreciate what "real" cooperativism was all about. He felt quite sure that his understanding was in no way deficient.

> Hell, when I was eight, nine, ten years old, Dad was secretary of a local
> co-op of small farmers in Scotland. We had no telephones, and if a railcar
> of coal – we called it a "wagonload" – came in, or a carload of twine
> came in, a message would go up to Dad, and I would relay it for the co-
> op all over the district. So I knew what a co-op was and how people
> could work together, and as far as the essence of a co-op was concerned,
> I had some of that in my blood. It was people getting together to solve
> their problems, exactly as they did when the Grain Growers Grain Com-
> pany got started, and I think that is where my sympathies naturally chan-
> nelled. But my hostilities developed over the people who were trying to
> use this valuable tool, and corrupt it by trying to make it a political tool
> instead of an economic tool.

To some extent, Mac's view conforms to the description of American cooperators as it was developed by economist E.G. Nourse in 1922. The typical American cooperator, he said, was "long on practice and short on theory," and his approach was to take "the essential facts of the market as he finds them, [and] seeks merely to put himself in the most attractive position with reference to it."[8]

The relationship between the cooperative movement and specific political parties has never been clear. Indeed, one of the Rochdale Principles is political neutrality. However, in western Canada at least, the anti-market, pro-regulatory, and interventionist attitudes so strongly entrenched in the pooling movement struck a resonant chord with the left wing of the political spectrum. To many in the grain industry, the relationships between the two were intimate and strong, and to Mac, the partisanship was excessive and at odds with what cooperativism was all about.

> One of the things that grew on me over my years in Canada was that the
> whole co-op movement in the west was an NDP movement – a CCF
> and NDP movement.
>
> I've known cooperators over the years who believe that their co-op was
> there to do business on their behalf and stay out of politics. I can buy that

and I can support that. But when it was so obviously an extension of the socialist structure, I just couldn't buy it.

I remember the head of Sask Pool's field service used to brag that he elected the CCF in Saskatchewan. He was a rabid CCFer and committed to social politics at that time. Sask Pool's view then was very much along these lines and they have never really shrugged it off their shoulders since. Well, that to me is just unacceptable.

I didn't think the future of western agriculture lay in political philosophy; it lay in the introduction of practical procedures to let the industry thrive.

To Mac, this political partisanship was not only contrary to what cooperativism should be, but also contrary to his own early experience: "The last thing that our local co-op in Scotland would ever have thought of was using it as a political tool. They came together purely and simply to serve the necessities of their farm supply situation: fuel, twine, animal feed, and so on. I remember one chap who was blind and he operated a two-acre poultry farm. It was amazing to see him work with his birds. They used to come and sit on his arms - and him a blind man. They were small operators, and it was just an ideal thing because they were able to buy in bulk, and going to the local outlets to buy all their stuff was going to be much more expensive than twenty-two of them getting together and buying it."

He preserved much of the essence of this kind of thinking right through his presidency, and "always thought about United Grain Growers as a farmers' movement that was doing the things a farmer wished to have done to improve his lot, and the essential part of it was the marketing of grain because that improved his lot the most and the soonest. But we also wanted to eliminate as many of the handicaps as possible: the grading, the pricing, the transportation, so we saw it as broader than just a grain handling and marketing business."

He found UGG's cooperative nature guided his decision-making as CEO of the company.

It got me past a lot of predicaments on the management side. Management people would come into my office and say things like, "You know we're having a problem up in the Saskatoon area. So and so is selling fertilizer cheaper than we are, and the guys are having a bad time. What should we do?"

I would just look at them and they'd start to grin because they knew

what my answer would be: "What would be best for farmers?" And lots
of times they would say, "But it is going to cost the company money."

Well, whose company is it? It's the farmers' company, and if it loses a little
bit of profit because it's to the benefit of farmers, surely there is nothing
too far wrong with that.

But you can't push this approach too far, because there is a legal responsibility on a director of a corporation to judiciously administer the assets
of that corporation, and if he starts giving them away to the shareholder-
customers, he is in trouble just as much as if he stole it himself. So you
had to watch it, but I was always prepared to give away a little bit on the
bottom of the balance sheet if I knew the direct benefit went into the
hands of farmers.

If the shareholders of United Grain Growers had not been farmers, I
might have had to take a different look at it, and that makes me wonder
a little bit about the company as it is today, compared with it as it was
then.

So Mac's self-image of "managing UGG," and his comfort with being
both CEO and president, conformed to his view of the proper role of the
cooperative movement in general, and the company in particular, as being
primarily engaged in business on behalf of its members, rather than pursuing broader social or political goals.

Whatever doubt some parties may have held about Mac's or UGG's
commitment to cooperative ideals, they were not shared by the Manitoba
government. In 1990, Mac was given the Distinguished Cooperator Award
for the year by then-Minister of Cooperative, Consumer and Corporate
Affairs Ed Connery. The letter advising him of the appointment said he
had been recognized as one of "a select group of individuals" who "through
dedication and perseverance have made things happen the cooperative way,"
and who were being recognized for their "contribution to the development of cooperative enterprise in Manitoba."[9]

As a farm organization, of course, UGG also had a responsibility to
participate in farm policy debates and to carry the views of its members
and supporters forward in forums where these matters were addressed.
However, not all of policy work Mac was called on to do was to his liking.
"There was," he said, "the other side of UGG – the farm policy field – and
that to me always had an aura of a 'never-never land' out there, because so

much of the conventional wisdom was garbage, just farm organization jar-
gon."

This comment very much surprised me because of the prominent leadership role he took in resolving a number of exceedingly difficult policy
issues. As we talked, however, I found that it was not so much policy work
itself he found so disagreeable, as the farm organization world within which
so much policy discussion took place. He found this world frustrating for
two reasons. First, it is very ideological – in the worst sense of the word,
meaning that facts often carry less weight than belief and presupposition.
Second, it is a highly political world – again in the worst kind of way, where
intrigue, self-interest, and power often play a more important role than
reasoned debate.

It was, however, a world where Mac's predecessor trod boldly. John
Brownlee had been active in farm organizations early in his career, and he
continued that activity when he became president of UGG. He loved to
debate, and he was good at it. But he did it to a fault. Mac recalled one
occasion when "at a Western Agricultural Conference here in Winnipeg,
the general manager of the United Farmers of Alberta, Wilf Hoppins, came
to me and said, 'Mac, isn't there something you people can do to stop John
Brownlee from running into a stone wall the way he did today? He stood
up there and he was just wasting his time and effort and undermining his
prestige, because he was not going to carry his point.'

"And those words stuck in my mind because John Brownlee was doing
it because he thought it was his duty. It was company policy and he believed in it and he felt an obligation to get up and debate it, but he might
just as well have been sitting down."

Mac was disinclined to follow Mr. Brownlee's example, but it bothered
him and he felt somewhat guilty about it:

> It may have been a cowardly thing to do, but I know there were times
> when I sat and listened to a discussion and knew the outcome was preor-
> dained and I would just say to myself, I'm not going to get up and talk on
> that subject.

> In fact, farm policy and farm organization work wasn't well served by
> me, even when I was a director of the Canadian Federation of Agricul-
> ture, because I could not stand up and say some of the things you were
> supposed to say. That was an area that really bothered me. I would see
> representatives of other organizations get up and make a "spiel" and I
> would be sitting there and I wouldn't have said anything. And I used to

think, Well now, am I doing my job by not getting up and speaking on this subject?

Mac tends to judge himself too harshly. The fact is that he believed the Canadian Federation of Agriculture (CFA) should be a forum for informed debate on agricultural policy issues, and for developing compromise positions which would benefit all farmers in all areas of the country. It would be as accurate to say that he was less accepting than Mr. Brownlee had been of the insincerity and the posturing, and often found himself upset by the positions that were taken to protect regional interests.

> On some things – for example, Feed Freight Assistance[10] or the movement of grain to eastern Canada – there was always the process of central Canada flexing its muscles and elbowing the west out. And there was always an element of bias and "one-sidedness" in the speeches. Somebody would get up and make a speech in favour of something, and I had to feel that I knew darn well that wasn't the case. And someone would get up and make a speech against it, and I would still have the feeling, well, you know that's not the case, either. They were both talking about an important issue, but sometimes they ignored the facts. They were always talking in terms of the current political thinking or belief on the subject and that used to drive me wacky.

> I read a piece in the paper the other day where Newfoundland is seeking further Feed Freight Assistance so it can be competitive with other provinces in raising poultry. Well, I have the greatest sympathy in the world for the people of Newfoundland who have always had tough times, and I know that they need business, they need work, they need jobs, and so on. But I just can't believe that hauling barley to Newfoundland from Manitoba is the way to remedy their problems. Transporting feed from the west to Newfoundland in order to raise poultry in competition with poultry that can be produced economically elsewhere and compete on a world-class basis is not good agricultural policy or good economics at all; it's just poor social policy. And that's the kind of thing we had to live with all the time.

He may also have been more realistic than was John Brownlee about what lay within his power to change, and of the kind of opposition he faced. Mac recalled Dave Kirk, executive secretary of the CFA, saying to him, " 'Never underestimate the power of Sask Pool.' And that power was sort of a basic element in the Canadian agricultural situation. For example, at meetings of the Wheat Board Advisory Committee, I was sitting there looking down the barrel not only at Sask Pool but at three Pool presidents and [National Farmers Union president] Roy Atkinson. I could only score if I had a really good point. If it didn't meet the acceptance of those four, I may as well forget about it. And lots of times, I did. I knew I was just knocking my head against a wall."

He also realized the near impossibility of reaching a national consensus on farm policy, describing it as "one of the ongoing, perpetual frustrations for Canadian politicians, because there isn't, except in very rare cases – and I can't even think of one example, off-hand – a policy which will be accepted from coast to coast, just because of the diverse nature of the country. What is right in one area is not right in another."

The divergent self-interests created by geography and agronomic diversity were, of course, the reason that national agricultural policy debate was characterized as much by power politics as it was by reasoned debate. In January 1966, the UGG board discussed what had transpired at a national conference on international trade organized by the Economic Council of Canada, and Mac reported that "difficulty was encountered in securing agreement that freer trade in agricultural products is very much in the interest of Canadian agriculture ... and should be a major objective of government economic policy. Representatives of the dairy producers in eastern Canada fought hard against the acceptance of that principle."[11]

They were, said he, "protecting supply management and subsidized production, which is perfectly understandable." However, he felt, the incessant protection of self-interest frustrated any real progress, because "if anything that you suggested that would improve agriculture in general was going to weaken the position that they built for themselves over the years, it couldn't go anywhere. If it didn't matter, you could get agreement."

Through the post-war period, the political strength of central Canada increasingly dominated the policy agenda. In April of 1966, reporting on the Canadian Federation of Agriculture's annual presentation to Cabinet, Mac told the UGG board of directors how western representatives felt that the greatest attention had been paid to the dairy section of the brief.[12] "Access to cheap western feed grain," he said, was "a major motivation for eastern interests because the price of feed grain was a big determinant in where livestock and dairy production took place." He explained the impact of this increasing eastern dominance on pork production.

> I don't recall the figures exactly, but at one time, something like thirty-four percent of hogs produced in Canada were produced in Alberta, because you could grow barley like crazy and you just shovelled it out of

the bin and into the hogs and then sent the hogs to market. About eleven percent were produced in Quebec. But over a period of twenty-five to thirty-five years, thirty-four percent of the hogs were produced in Quebec, and in Alberta it went down from thirty-four percent to thirteen percent.

In the Lac St. Jean area of Quebec, they couldn't grow even a fraction of what they needed in feed grain, so they were demanding barley at the same price as their competitors out here on the prairies. And when it came to a show-down vote on the price of feed grain and the accessibility of prairie feed grain, the BC people would swing around and work with eastern Canada. So they could out-vote us.

This was just "self-interest economics," with no spirit of cooperation, when you think about it, but politically, it flew. They knew what they wanted, and they got some pretty darn sweeping legislation in the form of the Feed Freight Assistance Act, and it was they who finally got feed grain on the open market so that they wouldn't have to purchase it from the Wheat Board.

This power of the eastern farm lobby was not only able, at times, to shut out any discussion from the west, but would co-opt western support for its positions. Mac recalled how, at "its annual meetings, CFA would often prevent discussion of resolutions which had come from, say, the annual meeting of the Dairy Farmers of Canada. We were simply bluntly told, 'These resolutions are not for discussion. They're the Dairy Farmers' resolutions which have already been discussed by the dairy farmers, and they are going to go to the government as they are.' So if the west had a viewpoint on it they wanted to express, they had no opportunity to do so. So they were not CFA resolutions, they were Dairy Farmers' resolutions, but they got carried to the government with all the weight of CFA behind them."

Western farmer groups tried to strengthen the western voice through the Western Agricultural Conference (WAC), a coalition of farm organizations centered, for the most part, in the prairies. Eastern groups immediately tried to stifle the WAC's voice:

We felt it a very necessary thing to put together a unified western Canadian opinion which sometimes included, and sometimes did not, the British Columbia Federation of Agriculture, but certainly included Manitoba, Saskatchewan, and Alberta. And once you got the thing hammered out in a meeting in the west, people were pretty well locked into having to support it.

So the CFA mounted an absolute campaign to eliminate the WAC because we had the audacity to put together a western point of view and take it down east and get it through because we had a united western front. It was almost laid on from CFA head office in Ottawa that "We'll dispense with the Western Conference this year; we just won't have one." It was just as simple as that, and there was no doubt about it, the CFA worked very hard with eastern interests to get rid of the WAC.

In eastern Canada, the milk marketing boards administered a supply management system that essentially removed dairy product supply and pricing from the market, and which was highly beneficial for dairy farmers. Of course, the removal of pricing decisions from the market was, as Fowke said, the very thing that many grain farmers wanted. Accordingly, there was a degree of philosophical sympathy between some western interests and CFA, which often undermined any attempt to present a common western front. Looking back, Mac said he felt that:

We should have been able to work with the Pools when there were disagreements between east and west, and get things done, but you always felt you were on thin ice with them. You never knew when they were going to pull the rug on you.

The trouble with them was they were playing a double game so often. They were working with the eastern people, and maybe that is where they purchased some of their influence: "If you support such and such, which will allow us to give Quebec or Ontario or some other area what they want, then we'll see that you get so and so." Well, we never tried to play that game.

I remember in one debate about policy and the CFA, [Saskatchewan Wheat Pool vice-president] Charlie Gibbings, who was the Pool's CFA representative at the time, said, "That is the way Sask Pool wants it, and if it's not going to be that way, we'll play our Quebec card." I forget the exact issue that it was, probably feed grain or Feed Freight Assistance or some such thing.

Not long before I retired, at the CFA annual meeting, Sask Pool voted with Quebec on their issue in order to get Quebec support on some of their stuff. And that just left me appalled.

As a result of the anti-market sympathies of most member organizations of CFA, UGG often found itself having to support positions with which it disagreed: "By the time I got to the meetings, there was often a conflict between what UGG believed and what CFA was saying. We always stayed in CFA because we always believed that if you're in an organization, maybe you can affect its decisions more than if you are outside it."

Mac summed up the frustrations he felt this way:

> My frustration was that here was the national body that should be aspiring to the greatest benefit of Canadian agriculture, and it really never was. It was tearing itself apart and hanging itself up on the politics of Canadian agriculture. That was the problem really - the frustration. I guess a good way to put it is that my desire - and I guess this is innate in me - was to see the greatest good for the greatest number. But that was not the atmosphere in the CFA. It was straight politics, closely related to provincial and federal politics, especially federal politics. On top of that, there was the underlying philosophical positions that created real problems.

> It's different now, but back in those days, you were simply a cooperator or you weren't, you were left wing or you weren't, you were an NDPer or you weren't, and left-wing thinking was dominant and that was the way the world went. Between the politics and the philosophy, the effectiveness of agricultural policy became a secondary consideration.

> However, all these things finally explained to me the meaning of an expression that I didn't understand at one time, that "politics is the art of the possible." At one time, it didn't make any sense to me. Now I know what it means.

Mac was a director of CFA from 1961 to 1968, and he remembers how acutely the frustrations affected him. "The CFA annual meeting was always my terrible experience of the year," he said, "and I used to get ulcers in January about the time of their annual meeting."

Mac altered the way that UGG participated in the CFA and the provincial farm organizations, not only because of the personal distaste he felt for some of its aspects, but for other reasons, as well. First, the demands of managing UGG grew steadily over the time he was president. In particular, trying to renew and rebuild the company's elevator system, and the difficulties this posed with so much uncertainty surrounding the rail system (see Chapter 7), became a major challenge. So Mac felt that, from this perspective alone, he could not do the job justice. Second, he wanted to give other UGG directors more exposure in these national forums, and wanted them to employ and develop their own skills so they could make a larger contribution to the company. Third, he felt uncomfortable, as a Saskatchewan farmer living in Manitoba, taking a prominent role in farm organization and farm policy discussions in Alberta. He felt particularly sensitive about Alberta because Mr. Brownlee had been an Albertan, had kept an office in Alberta, and had been so well known there. It seemed doubly presumptuous for him to try to take over Brownlee's place on the Alberta scene. Accordingly, giving some of the other directors a larger role in the policy field was a logical move.

> I deliberately encouraged Bob Brown, especially in Manitoba, to carry the load on the farm organization front, and nobody could have been better equipped for it because he had been manager of one of the provincial farm organizations, and he knew all the people and he knew all the nuances of the Manitoba situation, which was all new to me. So it was just ideal to have him around.

> Principally because of the success of Bob Brown, but also because of my apprehension about the Alberta situation, I moved in a different direction. There used to be a first vice-president and a second vice-president, but I asked the board to establish three vice-president positions, one in each prairie province, and I asked each provincial vice-president to carry the banner on the provincial farm organizations. Also, if UGG had a delegate to the CFA from the province, that vice-president would serve there too.

> So then I had three vice-presidents, each with a seat on CFA in some capacity or another, and I had the whole farm policy thing out in front of me and could keep on top of what was going on without it being too demanding on my time.

Mac also wanted to make one other significant change in UGG's governance, and so he "initiated and brought to the board the idea of having the Peace River area represented by its own director. Hugh Allen had been a board member from the Peace River area for a long time, and I could see the first time I went up to the Peace, it just wasn't going to jibe to have five directors from southern Alberta and none from the Peace. So we amended the company by-laws to provide for at least one – there could be more, but at least one - to represent the Peace River country."

Curiously, the issue Fred Dickinson had alluded to when he recommended Ortel Hoffas for a directorship in 1955 – the predominantly Anglo-Saxon composition of the board – came into play when Hugh Allen retired. There were two candidates for Hugh Allen's position, and they were "just like that," Mac said, holding his two hands at the same level. In the end, the selection committee recommended that position be given to a man who was not of Anglo-Saxon background precisely in order to broaden the cultural mix within the board: an example of "affirmative action" as it was intended to be, influencing a selection only when it lies between two candidates with precisely equal qualifications.

The three vice-president positions were established in 1966, and by this time, the major items on Mac's agenda for UGG were either completed or well under way. Also by this point, his leadership abilities were becoming more widely appreciated, both inside and outside the grain industry, as in 1967 he was asked to join the Great West Life board. He therefore found himself being called upon to take a role in a number of areas where change was occurring in the grain industry, and the scope of his activities expanded from UGG to the grain industry at large. It is to this broader role that we now turn in the next two chapters.

The Industry Leader: 1965 – 1975

6

When I first became involved in the grain industry in 1970, Mac was already acknowledged as an outstanding leader in both agriculture and in the Canadian business world. By that time, he was president of the Rapeseed Association of Canada, chairman of the Canada Grains Council, an honourary life member of the Agricultural Institute of Canada, and a member of the boards of directors of Great West Life and Canadian Pacific Limited. More significantly, he was also acknowledged, to use the words of one senior grain industry official, to stand "head and shoulders above his peers."

However, Mac's leadership had an unpretentious and self-effacing quality. The diffidence with which he accepted the presidency of UGG – feeling that he was "not going to show the world how to run a grain company" – he also carried into the industry at large. He had neither a burning goal he wished to see implemented, nor an overarching vision for the grain business. Nor did he seek the limelight as a great leader. He was, as he said, content to do whatever was at hand to the best of his ability.

During our interviews, Mac and I spoke several times about the leadership role he had played in the industry. Although it was clear he had spent some time thinking about it, he was also rather self-conscious talking about it. He somewhat paradoxically summed up our discussion this way: "I never aspired to be a great leader, but I always tried to be a good follower. In other words, I never felt, I'm the dominant person and I'm showing them how to do it. But if a good cause came along that I could believe in, then I was willing to help the thing along. If I have a quality of what some people would call leadership, it's a desire – and perhaps I have some ability – to nudge a process in the right direction. But I am not good at debating things in glowing terms on the floor of a meeting."

In contrast to Mr. Brownlee, Mac spoke sparingly at meetings, but perhaps the quality of his contributions was the better for his reticence. He recalled former Manitoba Pool president Jim Deveson's saying, "Well, that's settled it. Runciman has spoken."

His presidency of the Rapeseed Association of Canada (RAC) and his chairmanship of the Canada Grains Council illustrate both his leadership style and the way he earned the high regard in which he came to be held. However, the two experiences differed sharply for Mac himself. "I suppose," he said, "looking at things in retrospect, the greatest satisfaction - apart from any progress the company may have made - the greatest sort of development from the point of view of agriculture per se, would have to be the Rapeseed Association, which is now the Canola Council, and the greatest disappointment would have to be the Canada Grains Council."

The sharp contrast between Mac's experience with these two groups can be traced in part to the kind of changes that took place in farm opinion over the 1960s and 1970s.

Both the RAC and the Grains Council came into existence as a fundamental change was taking place in the thinking and attitudes of western farmers - a change which is still going on today, and which will likely alter the structure of the Canadian grain industry out of recognition. This shift in farm opinion involved the steady erosion of the relatively uncritical support for The Canadian Wheat Board and centralized marketing – support that had existed since the 1930s – and the corresponding increase in the number of farmers who wished to see a more market-oriented agricultural industry. Mac sensed the shift, and he began to give voice to what farmers were thinking, both in his speeches and in his reports to the UGG board.

It was not an unnatural shift for either him or UGG to take, because both held to a classic liberalism, favouring laissez faire and commercial freedom. In 1966, Mac delivered a talk to a local farm group in Carman, Manitoba, the Dufferin Agricultural Society, in which he expressed this philosophy:"Now one cannot define the farm problem and omit reference to freedom. ...

"I think the criterion for choosing between farm policy A and farm policy B should not simply be how much income each will generate. It is this plus the question of which allows the most individual freedom."[1]

In this talk, he was articulating a view he had held since he had begun farming as a young man in the 1930s. When we talked about that earlier period of his life, I sensed that he had been uncomfortable with the concept of centralized selling, and asked him about the reasons behind his objections. Was it the compulsory nature of Wheat Board marketing, or was it simply that he did not believe a central seller could dictate price?

"I wasn't really thinking about it in depth in those days at all," he replied. "I didn't really know enough about the background to make those kinds of judgements, nor did I have enough knowledge of economics or finance to provide any base for a decision. It was just sort of a basic instinct that I didn't want a central agency telling me what I was going to grow and how I was going to grow it and when I was going to sell it."

Despite these sentiments, he was quite supportive of the Wheat Board in the mid-1960s. This support was consistent with the position UGG had taken during Mr. Brownlee's tenure, and reflected the views of farmers as they existed when Mac took over the presidency. In January 1967, in a speech to the Ontario Soil and Crop Improvement Association, Mac reconciled his beliefs on individual freedom with the controls inherent in centralized marketing. He told them that "the farm policies the successful western Canadian farmer is looking for are ... policies that do not interfere with his decision-making rights. Sometimes, I admit, as [in] the case of the Canadian Wheat Board, he is willing to forego those rights since the price obtained through the bargaining power of the Wheat Board gives him more income stability. Most of the time, as is the case with the government-free beef and hog industries, he prefers to make his own marketing decisions."[2]

From the late 1960s on, he began to temper these views as he encountered a steady escalation in the criticism of Wheat Board marketing, and found farmers increasingly uncomfortable with the way this system affected their operations. In January 1969, he reported to the UGG board on a visit he had had from representatives of the Carman District Farm Business Council. "Their concern," he wrote, "centred around their need for markets" for feed grain. They could produce barley for eighty cents to eighty-five cents per bushel but could not sell it because "they have no access to markets." He went on to say that "more and more examples of this type of thinking are coming forward across the west. Originating as they do with progressive commercial farmers they must raise serious concern in the minds of those seeking to develop or influence grain marketing policies in Canada."[3]

In July 1969, he devoted a lengthy section of his report to the board to agricultural policy issues, and expressed his concern about where the increasing levels of dissatisfaction might lead:

If my interpretation of the present attitude of farmers is correct, they are ready to modify traditional concepts of government subsidies as the solution for farm income deficiencies. However, they deserve and expect acceptable alternatives. They appear ready to look to volume rather than price for income even though the realized income level may be unsatisfactory.

At the same time, farmers are developing a feeling that present grain marketing procedures are barring the way to high sales volume. ...

Although there appears to be increasing doubt in the minds of farmers as to the effectiveness of the Canadian Wheat Board as a marketing agency, it would be a disaster to see changes made in the marketing system which were rendered completely ineffective by the subsequent course of events. Chaos and confusion might result from which no valid conclusions could be drawn.[4]

In July 1971, he returned from a series of his regional board meetings through Manitoba and Saskatchewan with further evidence of farmers' growing discontent. He described "repeated expressions of a desire for more producer influence on The Canadian Wheat Board policies. Without outright criticism of the Board, questions about pricing policies, ways of shipping feed grains to compete with U.S. corn and the marketing procedures of the Board revealed a desire to assess the effectiveness of current Board marketing procedures."[5]

In Mac's view, the seeds of dissatisfaction with the status quo were sown in the 1950s by the backlog of grain on farms, and possibly even earlier by the British Wheat Agreement. Although the Wheat Board had opposed this Agreement, it was still the kind of arrangement the Pools and most of the farm organizations had espoused in the 1920s and 1930s in their support for a central desk selling system, bypassing the futures market and cutting out the middleman. That Agreement, however, had not turned out well for farmers.

This was followed by the restricted grain movement and high carryover stocks in the 1950s that caused Mac so much grief on his own farm. And this, he said, marked the point at which criticisms started to emerge and "there began to be a realization that we had to do something, (a) about markets and (b) about transportation." These difficult circumstances arose under the Wheat Board, whose operation was supposed to bring "orderly marketing." Although this concept was, as Vernon Fowke put it, "one of the most elusive and difficult of definitions to be encountered in a study of cooperative marketing,"[6] it nevertheless implied a steady movement of grain into the world market at the favourable prices a single desk seller could extract from buyers. For the farmer who was forced to wait until January before he could sell any wheat, it seemed – rightly or wrongly – that the system was not delivering what was promised.

The early criticisms were not sophisticated because farmers were not knowledgeable about world markets or even about how Canada's grain marketing system worked. They had not been required to learn very much about the grain market because they were largely shielded from its daily operation by the pooling system of the Board. According to Mac:

> Once a farmer hauled his grain into the elevator he figured he had done his job and it was somebody else's business from there on. As long as the Wheat Board and the Wheat Pool was looking after your interests, you were well served.

> I would never say that the Board or the Pools tried to deceive farmers about this, or consciously wanted to bring farmers under their control, but I think the very reliance they were encouraged to put on the Board and Pools stopped them from thinking for themselves.

> Once I got coming to Winnipeg for UGG board meetings, I began to get a view of the bigger picture, and I used to tell them, "If you want my opinion on these problems we have, it's that farmers should mind their own business." And when you tell an audience that farmers should mind their own business, it takes a little while for it to dawn on them what you are saying.

That farmers should take an interest in grain marketing and transportation beyond their own farm gate, and should have a voice in governing the industry that served them, was a fundamental article of belief for Mac.

> It bothers me to try to think about myself in analytical terms, but if I had a philosophy, it is that the guy out there on the farm who puts his life and his bucks into farming should make the decisions. And he has got to make them in an intelligent way. You can't have every impulsive farmer going off this way and that, but he should have an absolute controlling input into how his business is handled. It shouldn't be a bunch of guys sitting in offices in Ottawa, with indexed pensions and all the rest of it, running his business for him. And the like of the barley growers, and all the commodity groups – the flax growers and all the rest of them – they were starting to expound the needs of their particular industry.

The high stocks of the 1950s were dispersed by the first large sales to the communist countries in the early 1960s, only to reappear later in the decade. As carryovers grew, and the tight delivery quota situation of the 1950s repeated itself, the voices of criticism rose again.

As we will see again in Chapter 7, Mac recalls farmers generally blaming the high stocks on a shortage of railway boxcars. However, as some of them began to ask what went on beyond the local elevator, they found it was not boxcars that were lacking but sales. When they asked why sales were not being made, they came up against marketing policies.

As farmers showed an increasing tendency to "mind their own business" (in the sense Mac had intended it), UGG responded publicly with some answers to their questions. Not all the answers were complimentary to the status quo. Some of Mac's speeches took aim at governments that set marketing policy. For example, in a set of speaking notes entitled "Government Support of Wheat Prices," dated September 1967, he said that "Wheat prices have political overtones," and that this influences the CWB to retain high prices, which in turn result in lost sales. Wheat, he suggested, was unlike other commodities in this respect. "Are beef price fluctuations a regular subject of debate in Parliament?" he asked. "No!"[7]

In March of the following year, he gave a long talk to a Regina Chamber of Commerce Farm Forum on "What's Wrong With Canadian Wheat Markets?" His answer was that prices were not sufficiently responsive to market conditions: "The Canadian Wheat Board's price must bear a relationship to [the price on the Chicago Board of Trade] or Canada will not sell wheat."

"Unless Canada has a unique quality or quantity of wheat, we cannot sell wheat above what buyers think it is worth."[8]

In the view of some exporters, he went on, "The Wheat Board is not as elastic or flexible in its price policies as it could be simply because it is responsible to Parliament."[9] In other words, large carryovers and low grain movement arose more from marketing policies than from a lack of boxcars.

In this same speech, he also tried to dispel some of the old myths from the 1920s and 1930s about grain exchanges being dens of iniquity. An exchange, he said, "is simply a place where, in effect, *buyers and sellers from around the world meet to discover prices.* [It] is a place where sellers of wheat discover the price at which wheat will change hands. ...

"As an Abernethy farmer, I can make judgements about whether this is a destructive or constructive way to establish world prices for wheat. But a Grain Exchange does not do so. It does not make judgements. *It only serves as a meeting place where buyers and sellers meet, and where opposing forces of buyers and sellers discover prices.* "[10]

In 1969, the Palliser Wheat Growers Association (now the Western Canadian Wheat Growers Association) was formed. This was (and remains) a voluntary farm organization whose members were business-minded farmers, and whose philosophy was decidedly right wing. They wanted western agriculture to be run on a commercial basis, and were severely critical of the heavy regulation and centralization in the grain industry.

Palliser members began showing up in Winnipeg and Ottawa, asking questions about sales policies and the allocation of shipping orders and railway boxcars. To some, their aggressive search for information invited comparisons with the Territorial Grain Growers and early farm leader Ed Partridge's trips to Winnipeg in the early 1900s to find out how the Winnipeg Grain Exchange worked.

The formation of Palliser, visits from groups like the Carman District Farm Business Council, and, most importantly, discussions with UGG's own local boards, caused Mac to state more than once: "Are we perhaps on the threshold of a new era. An era when some farmers, instead of saying 'help me with production controls, marketing controls, subsidies and so on,' will be saying 'show me markets, take off the controls, and let me show you that I can manage and produce and make a profit with the best of them, no matter where they farm.'

"Now, I believe this may be overstating the thing a bit, but I am firmly convinced from my own experience that we have such farmers in our midst. And it will be a sad day if future agriculture policy in this country frustrates them rather than assisting them – strangles them rather than helping them."[11]

Such sentiments were not welcome to those who supported the status quo. It was unthinkable that the Wheat Board, which most farmers believed was "their" marketing agency and was there to serve their needs, should, in some way, actually inhibit access to market. However, as they learned more about the marketing system, they began to find that the CWB was less accountable to farmers than they had thought. In another talk to the Dufferin Agricultural Society in 1970, Mac told them just how the CWB's legislation was framed and what it said.

> The Canadian Wheat Board is responsible *to* a federal Minister *for* selling grain in the interests of producers. Responsible *to* the Minister *for* selling *your* grain. And the Minister is responsible to *Parliament* to see that this function is carried out.

The Wheat Board is a government agency not a producer-owned and controlled marketing board. True, it is financed completely by farmers but is not accountable to farmers. Both [Manitoba Pool president] George Turner and myself are presidents of farmer-owned companies and both can be voted out, or our operations questioned and we can be instructed to do this or that if the members so desire. We are obligated to explain, also, why and how we do such-and-such a thing in such-and-such way.

This, of course, makes it difficult to correspond with the Wheat Board. Who do you approach?[12]

A few weeks later, at a University of Alberta Seminar, he asked a similar question: "How do farmers formally enter into discussions with the Canadian Wheat Board? And the answer, I am afraid, is that there is no way legally unless it is through your member of parliament."[13]

Farmers had trouble communicating with more than the Wheat Board. In fact, the openness with which farmers' inquiries were met by the grain trade became a real issue in this period. Many of them thought they were not getting straight answers to their questions, and to some of them, the trade seemed to behave as if farmers had no business asking about their operations. But, rightly or wrongly, the Wheat Board was seen as being the least cooperative. Mac commented on this in January 1971 when he reported to the UGG board on his participation, along with a Wheat Board commissioner and two other grain company presidents, on a radio phone-in show. "In spite of some misgivings," he wrote, "the hour passed quickly and easily with almost all the telephone questions being directed at [the Wheat Board commissioner]. I think that reflects the desire of farmers for information from the Canadian Wheat Board about its operations. It also demonstrates, I think, the soundness of the new Board policy of responding to this demand by raising slightly the traditional veil of secrecy which formerly masked so many of its moves."[14]

By 1970 Mac began to call boldly for a change in marketing policy, saying that the Wheat Board had to be more responsive to the marketplace, and less concerned about holding out for the highest prices.

I believe the Wheat Board should have the freedom to sell wheat in volumes which will allow it to command 25 per cent of the world's export trade.

But I do not think its job should be to sell wheat at so high a price [that] it gives a wheat grower enough income to meet the extra cost of inflation plus tariffs.

It is not the Wheat Board's job to meet the price of inflation. And it isn't the Wheat Board's job to provide enough income to meet the cost of domestic tariffs. The Wheat Board's job is not to solve inflation or tariff problems.

[Wheat Board commissioner] Mr. Gibbings is doing the job we want him to when he sells grain. Since he sells grain on world markets he must move it at a price which will allow him to undersell somebody else. ...

It is the job of the Canadian Wheat Board to sell grain at the highest possible world price they can get - but sell it unhindered.[15]

This was not advice that either the government or The Canadian Wheat Board was initially inclined to heed. Both Canada and the United States thought price-cutting to clear stocks would run counter to farmers' interests (see previous chapter). But while politicians, trade officials, and policy analysts debated the issue, and the glut of the late 1960s grew, farmers were faced with the reality of full bins and restricted cash flows. In response, they began to seek other options to dispose of grain. This brought them up against another regulatory restriction.

Until the early 1970s, the CWB not only exercised a complete monopoly over exports of western wheat, oats, and barley, but also marketed these crops domestically. Farmers had always been able to sell grain to their neighbours, but the moment they tried to take it across a provincial boundary, it fell under the board's jurisdiction.

The most significant interprovincial trade was the movement from the prairies to mills and feed grain buyers in eastern Canada, and since the CWB's mandate was to market prairie grain, it made some sense that it should sell western grain to eastern buyers. However, the Board's legislation also brought grain moving between Manitoba, Saskatchewan, and Alberta under its control. This restriction may have made sense in 1935 when the CWB was first created. Most farms then were a half section or less in size, and farmers rarely moved their own grain more than seven or eight miles to the local country elevator. But taking grain across a provincial border was legal only if farmers intended to deliver to the Wheat Board at an elevator in the next province.

The obvious buyer for surplus grain in the prairies was the livestock industry, and as grain farmers began looking farther afield than their local community, they often found willing buyers in the next province. In seeking to make these sales, they were not interested in challenging the CWB's control of sales to eastern Canada; all they wanted was to sell within what is called the "designated area," which is largely the grain-growing area of the three prairie provinces. But when they did so, they found that it was illegal, and that they were restricted to feed customers in their own province.

In 1970, Mac appeared before the House of Commons Standing Committee on Agriculture, and, in his own non-confrontational way, raised the issue publicly. "I got that in at that Standing Committee on Agriculture, and without arguing for it or trying to make an issue out of it, I planted the seeds in the minds of the whole committee: Why the hell do we have this restriction? These committee meetings were a good opportunity for that sort of thing."

He was immediately attacked by the National Farmers Union (NFU). A few weeks later, he spoke about the incident to a University of Alberta seminar. Referring rather caustically to "the man who can't bring himself to consider the facts before taking a stand," he said:

I was the intended victim last week - via that, I suppose necessary disease carrier of the day, the public relations press release. The attack came from the vice-president of another farm organization, who by cleverly disregarding what he knew I had actually said, tried to make it appear I suggested removing all interprovincial barriers to the movement of grain in Canada. The author of the press release thereby tried to show this would destroy our orderly method of grain marketing and this gave him an opportunity to show himself as more warmly and worthily concerned about grain marketing than anyone else.

What I actually said was in reply to a House of Commons Standing Committee on Agriculture's question ... I had the audacity, some people would call it, to ask "why" grain isn't allowed to flow freely in the designated area.[16]

Although the restriction was becoming increasingly unworkable, the NFU's reaction was typical of those who were uncritically supportive of the Board's powers. "I can recall [Sask Pool vice-president] Charlie Gibbings saying that it would be the end of the Board if that regulation were ever relaxed," said Mac.

Mac actually did have an answer to the question he raised in front of the House of Commons agriculture committee, but it was not a very satisfying one. He told the University of Alberta seminar that he had "asked a number of people in the Wheat Board [why this regulation exists] and nobody could answer me. Finally the solicitor to the Wheat Board advised me it was to drive all grain into the Wheat Board's hands. I didn't ask 'why' again, I just gave up."[17]

The feed grain marketing issue did not remain confined to the prairie area, but expanded to national proportions because of its impact in Quebec and Ontario. As stocks grew on prairie farms, prices hit disastrous levels. Barley traded in the prairies at three bushels to the dollar, while the same grain was sold by the CWB to Quebec and Ontario farmers at two and three times that price. Eastern farmers saw themselves as being held to ransom, and the issue became one of the most bitter and divisive in Canadian agricultural policy debates.

As so often happens when government intervenes in the marketplace, off-setting and contrary government policies had developed. Whereas the CWB artificially held up the price of Canadian feed grains in the east, freight subsidies, through the Feed Freight Assistance program, were designed to bring them back down again.

At the height of the debate, Mac delivered a talk to the Barley and Oilseeds Conference in Winnipeg, which outlined where he and UGG stood on the issue. "To my mind, he said, "there are really only two ways to get equitable pricing.

"The alternatives are either total Wheat Board control or no Wheat Board control over domestic feed grains."[18]

Total control, he pointed out, had been suggested by the National Farmers Union, and would involve "prohibition of farm-to-farm sales and farm-to-feed mill sales within the prairies except on the basis of Wheat Board prices." UGG opposed this completely. "The trouble is that, even if such complete Board control were desirable [it] would simply not be enforceable."[19] After an acrimonious fight - much of which was carried on in the national farm organization forums Mac found so disagreeable - control of domestic feed grain marketing was taken away from the CWB, and turned over to the private trade.

The restrictions on farmers' ability to truck their grain across the prairie provincial boundaries disappeared and in 1974, looking back on the debate, Mac was blunt about the regulation as it had existed: "One move – that of removing the Saskatchewan boundary restrictions – has caused no problems whatsoever. This was always a bad regulation – with no purpose, except apparently to drive grain into the Wheat Board['s] hands (except that the Board couldn't accept it when so driven). It was a nonsense regulation that tended to create instability in livestock areas, depress off-board prices in surplus areas due to lack of competition, and make law-breakers of a good number of people who couldn't see any sense in the regulation.[20]

The importance of decreasing regulation, and of having prices and selling policies driven by market forces rather than by politics, were constant themes in Mac's public statements over the last decade of his presidency. At a Rapeseed Marketing seminar in Winnipeg in January 1972, he said:

> Prairie farmers have learned the hard way these past few years that they ... must not leave the marketing of their crops to the government or to the rest of the industry.

> They have learned the hard way that too much government control of their business means eventually their business will be run in the interests of the other 93 per cent of the voters rather than themselves.

> They have learned the hard way that too much dependence on government-run programs means that, in an urban and eastern Canadian dominated society, it is unwise to sit like ducks on a slough, and wait to be blown out of the water when a particular farm program budget gets slashed.

> They have learned the hard way that the more people depend on political activity for their prosperity, the more they give up their individual freedoms. ...

> And they have learned the hard way that politicians have no knowledge of market forces and how they work, and no farm policy is worth the paper it is written on unless market forces are properly considered.[21]

The feed grains policy was the first major policy decision taken in the western grain industry to reverse the trend towards centralization, regulation, and intervention that had begun in the 1920s. It was to be an additional fourteen years before the next major step occurred in the form of the repeal of Crow's Nest Pass Rates in 1984. But the shift in farm thinking was well underway by 1970, when Mac told a University of Alberta seminar that "discussion about the merits of the Wheat Board method of marketing is going to continue to increase in tempo, and I suspect the camps are going to get more divided as time goes on."[22] He could scarcely have known just how prescient this remark was to be, nor how long, bitter, and increasingly divided the debate was to become.

It was against this background that both the Rapeseed Association of Canada (RAC) and the Canada Grains Council came into existence. However, the experience of the two organizations, not only for Mac, but for the whole of the grain industry, could scarcely have been more different. The story of the RAC was the story of the future direction the grain industry was taking: towards diversification, away from regulation and centralized control, and into a more commercial environment.

The story of the Grains Council, on the other hand, looked backwards. Its every move seemed to heighten the growing tension between farmers who were increasingly frustrated by the status quo, and the CWB and its supporters, who would hear no criticism of either the Board or the highly regulated control of transportation and handling.

The Rapeseed Association of Canada, now the Canola Council of Canada,[23] was started in 1967, six years after Mac became president of UGG. It is to Jim McAnsh, a grain industry retiree who had begun his career in the 1920s as a journalist for the *Manitoba Free Press*, that the greatest credit is due for the formation of the association. It started at an annual grain industry conference whose locale alternated annually between Winnipeg and Minneapolis. Mac said the idea "grew out of Jim's participation in the 1966 Barley and Oilseeds Conference in Minneapolis, where he got them to pass a resolution that rapeseed needed some specific assistance and should have an agency of its own."

A subsequent conference was held on March 14 and 15, 1967, in Winnipeg, to discuss the practicality of the project and to take the first steps towards realization. The concept had an avid supporter in Mac, who chaired the March meeting. In his opening remarks, he outlined the importance and the challenges of rapeseed. "For the producer in 1966," he said, "[rapeseed] meant a farm income of 50 million dollars from 1.4 million acres of crop land. If we produced 4 times last year's yield, it would mean 200 million dollars of earnings to farmers and the country.

"You gentlemen, better than I, know that a growth potential such as that can only be realized if we attain [certain specific] objectives."[24]

He went on to enumerate these objectives: improve the quality of rapeseed meal, and both the quality and yield of oil; improve the agronomics of rapeseed; educate farmers about the futures market; and increase sales domestically and abroad.

Mac reported to the UGG board on April 19, 1967, that, although some of the organizers had feared the conference would fall flat for lack of interest, more than 180 delegates had registered at the March meeting, representing industry participants from all parts of the country, including farmers, crushers, and food manufacturers. The formation of an organization to promote the use of rapeseed was agreed to, and a provisional board selected. A meeting was slated for April 27 to hand over the duties to a permanent board. Mac was clearly eager that UGG should continue to participate in the proposed organization, and he was able to secure the approval of his fellow directors for the company to stay involved.

In July, he reported on the April meeting and apprised the board that he had been selected as the first president of the new organization. Five standing committees had been formed: the executive; and four working committees on finance, trade development, traffic and tariffs, and research.

What to name the organization became one of the first items of business. Four names had been suggested in the application for a charter, two of which used the word "council," and two, the word "institute." A letter the new board received from the government might be a classic example of the regulatory tendency to split hairs. The word "council," it said, "would appear to have an official connotation," which "might lead the public to believe that the corporation incorporated under such a name is a crown agency." This, it said, was against policy. "Institute," on the other hand, "is restricted to societies or organizations instituted to promote literature, science, art, education or the like." Ottawa "subsequently advised that Rapeseed Association of Canada would be acceptable" and so it became.[25] "What I get a kick out of," Mac said later, "is that, after originally being rejected, today it is the Canola Council."

As of July 19, 1967, the membership in the RAC stood at forty-two individuals and organizations, and Mac reported that "A strong drive for additional members, with special attention to the enrollment of rapeseed growers, was planned."[26] Grower participation was particularly crucial as far as he and Jim McAnsh were concerned: "If you go back to the minutes of the Rapeseed Association in the early days, we harped and harped on the issue: How can you get the growers to come in and realize that this organization is intended for their benefit and the benefit of their industry?"

It was two years before this dream came to fruition, at a meeting of farmers in Tisdale, Saskatchewan. This meeting, Mac recalled, "was the turning point" for farmer involvement. He did not attend the meeting, but Jim McAnsh (who by this time was the executive director of the RAC) did, and he wrote to Mac that "the second half of my trip, Winnipeg and west, was quite a contrast and a great relief after the frustrations of the Ottawa Agricultural Congress. The highlight was the meeting of rapeseed growers at Tisdale where close to 300 farmers were enthusiastic enough to launch a Saskatchewan Rapeseed Growers Association and then we had another good meeting at Melfort on the next night."[27]

Manitoba soon followed suit. Through a series of meetings held at the University of Manitoba, and at Dauphin, Brandon, and Swan River, a group of farmers had been nominated to an organizing committee of the Rapeseed Growers Association of Manitoba. This association was to be similar to the Saskatchewan organization.

Mac's concern for gaining farmer members grew straight out of his early experience with the local cooperative in Scotland, his interest in the pioneers of UGG, and his philosophy that farmers must have "an absolute controlling input" into the businesses that served them. "What would be best for farmers?" he used to ask UGG management, and, reflecting back on the Rapeseed Association, it is apparent that this view informed his activities outside as well as inside the company.

The Rapeseed Association took up a good deal of Mac's attention during the four years he served as its president, and the work began immediately. The executive met in Vancouver in July of 1967 and set an ambitious program of action: publishing a brochure describing the Association; initiating research to evaluate rapeseed meal; establishing a committee of technical advisors on industry problems; forming a subcommittee to examine herbicides, pesticides, handling and cleaning of rapeseed, and similar problems; lobbying for the elimination of federal excise tax on margarine; and selecting delegates to two upcoming conferences on rapeseed.

Very few of the president's reports over the following years failed to contain at least one reference to the activities of the Association. Many of these were quite lengthy, as Mac described how the RAC was implementing the objectives laid out at the founding meeting. Perhaps some of its most intense efforts were directed towards market development. Between 1968 and 1971, Mac's reports recorded, among other things, missions to Japan and Taiwan, promotion of rapeseed meal in livestock feeds, hosting trade missions and other delegations from the UK and Japan, a gift of rapeseed to Peru to promote its use, and preparation of a booklet (in several languages) on the use of meal.

One of the key advantages of rapeseed oil to the consumer was its low percentage of saturated fats. However, the presence of what are called glucosinolates and erucic acid posed problems – the former with getting rapeseed meal accepted as animal feed, and the latter for acceptance of the oil as human food. These obstacles became apparent quite early, but it was some years before an entirely new strain of rapeseed, free of these substances, was developed and dubbed "canola." The Rapeseed Association became known as the Canola Council of Canada, and the salutary qualities of canola oil led it to command a large percentage of the edible oil market.

It was an impressive Canadian effort, jointly pursued by the private and public sectors, which paid handsome dividends at the farm level. Rapeseed acreage rose from around one million to one and a half million acres when the Association first started, to an average of more than five million acres just before Mac retired. Over the same period, exports rose even more dramatically from about 300 thousand tonnes to between one and a half million and two and a half million tonnes. Today, canola acreage fluctuates between six million and eight million, with exports between three million and four million tonnes. In recent years, canola has rivalled wheat in net cash returns to farmers.

Mac wanted to step down as president of the Association at its third annual meeting in February 1970, but was asked to stay on for a further six months, and then an additional six, eventually relinquishing the post at the next annual meeting in February of 1971.

His comments reveal several reasons why he found such satisfaction in his work with the Rapeseed Association.

> One of the greatest satisfactions was that you were always accomplishing something. Another was the way in which everybody was involved: farmers, plant scientists – everybody was in it. And what was so wonderful was that it was industry people doing it, not government.

> We went from a few thousand tonnes to millions of tonnes, a market for it, a system to handle it, a pricing structure: the whole thing, and it just flows like a stream of water, because every segment has to make its part work.

> But what I think came out of it as much as anything - and it was also one of the benefits (some people would say one of the few benefits) of the Canada Grains Council – was that it got people who had never talked to each other before into the same room sitting around the table discussing common problems, and they got to know each other a bit and they got to understand each other's problems, and those two organizations – the Canada Grains Council and the Rapeseed Association – developed an industry attitude that had always been lacking before. It had always been "we and we" and "they and they." Finally it got around to being something bigger just "we."

The pragmatism, cooperation, good personal and professional relationships, and sound accomplishments of the people who worked so hard in the Rapeseed Association, and the growers who turned to rapeseed, are the things Mac recalled with pride. Simply noting these things, however, does not tell the full story of the grain industry's interest in, or success with, rapeseed.

The rapid growth in rapeseed production took place against the background of the paradigm shift in farm opinion, and the issues surrounding Wheat Board marketing, referred to earlier in this chapter. These circumstances created two motives for people to take such interest in rapeseed. The first was that it provided an alternative crop at a time when wheat was simply not moving to market. Mac knew such options were necessary for farmers to realize a decent cash flow, because he could recall his own experience of having to store wheat on the farm, and waiting, in the worst case, until mid-January for a marketing opportunity. He said, "I always felt very comfortable about advocating rapeseed, and I spoke repeatedly in speeches about the need to diversify to the extent possible in Saskatchewan, rather than being so totally dependent on wheat."

At the same time, the growing dissatisfaction with the centralized marketing system of The Canadian Wheat Board provided a second motive for turning to rapeseed: an escape from the heavy control under which an increasing number of farmers were chafing. As Mac put it, "You didn't have to deal with somebody sitting up there and saying, 'It's not very convenient, but by God it's handy for me, so you'll do this, and you'll do that.' That's the unfortunate tendency in a highly regulated system, at least as far as I see it."

And not only farmers, but industry people, too, welcomed the opportunities that rapeseed provided. Some years later, in a talk to the Western Canadian Fertilizer Association, Mac pointed out that "the increased volume of oilseeds, the addition of domestic feed grains, and rapid increase in volume of specialty crops [have] given a marketing responsibility to the grain trade that we have not had for almost forty years ... and I tell you quite proudly we are [coping] with it."[28]

As rapeseed grew in volume and importance, it inevitably became a major bone of contention between pro- and anti-central marketing forces. While many farmers were pleased to have a major crop that could be traded on the open market, others who favoured central selling wanted to see the new crop brought under CWB control.

Mac deplored the fact that so much of this debate – and the debates over feed grains, transportation regulation, and the value of central marketing itself – became so dogmatic. In December 1973, in a talk to the Alberta farm organization Unifarm, he pleaded with the agricultural community, "Let's Not Solve Farm Problems by Doctrine," and he lampooned extremists on either side of the great "orderly marketing" divide. "Farmers are being forced to choose one side or the other, and some of them are taking pretty opposite stands," he said. "I hear one neighbour [of mine in Abernethy] believes if we can just put rapeseed, flax, rye, beef cattle, hay bales and honey bees under one great marketing board farmers would have no more income problems. He also believes the earth is flat.

"Of course, there is another neighbour who believes if we eliminated the Wheat Board, got rid of all the hog and chicken boards and opened everything up to a Hong Kong-style free trade area, our problems would all be solved. He plans to put the pressure on for this as soon as he gets his perpetual motion machine in working order."[29]

Doctrinaire approaches to problems, he said, provide solutions for politicians, but split farmers into philosophical camps and shift the focus away from real problems.

The tension between farmers who favoured leaving rapeseed on the open market and those who wanted it brought under the Wheat Board eventually resulted in a plebiscite on the question. For the most part, UGG stayed out of the plebiscite debate, but Mac commented on the process after the voting. At the Winnipeg rapeseed marketing seminar in 1972, he referred to one of the studies done during the debate, which he thought to be a good study, except that "because numbers weren't used – dollars and cents – we ended up in a publicity donnybrook where the issue was not an economic question but a religious one. Growers in the middle had no option but to join one philosophical camp or the other."[30]

In a speech to the High Energy Grains and Oilseeds Industry Conference in Calgary in January of 1973, he dealt with the subject again, noting how much of the debate was conducted by those who had no financial stake in its outcome.

> Oddly enough the request to have rapeseed come under the Wheat Board has never come from organized rapeseed growers. ... I have not heard any one of the three prairie organizations recommend that rape marketing should come under the Wheat Board. ...
>
> Unfortunately, all the (for want of a more precise word) propaganda has come from groups who don't represent rapeseed growers. And I include here the Wheat Pools, U.G.G., Palliser Wheat Growers and a number of other organizations. ... But to me, for a general organization to propagandize how rapeseed should be marketed makes about as much sense as the Alberta Rapeseed Growers Association promoting a new beef marketing system, or a U.G.G. Local Board suggesting how big an annex Alberta Wheat Pool should build at a point.[31]

Looking back, he was more emphatic, and considerably less diplomatic, commenting that "the perfect illustration of the political and left-wing philosophy at work was what happened when they were having the vote on the marketing of rapeseed, and they said that all permit holders should vote. Now, why in hell, if I'm growing rapeseed, should you, who never grew rapeseed in your life and don't intend to grow rapeseed, have a vote in deciding how I am going to sell my product? That griped me intensely. I don't know what I would have done – I think I would have quit – if the plebiscite had gone in favour of Wheat Board marketing of rapeseed, I just felt that strongly about it, because it was absolutely unjust to the people who were making the commitments to the growing of rapeseed."

In his Calgary speech, he went on to refer again to the same controversial study, and again deplored its failure to provide any quantitative analysis: "So what are we left with? Words. And words are wonderful things for philosophically inclined groups to play around with ... and play on the 'grass roots' emotion and biases because the 'grass roots' doesn't have the numbers to go along with the philosophy."[32]

In the early 1990s, several economic studies analyzed, after the fact, the impact of a brief period when the US border had been opened to barley movement. The findings of those economists who favoured the CWB differed sharply from the findings of those who did not. If Mac had still been involved in the industry when these competing studies were done, he might have had less faith in so-called "objective" analysis. The argument about the relative merits of single-desk versus open-market selling is still a "religious" one, notwithstanding the advent of very sophisticated analytical techniques.

Of course, what we all have to recognize is that ultimately, all our assessments of economic issues have an ideological component, in the sense that they are based to some extent on our value judgements about issues like individual versus collective responsibilities, and on the degree to which the distribution of goods and services ought to be governed by the market or by the state. The way we interpret our experiences is governed by our a priori judgements on these questions to a greater degree than perhaps we might realize or acknowledge. However, the kind of ideology or (to use his word) dogma that Mac deplored was the kind that ignores facts, and proceeds from values to conclusions without stopping in-between for adequate thought.

In retrospect, Mac tended to view the experience of the Rapeseed Association as a triumph for private initiative, as a demonstration of the fact that individuals, private capital, and government could work together within a free-market setting to achieve a common goal, and as a refutation of the most egregious claims for central desk selling. He brought these thoughts together in the following way.

> The final argument in my book is this: If the Wheat Board's single desk selling is so essential to the health of an industry, how on earth did canola get to where it is today? Because it never had a central selling agency. It depended totally on the open market and it has been nothing but a success story and the open market moved all the product.
>
> In fact, rapeseed has proved it. It wasn't a marketing board commodity, and yet they went out and they found markets, and they found people who could develop those markets. And I come back to what I think is an excellent organization and an excellent model.
>
> What baffles me is the continuing argument that a single desk seller will always get you a better price than multiple sellers. I think it's not necessarily so, if multiple sellers can go out and find markets that the other fellow didn't find. I think that has been the secret of the success of canola. There was always somebody out looking for ways to make a dollar by finding a new market. Who could make a dollar by finding a new market for Wheat Board wheat? It just won't work.
>
> I'm not carrying a particular penchant for the open market, I am just trying to judge what happened. The canola industry just went from nothing to great success based on an open market getting rid of its product and it got rid of it year after year after year. And even today, with record acres and production, apparently it is all going out into the world market.

Through the first half of the 1970s, the CWB changed its marketing philosophy and became much more responsive to the market in its pricing. Adopting a much more aggressive selling policy, it moved grain in record volumes, and this tended to take the focus off the debate about grain marketing.

However, by the end of the 1960s, the federal government had a bundle of grain issues that were festering and needed attention. On the marketing side were the problems that Mac had encountered both on the farm and as president of UGG: high carryovers; congested elevators; expensive government storage programs; and a nascent discontent with CWB marketing. There were also problems with the grain transportation and handling system: prairie rail branch lines; railway losses on the Crow's Nest Pass Rates; an outdated country elevator system; and logistical breakdowns. The federal Liberals, therefore, developed a proposal to tackle them, which entailed the creation of a National Grains Council to advise government on the best approach. The first public announcement that the government intended to establish such a body was made by Liberal leader Pierre Trudeau on June 2, 1968, in an election speech in Winnipeg. The proposal was contained in a policy statement released during the election campaign. Mac quoted from this statement in a talk to the Manitoba Farm Business Association in 1972: " 'There must be a forum established where representatives of [governments, farmers, grain companies, exporters, railroads, and others] can meet and play their part in planning action. In consultation with industry, this Government intends to establish a National Grains Council in order to involve ... the various elements of this great industry.' "[33]

The policy statement laid out four purposes for the Council: to make recommendations on "any existing or proposed program or development" in the industry; to assist in the promotion of exports; to assist in the promotion of research; and to improve liaison between government and industry.

Curiously, the idea of such a body had been developed by UGG in the 1930s, and a document bearing the impressive title of "Proposals for the establishment of the CANADIAN WHEAT INSTITUTE as a National Body to Conduct Work in the Interests of CANADIAN WHEAT" exists in the UGG archives at the University of Manitoba. This document, although adumbrating in every detail the mandate eventually adopted for the Council, was not the source of the idea for those who advocated it. Mac's recollection is that the concept of a council was introduced into the Liberals' election platform by some prominent members of the party from the Winnipeg grain establishment. He remembered that "[National Grain president] George Heffelfinger was one of its promoters. George was a leading Liberal light at that time, and he was quite enthusiastic. Charlie Kroft, who had been with McCabe Grain and was still active, was another. And [Manitoba Pool president] Bill Parker was another mover. Bill was also a Liberal, and he was quite enthusiastic about it. I very willingly supported it, and there were one or two others. Then Trudeau came to Winnipeg during the 1968 election campaign, and there was a huge rally at the International Inn where he announced it and it became an election promise."

The new organization came into existence as the Canada Grains Council (CGC), and seemed to offer the entire grain industry possibilities that were being realized by the Rapeseed Association for the single crop. In fact, Mac's hopes for the Canadian Federation of Agriculture, the Rapeseed Association, and the Grains Council were all, in a general way, the same: that they might be forums where policies could be found for the betterment of Canadian agriculture as a whole. CFA, as we have seen, was a disappointment and, as things transpired, so was the Council – in fact, as he said, the greatest disappointment of his career. "I guess," he said, "I was just so politically naïve in those days that I couldn't see the problems that would arise."

Mac's first mention of the Canada Grains Council to the UGG board is in the president's report of October 31, 1968: "Under the auspices of the Minister of Agriculture [Bud Olson] and the Minister of Trade and Commerce [Jean Luc Pepin], a meeting, including representatives of all branches of the grain industry from across the nation, was held in Winnipeg on October 16 to discuss the structure and organization, the possible terms of reference and financial arrangements for the proposed Council."[34]

His next report on the Council, the following April, provides some measure of the degree to which his leadership qualities had been recognized beyond the grain industry itself. At that time, "at a meeting with the Honourable J.L. Pepin, the Honourable H.A. Olson, and the Honourable O.E. Lang in Ottawa on January 28, I formally accepted the chairmanship of the Canada Grains Council. My acceptance was based on the conditions approved by this Board when we met unofficially on January 24 to discuss the request of the Ministers that I serve as Chairman of the Council at least during its formative stages."[35]

A meeting of the Council, "with twenty-seven member organizations participating,"[36] took place on February 3 to review the proposed terms of reference and organizational structure of the new body. The meeting approved an impressive mandate for the Council: to coordinate work on improving market share; to improve coordination of programs in the industry; to make recommendations on any proposal, development, or program referred to it by ministers, or which the Council itself decided to review; and to formulate recommendations which represent a consensus within the industry.

While the federal government supported the Council financially, no government body - including The Canadian Wheat Board - was permitted to become a full member. However, government organizations were expected to provide expertise where needed, and were permitted to serve on committees of the Council when appropriate.

The Council got off to a reasonable start in its work program, when "its first major project gave it a little credibility and acceptance. Bill Parker was right behind this one, and that was a review of the Canada Grain Act, which had not been reviewed since 1931 and still spoke in terms of 'wagons' delivering at country elevators and things like that. It was a good revision of the Canada Grain Act and we went to Ottawa on different occasions to appear before the House of Commons Standing Committee on Agriculture. It gave us a good chance to show that we knew what we were talking about, and the committee accepted our recommendations."

However, a body with such a wide-ranging mandate might be expected to attract opposition from some quarters, and it was not long before it found itself embattled on a number of fronts. "The Canadian Wheat Board was always an enemy of the Council because they saw it as encroaching on some of its policies," Mac explained. "Bill McNamara gave it token support because Jean Luc Pepin was his minister. But they never did want to see the Council succeed, and they were totally opposed to any Wheat Board money going into it."

Although not openly opposing the Council, the Wheat Board kept up pressure against it by frustrating its initiatives. In April 1972, Mac reported how one Council committee's proposal to study problems with freight and storage of grain had been thwarted: "In its initial investigations the committee learned that the matter was being investigated by the Canadian Wheat Board and no further active study of the problem by the Council would be required."[37]

In July of 1973 he spoke about research on high-yielding feed wheats that was being pursued by the Board, and told the UGG board how "much of the interest of [the Wheat Board's] report lies in the fact that the work being carried on by [the Board] has been advocated and pursued by the Canada Grains Council for some time as part of its program. The Wheat Board which now assumed the role of leader in this work never gave more than lip service to Council efforts in these areas."[38]

Mac recalled the attitude of the Wheat Pools towards the Council as being mixed. Manitoba Pool president Bill Parker, as he said, was one of those who pushed for the Council, and Alberta Pool president Gordon Harrold had also been supportive. Initially, said Mac, "they could see the need, and they went along with it." However, "they were among the more difficult to accommodate," and that difficulty grew with time. Eventually, their problems with the Council became insurmountable, and they withdrew their membership.

The Pools' apprehensions came from three sources. The first was the industry's chronic battle of "free market versus regulation." Mac's president's report of October 1969 highlighted this issue in what is almost a side comment, but he was still hopeful that things would be worked out: "The Council and the Board of Directors seem to be settling down to reasonable working relationships although a few stresses and strains are still in evidence. The CFA and the Alberta and Saskatchewan Pools are still on the defensive looking for ulterior motives on the part of this 'trade dominated' organization. ...

"I expect that once the work of the Council becomes further advanced and results more evident, we will find a better understanding developing among members and a sense of trust and mutual purpose which may be lacking at present."[39]

The second matter that bothered the Pools – and with a good deal of justification in Mac's mind – was the personality of the then-president of the Winnipeg Grain Exchange, Ernie McWilliam. Mac recalled McWilliam as being "very abrasive, and that is why the National Farmers Union walked out. The Pools were pretty itchy, and I had sympathy with them on that one. He was just far too abusive and absolutely fanatical in his support of the open market, and anti-Wheat Board. He just antagonized people. He could talk well enough to get up on his feet at any point in time and make a pitch. But some of the stuff he pulled! He caused me many a restless night."

However, the most serious issue as far as the Pools were concerned, and which eventually led them to resign from the Council, was a disagreement over its role in policy development. The president's report of November 1970 documented an early example of this disagreement. In the preceding May, the government had released an important and widely debated report of a federal Task Force on agriculture. The Council had formed a subcommittee to study the report and bring forward an assessment to the board of directors. Mac's report is worth quoting at length, because it documents the nature of the tension over policy issues that existed between the Pools and the Council, and the way both sides reacted to it.

> A review of a sub-committee report on the marketing aspects of the Task Force report was started but, before its completion, Mr. Turner of the Saskatchewan Wheat Pool queried the value of the exercise to the Board. He said SWP was not prepared to come to the Council to discuss items considered by them to be in the policy area. He was supported in his statement by Alberta Wheat Pool and The Canadian Federation of Agriculture. Discussion then ensued on the advisability of the Council being involved in policy advisement.

> It was finally decided the Task Force Committee report would be distributed to Board members, but would not be sent to government or the Council members and there would not be general endorsement of the report by the Board of Directors. It was further decided the Secretary General should attend the Canadian Agricultural Congress, but that he

should be an observer only and not make any policy statements at the conference.

The import of these decisions, in effect dictated by a minority of the Board of Directors, has since given rise to serious concern in the minds of many Board members. Early clarification of the situation is essential and may well lead to disintegration of the Council in one way or another. Saskatchewan Wheat Pool openly threatens to discontinue membership if the Council gives any consideration to questions which it designates as being in the policy area. Support of this position by Alberta Wheat Pool and The Canadian Federation of Agriculture is implied. Other members will refuse to participate in the work of the Council if a minority group is to dictate Council policy. These questions may be considered on November 9 and 10 when the Board of Directors and Council are to meet.[40]

The tension reached the breaking point a few years later when the Council undertook an evaluation of a series of government-commissioned reports on transportation and handling. Just how these studies came to be done, and why the Council was asked to review them, is an important part of its story.

The problems in the transportation system, which some of the more perceptive people in the industry began to recognize in the 1950s, were made evident to everyone near the beginning of Mac's presidency, with the first large sales to the Soviet Union and China. The inadequacies of a system more than two decades out of date had prompted the formation of an ad hoc group of the most senior people in the industry, which called itself simply the Grain Transportation Committee (GTC). Its purpose was to provide a forum where transportation and marketing issues could be discussed confidentially by the most senior company representatives in the grain industry, and where operating decisions could be taken to ensure that grain would move to meet sales. Because of the seniority of the Committee members, commitments could be made with the assurance that the operating people in the individual organizations would comply with the Committee's instructions.

As they dealt with the problems of meeting large sales with what was, as Mac later called it, an "almost inoperative" system, the GTC recognized that some serious work had to be done to prevent the problems from recurring. They appointed a working committee called the Grain Transportation Technical Group (GTTG), comprised of transportation specialists within the industry, which was instructed to examine the system and recommend improvements.

A few creative people recognized that the existing system for ordering railcars of grain to move from country elevators had been designed for a different time, and new methods were needed to control grain movement if the system were to function effectively. By bringing some of the best brains in the industry to study the problem, a new system was developed, called the Block Shipping System.

While this work was going on within the industry, the MacPherson Royal Commission on transportation had identified the Crow's Nest Pass Rates and branch lines as two major problems affecting western grain and creating significant financial burdens on the railways. When the first National Transportation Act was passed in 1967, branch lines were identified as "an imposed public duty," and therefore were eligible to receive subsidies. The grain rates would have been treated similarly, but such was the outcry in Parliament over the audacious suggestions that the Crow was a "burden" and was a losing proposition for the railways, that the relevant sections of the bill were voted out. The same legislation transformed the Board of Transport Commissioners into the Canadian Transport Commission, which was given a research role as well as its traditional regulatory and judicial functions. Accordingly, it received substantial funding and staff to examine these two key grain transportation problems. It barely had a chance to undertake this work.

The formation of the Canadian Grains Council was not the federal government's only initiative to tackle the problems besetting the grain industry. Its next step was to assign responsibility for grain issues to a separate minister, Otto Lang, who was appointed Minister without Portfolio Responsible for The Canadian Wheat Board. Prior to this, responsibility for the Wheat Board had always been combined with some other portfolio, usually industry and commerce.

Then, in a move which in retrospect was not entirely consistent with the creation of the Council, the government set up a small, interdepartmental advisory body responding to Lang, called the Grains Group. It was a situation ripe for conflict. Predictably, the Grains Group became a major foe of the Council, and opened another front on which the Council had to fight for position. Mac's reports to the board document the Council's increasing frustration with the new body and its attitudes, and the increasingly hostile relationship with the Grains Group – and, indeed, between the Grains Group and the entire grain industry.

In January 1970, he began on a positive note, reporting to the UGG board on a meeting on the 12th of that month between the board of directors of the Council, and Mr. Lang and his new Group. "A very encouraging exchange of views took place and the prospect of a good working relationship with this group being developed on a continuing basis is excellent," he wrote.[41] It was downhill from this point on.

By this time, wheat stocks had risen to the point where Canada was carrying over very nearly a full year's production at the end of each crop year. This huge carryover was depressing prices and clogging commercial storage space, and the Grains Group had hatched the idea of a one-year reduction in wheat acreage to reduce stocks.

In April, Mac reported on two meetings between Grains Group representatives and western farm organizations, one in Saskatoon and one in Ottawa, "to discuss the proposed plan to retire land from wheat production" in 1970.

"In both meetings," he said, "after an introductory statement by the Minister, frank discussion took place with plenty of opportunity for everyone to state their views. The farm organization people expressed reservations about some elements of the proposed program. Alternatives were suggested for certain provisions without much apparent acceptance by the Minister and the Grains Group."[42]

Mac's opinion was that the proposal had been only marginally influenced in one small detail by the two days of discussion. The government, he said, wanted this kind of consultation merely to secure "better acceptance" of new programs by farmers and their organizations. This, it should be noted, was not long after the federal Liberals had introduced the slogan "participatory democracy" into Canada's political vocabulary to indicate that a new relationship was to be created between the government and the governed. Mac's report picked up on the phrase: "Whether this use of 'participatory democracy' will work remains to be seen. On the basis of these two meetings, I seriously doubt it. The question is quite important as there is every indication that the communication and consultation approach is to be part of the operating method of the Grains Group to provide the form, if not the fact, of participation in the formulation of its policies."[43]

By April, relations had deteriorated to the point where the Council felt it had to reassess its role vis a vis the Grains Group. The executive met on the 14th, and the July president's report noted:

> The original concept of the Council, as reflected in the terms of reference and by-laws, is that of an industry organization working in partnership with government rather than as an independent body.

However, since the advent of the Grains Group, its members had developed an attitude that the Council had special responsibilities to government to divulge its plans for activities including market development and research without the Group sharing its plans in these areas because of the need to preserve confidentiality. This led to a most unfortunate situation as time after time when the Council advanced a proposal for work on a specific project word came from the Grains Group that it was interested in the same area and deemed it advisable for the Council to leave it for their attention.[44]

The Grains Group not only usurped many of the functions that Mac and some other early supporters of the Canada Grains Council had foreseen as part of its role. It also appropriated some of the ongoing work being done by the Grain Transportation Technical Group and the Grain Transportation Committee. In the mid-1960s, shortly after the GTC was formed and the GTTG began its work, a major grain industry conference had been held in Minaki, Ontario, where the activities of the GTTG began in earnest, and the development of the Block Shipping System pushed forward. The Minaki Conference had been a watershed event in the grain industry and, according to a former senior executive of the Grain Commission, Earl Baxter, created a real sense of excitement. At long last, it was felt, the industry was taking hold of its major problems and dealing with them successfully.

All that ended when the Grains Group was set up. According to a former member of the GTTG, they were called together by the Wheat Board and informed that they were being disbanded. Henceforth, transportation and handling research would be taken over by the Grains Group.[45] Whether or not this story is an accurate reflection of the message conveyed to the GTTG, the fact is, for good or ill, the Grains Group began working energetically, and the work underway within the industry ground to a virtual halt.

The money and staff that had been assigned to the Canadian Transport Commission to study grain transportation problems were transferred to the Grains Group, and a major set of studies of grain handling and transportation was undertaken. These studies started as a few people in the grain industry and in government began to recognize that the elevator and branch line system was twenty-five to thirty years out of date, and therefore had to be rationalized and modernized. In contrast, other bulk commodities such as coal and potash were moving much more efficiently in large volumes in "unit trains"; i.e., trains with fifty to one hundred railcars which remained coupled together and moved as a "unit" from the point where they were loaded to the destination where they were unloaded.

Coal and potash seemed to offer examples of the kind of transportation system appropriate for moving grain, and its application seemed to be obvious. A few simple calculations showed that, to make unit trains work, the country elevator system would have to be reduced from approximately 3000 elevator facilities to no more than a few hundred, and possibly as few as twenty.

The Grains Group's transportation specialist, Bob Shepp, delivered a speech in Winnipeg in 1970 which spoke of "twenty inland terminals" replacing the existing elevator system, and the fat was immediately in the fire. If ever there was a speech that inflamed an industry, it was that one, and the speech and the inland terminal concept were attacked from every possible quarter – right and left, governments and industry, cooperatives, private elevator companies, and farm organizations. Eventually, even the United Church got in on the debate, condemning inland terminals as destructive to local communities.

Those who saw the large inland-terminal style of elevator as the trend for the future were eventually proven correct, and by the 1990s, exactly that kind of system began to emerge. However, in 1970, for a number of reasons - technological, economic, social, and political - immediate development of such a system was not possible. Nonetheless, the Grains Group's technocratic mindset embodied an attitude of "knowing best" what was good for others, and those who embraced this view thought it the government's duty to impose an "optimum system" of their own design on the industry.

As everyone waited to find out what the government was going to come up with, the fear of nationalization of the entire system was in the air. And it must be admitted that to some players – in and out of government – it sometimes seemed to be the only approach that would allow the kind of major changes that apparently were needed.

However, this view did not prevail. The majority of participants in the discussion felt that grain handling and transportation were functions best left in private hands, and began to make efforts to understand the factors preventing a modern system from coming into being. Those within the Grains Group who favoured this approach argued that the industry was hamstrung, not by an ignorance of what that "optimum system" was, but by a lack of market signals, and by an overly tight system of regulation, both of which frustrated the modernization process. They pointed out the political impossibility of government's imposing its view of what the grain handling and transportation system should look like, and that it would not be acceptable to farmers or industry.

The arrogance in the Grains Group caused a great deal of concern in the industry, to the point where, as Mac recalled, "we were scared stiff of their attitude. Mind you, it's understandable in a way too. Here were some young people full of initiatives in areas that were conundrums for a new minister, and no minister ever has the time to do all the detailed work, so he turns somebody loose on it. Otto Lang turned them loose, but they turned out to be a loose cannon on the poop deck. They were going to reform the world. They were just going to reshape the world and they thought they had the authority to do it, and it was going to be run totally from Ottawa."

Concern over the future direction of grain policy brought a halt to the cooperative efforts of the industry in the Council and the Grain Transportation Committee, and to planning work carried out by the grain companies. In April 1971, Mac was invited by the secretary-treasurer of the municipality of Russell, Manitoba, to attend a meeting on elevator closures. His report on the meeting to the UGG board in July stated that "the purpose of the meeting was to find out what the policies and plans of the grain companies are for the future of the elevator system. ...

"In a letter of reply to the invitation, I stated that the timing of the meeting was poor because no grain company could have a policy on elevator closing, or any other approach to rationalization of the elevator system in western Canada, until the report of the Grains Group was available."[46]

The Grains Group's steamroller did eventually come to a halt, and in retrospect, said Mac, "I think it was their extremism that created the furor that stopped Otto [Lang] in his tracks."

The Liberals elected under Pierre Trudeau in 1968 were, of course, of a very proactive and interventionist frame of mind, with a strong, even inflated, belief in the role government could play in addressing social and economic problems. The formation of the Council and the Grains Group, while not entirely consistent with each other, was typical of the aggressive and vigorous, but perhaps not carefully thought out, way in which that government set about attacking problems. As a young man working in the Grains Group at the time, I can recall being captured by this spirit. There was a feeling that they could and would resolve problems that had eluded their predecessors. Unfortunately, however, this was accompanied by a strong undercurrent of contempt for the people in the industry who, it was hinted, lacked the brains or resources to resolve these problems themselves.

The first sign of a less aggressive attitude occurred when the studies on transportation and handling were released to the industry, and Grains Group representatives began a series of consultations on them. UGG received a confidential letter from Otto Lang, dated August 25, 1971, forwarding the reports and requesting a meeting with Grains Group officials. The meeting occurred on September 21, and Mac's report to the board on September 22 records the results. He put his finger squarely on the conundrum that activist governments face when their enthusiasm for change outruns their constituency's willingness to accept it.

> We had been prepared for a softer line from the group by a sentence in Mr. Lang's letter: "Any contemplated changes to the existing system must be clearly beneficial to the producers who will have the option of decid- ing whether or not these changes will occur." And by statements in the discussion paper such as: "It is clear that the producers themselves must indicate their desire to change from the present system before change can occur; moreover there must be clearly indicated benefits to the producers by making such a change. In the event that changes are desired there will probably be a need to consider programs for producers, communities and labour related to any adverse effects incurred by changing from the cur- rent transportation and handling system." We did not, however, expect the complete lack of direction expressed by the Grains Group repre- sentatives. It seems the word is now out to avoid any politically unpopu- lar action on this whole question and, as a result, the group is completely at a loss to know what course of action to follow from now on. Members of parliament are starting to ask when a report may be expected, what recommendations the group will make and, on the basis of current mate- rial, the minister has nothing to offer as an answer. ...
>
> It seems that the stage is set for a major move into elevator rationalization but everyone involved, and especially the government, is saying "after you please". What is needed is positive leadership. Because of its regula- tory powers, the government obviously feels responsibility in this area but it is not prepared to accept the political liability of an initiative at this time. They would be most happy to see someone else, preferably the grain industry, make the move. But why should it accept the burden of a course of action which will be unpopular in the country.
>
> It seems that a position of stalemate has been reached.[47]

Being brought to a halt (and, perhaps significantly, also coming up to an election), the federal government then turned to the Canada Grains Council to finish what it had begun. Suddenly, rather than attempting to thwart the Council from gaining influence, the government chose the Council as a vehicle to deal with a difficult issue and to determine the next steps.

It was an ambiguous decision. Did the government really wish to pass the initiative back to industry? Or did it simply want to dump what seemed to be a troublesome issue on someone else's plate? Likely, as with most such decisions, the motives were mixed.

Some months passed before the reports were finally made available to the Council for its consideration. Mac's report to the UGG board in July 1972 recorded the event.

> A confidential letter was received from the Honourable Otto E. Lang requesting the Council to take the responsibility for organizing an appropriate committee to consider various aspects of the future of the grain handling and transportation system. The activities of the committee would flow from the indications in the various reports prepared for the Grains Group. ...
>
> The role of the Group would be integrated with the committee established by the Council, but would not be immediately involved in the work of the committee, except under the Council's direction and guidance.
>
> Some concerns were expressed:
>
> (1) The Council should not be pressured for instant results. ...
>
> (2) The Council committee should act independent of government. ...
>
> (3) ... the actual program of modernization must be acceptable to and carried out by individual grain handling organizations.
>
> (4) ... producer representation ... should be solicited. ...
>
> (6) It was recognized that [the] findings of such a committee might be counter productive, e.g., no consensus could be reached.[48]

The Council established the requisite committees, and they set about doing a complete review of the thick package of Grains Group reports. The work started in late 1972 and continued for about two years. When the Liberals went back with a minority government that year, the fear of nationalization abated somewhat, and the Council's work was instrumental in re-engaging the grain industry in the long and protracted debate on transportation and handling, which was to include two commissions of inquiry and a seemingly endless parade of special studies.

One of the initiatives undertaken by the Council was a study entitled *The State of the Industry.* This started as an effort to analyze the industry, to define the problems more precisely, and to set the stage for where things should go. It did rather more than that.

Unexpectedly, the study became an in-depth analysis of the historical reasons why the transportation and handling system had so stagnated. It described how the central desk selling system of The Canadian Wheat Board had resulted, almost unintentionally, in an increasingly centralized and regulated system. While not outrightly critical of the Board or central selling, it identified the way the marketing system blocked market signals, and held grain off the market. It concluded that these actions had combined with regulation of handling tariff and rail rates to frustrate attempts to modernize the system. Its most radical step was to identify forthrightly the Crow's Nest Pass Rates as part of this complex, and one of the roots of the problem. The report was, therefore, critical of all the things the supporters of regulation and centralized marketing held dear, and which they had been so successful in creating and defending for close to thirty years. The report recommended the development of a more market-oriented industry and a reduction in regulation as the best ways to resolve the transportation and handling problems. To Mac, it was "one of the most incisive reports ever produced on the western grain industry."[49]

Getting it accepted and made public was an exercise in diplomacy which he, as chairman of the Council, accomplished by shepherding the report carefully through a minefield of ideological interests that did not want such things said. The president's report of July 1973 contains a very mild description of a meeting I was privileged to attend, and recall as one of the most fractious and tense meetings in which I have ever been involved.

> The committee, after sitting from 9:00 a.m. to 7:30 p.m., found itself unable to complete its consideration of the report and agreed to submit written comments on the portions not dealt with.

> The broad cross-section of interests represented on the committee finds it difficult on occasion to reach common ground but, with a few minor changes in the text, it is hoped that general acceptance of its contents will be forthcoming.

> The sensitivity of some members of the committee on some of the points covered in the report is remarkable and leads to most of the difficulty

encountered in reaching full acceptance, but members do seem to find it possible to discuss even the most delicate subjects in a way which I don't believe would have been possible even a few years ago.[50]

"Remarkable sensitivity" was a remarkable understatement. The report was controversial in the extreme and generated as much reaction as had Bob Shepp's "twenty inland terminals" speech three years earlier. This time, however, reaction was mixed, with some people supporting the analysis contained in the report and some virulently opposing it.

It was during the evaluation of the Grains Group reports, and while the *State of the Industry* study was underway, that the Pools resigned from the Council. Without them, its membership was no longer representative of the grain industry. Of course, it was inevitable that the issue of the Crow's Nest Pass Rates would surface as the industry and the government struggled to come to grips with the transportation and handling problems, and as more and more people in the industry began to doubt the wisdom of retaining them. As far as the Council was concerned, therefore, being designated to carry on the Grains Group work was a very mixed blessing. For a period, it became the forum for discussion and resolution of the most important issue of the day. But, in the end, it was a victim of the long and bitter fight over the grain freight rates that lay at the core of the transportation and handling problems.

Mac was chairman of the Council for four years, from its inception in 1969 until 1973, and over that time, he saw its position steadily eroded. Embattled by the Wheat Board and the Grains Group, and losing three of its key members, it went from a potential forum for the grain industry to resolve long-standing problems, to a relatively ineffective and unrepresentative body, and it is not hard to see why his chairmanship of the Council turned out to be his most disappointing experience. He summarized it this way:

> There were two things that completely emasculated the Canada Grains Council. The first was the formation of the Grains Group in Ottawa. The government created the Grains Group just after the Council came into existence, and it took over many of its functions, and it was just a matter of Ottawa civil servants making damn sure that there wasn't going to be an upstart outfit in Winnipeg that would take some of their influence away. It was as simple as that.
>
> And the second thing was the creation of the Canadian International Grains Institute [CIGI].[51] It took over a function that had been foreseen

for the Canada Grains Council: the education and the dissemination of information to customers. The Wheat Board did not want to contribute money for something that was being influenced by the Canada Grains Council, and a lot of the money for CIGI comes from the Wheat Board.

So by the time you took the Grains Group out and the International Grains Institute out, it left a fairly hollow shell for the Council itself.

I still think there was a place for it and a function for it and a justification for it, given the things it might have been able to do if government hadn't decided it would do them itself. And sometimes would do them after the Council initiated the concepts! That's what was so galling about it. I just don't think it ever has achieved its potential because there were always political forces making sure it would not.

If the Canada Grains Council had been allowed to do the things that it could have done well – and were being done for rapeseed by the Rapeseed Association – it could have been more successful. But I guess the Rapeseed Association got away with it because it was so inconspicuous and self-financing. That gave it independence which the Canada Grains Council has never enjoyed.

The contrast between Mac's experiences with the Rapeseed Association and with the Canada Grains Council could not have been more stark. Where he encountered cooperation among industry players and government in the RAC, he experienced discord and factionalism at the Canada Grains Council. Where the participants approached the industry's problems with openness in the Association, they approached them with dogmatism in the Grains Council. Where there was a genuine desire to work together in the one, the other was characterized by intransigent and uncompromising attitudes. Where government people collaborated with the RAC in approaching problems, there was rivalry and conflict with government at the Grains Council.

There were two key reasons for these differences. The first was that the Rapeseed Association was primarily concerned with practical operating matters: market development; varietal research; development of products with better end-use qualities; and technical issues related to the production and handling of rapeseed. The people who directed the Association and the people who worked on its projects tended to be drawn from the operating side of the member organizations or, like Mac, wore management hats when they were at the table.

On the other hand, once it had been handed the transportation studies of the Grains Group, the Council was confronted with a highly emotional and politically charged set of policy issues. These issues had been debated almost since the beginnings of agricultural development in the west. Conflict was therefore almost inevitable.

The second, and somewhat related, reason arose from the shifting climate of opinion Mac encountered in his first decade as president of UGG. The cooperative wing of the farm movement had won its battles during the 1920s, 1930s, and 1940s: the formation of the Pools; their rescue from bankruptcy by the provincial governments; the legislation of the Crow's Nest Pass Rates and their extension to all elevator points, rail lines, and ports; the formation of the Wheat Board; and the cessation of futures trading in wheat on the Winnipeg Grain Exchange. By the end of the war, all these things had been accomplished, and the industry, by and large, was structured in accordance with the philosophy of those who were critical of the market and who wanted a centrally controlled and highly regulated system.

However, a new critique was emanating from the farm community, having its origin in the 1950s as farmers began to experience some of the negative effects of the centralized and regulated system: sluggish grain sales; reduced cash flow; and an unresponsive and stagnating grain handling and transportation system. This critical spirit grew stronger and more informed during the 1960s, and it eventually found its voice in the Palliser Wheat Growers in 1970.

By the early 1970s, therefore, the Pools, the Wheat Board, and the left-wing farm organizations like the National Farmers Union had, almost paradoxically, become the "conservative" wing of farm opinion, protecting the status quo they had worked so hard to establish decades before. The radical voice of change now emanated from the other side of the debate: the right-wing, pro-market farmers, who began to do the innovative and critical thinking. It was they who began to analyze the problems that centralization and regulation were bringing. And the solutions they proffered were market solutions: free up the system; let us have the incentives and innovation free markets bring; let us take a commercial approach to problems, rather than a regulatory one.

The RAC was one of the vehicles for this new spirit. Here, those who sought to preserve the status quo held no authority. Rapeseed was an open market grain, and the effort made in the plebiscite to bring it under the Wheat Board had failed. The crop was grown, promoted, and sold by people who were comfortable with, and supportive of, the open market, and as they encountered the challenges of a growing industry, they addressed their problems from within this shared point of view.

In the Grains Council, however, every question and every problem were seen by the participants from two quite different perspectives. The market should decide which railway branch lines should be abandoned; the government should decide which railway branch lines should be kept. Deregulated freight rates will allow the market to develop an efficient system; freeing freight rates will only unloose an oppressive railway monopoly. Grain shippers should access scarce railcars in a free transportation market; only controlled access to transportation will ensure that all farmers are treated fairly.

On neither side of the debate were these views held dispassionately. When the Council inherited the transportation file from government, they were handed an emotional and political time bomb. The task of reviewing the Grains Group's studies rekindled debate on virtually every issue that had been bitterly fought for at least two decades prior to the war, and the defenders of the status quo saw themselves as the guardians of the received wisdom that had shaped the system to its current form. That received wisdom was suddenly being challenged by studies like the *State of the Industry* report, whose analysis identified as problems the very things the cooperative movement had seen as beneficial and which they had fought so hard to create.

It is clear that the dogmatic attitudes encountered in the Council were not exclusive to organizations on either side of the ideological debate. Nevertheless, from Mac's point of view and from my own, it was the protectors of the status quo who seemed to be the least cooperative when it came to the Council's work. It may, of course, be argued that Mac's perception of the left wing's intransigence arose from his own philosophical leanings. However, this judgement is not supported by the evidence. It was his fairness and generally non-partisan leadership, and UGG's "middle ground" position, that led him to be chosen to chair the Council in the first place. And while Mac came to be a spokesperson for those who sought change, and became increasingly critical himself of the status quo, he was not comfortable with ideologues of any persuasion. He always had a healthy respect for his opponents' point of view, and he arrived at his position not from an ideological perspective, but from a pragmatic and experiential one. Moreover, he always retained the respect of those with whom he differed, as his experience with the likes of Bill Parker and Jim Deveson attests.

Despite this analysis of why Mac's experiences with the Rapeseed Association and the Canada Grains Council stood in such contrast, there still seems to be an irony in the way the two organizations evolved. In the rapeseed business – controlled by the private sector that the cooperative movement had condemned as individualistic and completely self-interested - the cooperation between industry, farmers, and government proved most effective. In the Council, those who had for decades espoused the ideals of cooperation and collaboration proved unable to work together. In Mac's view, it was because of their inflexibility and their unwillingness to compromise that the Council's effort was destroyed by factionalism and power struggles. At the end of the day, they were the first to leave when they did not get their own way.

The situation in the grain handling and transportation system reached crisis proportions in the early 1970s. A total breakdown loomed because the railways refused to purchase new equipment, claiming that the legislated freight rates simply made it financially impossible for them to do so. Later, there came to be a grudging acceptance of the validity of this position, and a consensus emerged that the railways should be made financially whole in the movement of grain. However, this consensus was still to come when the Council was establishing itself, and in 1972, the government felt forced to step in with the purchase of 2000 new hopper cars – although in those days, it did not take much forcing with an interventionist government not bothered by deficit financing. This, however, was only a stop-gap measure, and it soon became apparent that permanent solutions were not going to come from the Grains Council.

In 1974, the newly elected majority Liberal government seized the initiative back from the Council, and established two commissions of inquiry to deal with the transportation issues. And it was during the late 1970s, as this debate intensified, that Mac emerged not only as an industry leader, but as an industry statesman, as well.

The Statesman: 1970 – 1981

7

It is a cliché worn thin to speak of periods of "great change." In fact, intense change has been more the rule than the exception in western agriculture, with each generation having to cope with its own particular upheaval: the opening of the west prior to the turn of the century; heavy immigration and settlement in the period prior to the First World War; explosive growth in acreage devoted to grain production in the post-war period; the creation of large cooperatives using price pooling and centralized marketing in the 1920s; the devastation of the 1930s; the revolution in farm-production techniques through mechanization and chemicals following the Second World War; and the intense debate on transportation and marketing of the 1970s. Resolution of these latter issues has not yet been achieved, and already the industry seems poised for another major transition towards globalization, privatization, market fragmentation, and massive corporate reorganization.

So, was the period of Mac's presidency more tumultuous than any other? Very likely not, but its greatest challenge arose from having inherited a set of transportation and marketing policies – and, more particularly, a grain handling and railway system – largely designed and built in the 1920s and 1930s. The issue of modernizing the grain handling and transportation system dominated the agenda over the last half of Mac's presidency, and seemed to create a set of almost intractable problems: superfluous branch lines; a badly out-of-date elevator system; operational inefficiencies; freight rates that were a losing proposition for the railways; periodic tie-ups in transportation; and disputes over how the Wheat Board allocated railway cars. "To me," Mac recalled, "rail rationalization was our major project for a long period of time, and if I agonized more over any one issue over an extended period of time, it was this one."

He believed that the story of his involvement with the handling and transportation problems, more than any other part of his career, had to be told. He wrote:

> At the time I became president, there was a growing recognition, certainly among those engaged in the gathering and transportation of grain for export, that changes had to be made in the existing system. Among the first to "go public" on this issue were Bert Baker, General Manager of Alberta Wheat Pool, and Donald Gordon, President of Canadian National Railways. At the opening of the Symington Yard in Winnipeg, Mr. Gordon stated in no uncertain terms that low volume branch lines had to be abandoned if the railways were to move grain efficiently and economically.
>
> Mr. Baker made the same sort of case for major changes to the country elevator system. In a talk given to an agriculture course in Lethbridge, Alberta, he called for the elimination of some shipping points and a considerable reduction in the number of elevators so that larger handlings could carry the rapidly increasing cost of newer and more modern facilities.[1]
>
> While some industry people accepted this view, it was not an easy sell to farmers and politicians who had ingrained attachments to the status quo and strove to maintain it.[2]

UGG was one of the more forward-looking organizations in the industry, and it was soon to see - and more importantly, to join people like Bert Baker in publicly acknowledging - the need for such changes. Their message, however, was decidedly not welcome. Mac recalled that "when Donald Gordon said it in public in that speech in 1962, he really laid it on the line, and the reaction, of course - the formal or official reaction - was to be aghast at this terrible thing. And yet eighty percent of the people who were acting shocked knew damn well it had to happen, but they didn't want to say it in public. All scared of losing a bushel of grain up the driveway."

This fear was not groundless. Rural communities had a deep and emotional attachment both to their local elevators - the "prairie sentinels" dotting the landscape - and to the railway branch lines, which were seen as the very lifeline of small towns.

These attitudes made it difficult for the grain companies and railways to make the necessary changes to the grain handling and transportation system, and made the transportation debate as political and emotional as anything Mac had encountered in the Canadian Federation of Agriculture. Even so, he did not find the debate to be in the same "never never land" as the CFA policy discussions.

"It was," he said, "a different field altogether, because there was a background of economic necessity to it. The continuing success of the commercial operation of the company depended totally on getting something done about branch lines and removing surplus elevators, and the consolidation and updating of the system.

"So I never had any trouble getting up and sounding off about the elevator system, the rationalization of the elevator system, the rationalization of the rail system, and all the rest of it, because these were things I came to know something about and I believed so soundly they had to be done."

Although this is Mac's story, I can think of no better way of illustrating why he "agonized" so much than to tell of my own reaction the first time I set foot in a country elevator. It was in 1970, and being by birth neither a westerner, nor from a farm background, I was unprepared for what I was to see.

As I first walked into the elevator, I felt as though I had entered a living museum. My most vivid recollection is of the large, hand-carved, wooden levers protruding down near the back of the elevator. These, I was told, controlled the slides and gates that allowed grain to flow from overhead bins. An old boxcar was parked at the back, ready to be loaded. There was no running water and the washroom consisted of a small outbuilding. The manager weighed the incoming farm truckloads of grain with a manually operated scale, hand-writing the weight on the grain "ticket" to record the delivery. I had seen more modern equipment as a high-school student nearly fifteen years earlier, weighing truckloads of construction materials. All in all, I felt as if I had stepped back into a scene from the 1930s, which, in a very real sense, I had. I learned later that I had not visited the most modern of facilities, and the newer models would not have cast quite the same impression. But I had been introduced to what was probably an average elevator at the time.

I intrude into Mac's story with my own recollection only to describe in as graphic a way as possible how the problem faced by the grain industry in the early 1970s presented itself to the outsider. At UGG's delegate report meetings in 1976, Mac put it bluntly: "We have an elevator system, much of which is over 40 years old and very expensive to operate."[3] While the newer elevators looked less strikingly like museum pieces, and were as much as twice the size of those built in the 1930s, they still fell far short of what most people outside the grain industry, and the more thoughtful people inside, believed was required for a modern bulk-handling system.

The railways were as antiquated as the elevator system. Grain still moved by boxcar, the common-purpose car that had been the mainstay of the railways' fleets before the war, but which, in other industries, was quickly being replaced with specialty cars. Boxcars were never suited to hauling grain because, with a side-mounted door, they were exceedingly difficult to load and unload. The loading problem was solved by constructing, for every trip, a temporary wooden "grain door" just inside the car door, with a gap left at the top to insert the spout from the elevator. The outer door of the car slid shut over the grain door. The construction of the temporary door was called "coopering" the car, which was, as Mac said, "a tedious and wasteful process because every grain door was destroyed when the car was unloaded at the terminal elevator." Moreover, because of the continuous nailing into the door posts of the cars, "some of the old boxcars got so there was nothing left to nail the darn things to."

When the car reached a terminal elevator, the grain door had to be broken open, against the pressure of the contents of the car, so the grain could flow out. The grain piled in the ends of the car then had to be shovelled out. For many years, all this was done manually, but later, a machine called a "dumper" was developed, which actually lifted and tilted the car, back and forth and end to end, to allow the grain to spill out the side door.

The rail network was no more modern than the rolling stock. Even in 1976 – fifteen years after Mac became president – he was able to tell a Regina audience that "we have a rail system hopelessly expensive to operate and maintain as it is. We have a rail system little different from that of the 1930s, when horses pulled the grain to market. With so many miles of branch line in such sad repair, there is a risk trains will not be allowed to run on them."[4]

The shift from rail to truck for local, short-haul collection and distribution had removed virtually all traffic from these branch lines except for grain. Mac had seen the way cars and trucks were supplanting trains as the chief mode of local transportation even when he was living on the farm. "To get from Abernethy back to the farm in the winter time," he remembered, "we had to drive out of town, go north to Highway 10, go to Balcarres, and go south and back to the farm. As you were driving out of Abernethy to Number 10 highway, you were liable to meet McGavin's bread truck, you were liable to meet the mail truck, you were liable to meet groceries, fuel – all the things that used to come to Abernethy by rail were coming in by road. And that had changed, but grain wasn't supposed to change."

With small and closely spaced elevators, railway cars were still distributed to each country elevator a very few at a time, and the railway sidings beside the elevators were short, usually accommodating no more than a half-dozen cars at the most. Farmers still delivered in small trucks and, indeed, the platform scales on which the trucks were weighed were seldom long enough to handle semi-trailers, even though such equipment was beginning to come into use.

The newer elevators were being built progressivly larger, but the overall system was not designed for fast and efficient movement of a bulk commodity, even by the standards of the time.

A report prepared in 1970 by the management staff of UGG illustrated both the nature and extent of the problem faced by the company in modernizing its system. The report gave the age structure of the UGG elevator system in 1970 as follows:[5]

Age (years):	Built between:	Number of elevators:
Over 60	before 1910	9
50 – 60	1910 – 1919	71
40 – 50	1920 – 1929	233
30 – 40	1930 – 1939	76
20 – 30	1940 – 1949	35
10 – 20	1950 – 1959	100
Under 10	after 1959	62
Total		586

So almost half the elevators then operating had been built from 1920 to 1929; about one in eight was even older; and only just over one-quarter had been built in the most recent twenty years. The report pointed out that, at the current rates of construction of new elevators, it would take the company ninety-two years to replace the current system, or forty-one years if it only replaced half. It was not an encouraging observation.

UGG's system was quite typical for the industry at that time. The number of country elevators reached its peak of just over 5700 in the first half of the 1930s. All but a handful of these had been built prior to the 1929 crash, and about half of them in a period of most rapid expansion in the 1920s. By 1961, this number had only shrunk to 5300, and over the first decade of Mac's presidency, it went down to only about 4800.

The slow pace of change could readily be accounted for up to 1945 as the Depression and the war stifled development. However, after the war, while agricultural production was almost revolutionized with mechanization, chemicals, and fertilizers, and while other industries changed dramatically with new technological applications and increasing economies of scale, grain handling and transportation remained virtually unaffected by these same trends.

With the limited consolidation that had occurred, the roughly seven-mile spacing originally found between elevator points hadn't materially changed. During the 1970s, it became almost a cliché to say that the grain handling and transportation system was designed for the horse-and-buggy era.

It is essential to know why things had so stagnated, and why it was so dauntingly difficult to introduce change, in order to appreciate the depth of the problem the grain industry faced during Mac's presidency. At the core of this stagnation were four factors: grain marketing and storage policies; the quasi-regulatory role played by the CWB in setting grain handling charges and in managing transportation; the Crow's Nest Pass Rates on grain; and, last but not least, a bundle of attitudes and beliefs among the farm population. These four factors were interwoven into a web of constraint that made it impossible for any one party - railways, elevator companies, or farmers - to make changes without substantial cost (and no offsetting benefit) to their own operation.

Marketing policies were the starting point. In the post-war period, holding stocks off the market was seen as a key element of price stabilization and support in both the United States and Canada. These marketing policies, combined with a series of particularly good crops, had resulted in massive carryovers and chronic "congestion" of country elevators, which meant that country facilities were stuffed to the rafters with wheat.

The carryovers were moved into commercial storage rather than carried on the farm in order to provide farmers with some income. Farmers received an "initial payment" for wheat and barley received into primary elevators, and therefore the farmer realized an income to the extent that storage space was available. However, as a means of providing income, this strategy was soon swamped by large crops and restricted markets.

During this period, the CWB effectively controlled the grain companies' revenue from handling grain under an agreement that set charges on each bushel of grain farmers delivered. Ostensibly, the charges levied consisted of an elevation charge set by the Board of Grain Commissioners, and an administrative fee paid to the elevator companies for handling the grain on behalf of the Wheat Board. For practical purposes, however, the CWB charge was the effective handling fee, and the Board felt an obligation to minimize farmers' handling costs. Mac recalled how "Bill Mac [Wheat Board Chief Commissioner William McNamara] would say, 'Things are pretty tough out there on the farm, you know, we've got to help those guys out as best we can.'"

With its monopoly power, the CWB virtually dictated the tariffs the companies could levy. Because it kept such a tight lid on these charges, the revenues achieved under the handling agreement generally were not high enough to cover the costs of either sustaining or renewing the elevator system.

While handling revenues were kept down, storage revenues were not. With the CWB holding back grain from the market, but taking as much into storage as possible to provide farmers with some income flow, the average carryover stocks at the end of the crop year during the 1950s often equalled a full year's production. The government responded with a subsidy program under the Temporary Wheat Reserves Act (TWRA), which reimbursed the Wheat Board for the storage of all CWB-owned wheat stocks in excess of 178 million bushels. Grain companies' revenues came from both storage and handling, and although the Wheat Board kept a tight lid on their handling costs, storage tariffs were set by the Board of Grain Commissioners, which had a more pragmatic view of the companies' revenue needs. Moreover, because these charges were less visible to farmers, and were being picked up by the government anyway, there was less pressure to keep storage costs under control. As a result, storing grain at government expense became a more lucrative proposition than grain handling.

The marketing strategies that created high stocks, the storage charges that rose more quickly than handling tariffs, and the TWRA subsidies that shielded everyone from the costs of these policies had a number of perverse effects. Among these was encouraging grain companies to construct "balloon annexes" – large bins adjacent to existing elevators – which were quickly filled with grain. Mac later became extremely critical of the TWRA. He thought it "did an immense amount of harm to the elevator industry and to farmers. It made us into a storage-conscious industry (and we didn't realize what was happening and what was wrong) and it sapped our thinking.

"[The TWRA helped] no one but grain companies - and not even them because it was building useless storage that wasn't even needed."[6]

The subsidy program also paid storage and carrying charges for grain in "temporary storage facilities," and in this manner, a good number of curling rinks were built in western Canada at public expense.

In Mac's view, marketing policies were the crux of the problem.

> The Wheat Board had a great deal to do with the slowness in starting rationalization of the country elevator system, because they paid storage on grain in the country and they made it more profitable to store grain than move it. There is just no doubt in my mind that this could have been done differently.

> I think it was all part of the CWB's philosophy of holding out for the last cent. You don't sell grain when the price is down; you hold it until the price goes up and the farmer makes more money. But this philosophy doesn't say what he lives on in the meantime. I heard Bill McNamara tell the Wheat Board Advisory Committee, "Well, we can't get the price right now, but they are going to have to come to us one of these days and maybe we will get the stuff moving."

The more thoughtful and active farmers began to notice all this and objected to it. They were quite unforgiving of the fact that the grain companies were themselves caught in a bind. Mac explained that:

> The grain stored in rinks and balloon annexes and so on was one of the sorest points with the Palliser Wheat Growers Association. When they first started up, they used to blame the grain companies for doing this, because they were making a lot of money. And one of the hardest things to convince them of was that we would be much happier to be moving grain than piling it up like that, but that was the only way we could make a dollar, because the Board of Grain Commissioners was far more realistic about our revenue situation than the Wheat Board. They gave us more money on the storage side than the Wheat Board gave us on the handling side. So we were forced to do it.

> Actually, we were doing it for two reasons: it was the only way we could make a dollar, and it was the only way the farmer could deliver any grain.

Because of the congestion caused by high stock levels, a farmer could deliver grain into an elevator only when a boxcar arrived to take grain out. As we saw in Chapter 4, farmers were, therefore, often forced into the kind of situation where even the opportunity to deliver on the "initial quota" had to be shared informally at the local level.

Neither farmers nor grain companies had much control over the arrival of boxcars. Grain movement was broadly controlled through shipping orders given out by the Canadian Wheat Board to the grain companies, which then distributed them among their individual elevators. Theoretically, this provided the railways with guidance as to where to place their cars. However, these "general shipping orders" were frequently overridden by more specific shipping instructions from the Board. Moreover, there were always far more shipping orders outstanding than the railways had cars to place, or than there were actual sales outstanding. With a large number of shipping orders always outstanding, the railways had a great deal of flexibility in where they could place boxcars for loading, and so they distributed cars pretty much in a manner they found convenient to themselves. Individual elevators, therefore, were almost completely at the mercy of the CWB and the railways in moving grain out of their facilities.

The system also restricted the farmers' ability to deliver grain when and where they wished. Not only was there a quota system that regulated the timing of deliveries during the year, the regulations also required each farmer to select only one delivery point at the beginning of the crop year. Once this point was selected, a farmer was not allowed to deliver grain anywhere else. The effect of this regulation was particularly pernicious when one company closed an elevator at a competitive point. "A farmer could get locked into a Pool point, when he had no intention of delivering to the Pool," Mac said, "but he couldn't deliver it anywhere else because his permit book would not allow it. I don't think you could get away with something like that today."

The net effect of the marketing and storage policies was to frustrate the grain companies' ability to consolidate their systems. It became almost impossible for a grain company to close a group of small elevators and consolidate the operations in a more modern facility at one point. Closing elevators meant losing storage revenue, and losing the ability to ship grain under the CWB railcar allocation formula. In fact, the importance of storage revenue sometimes impelled grain companies to keep country elevators licensed and full of wheat, even after they had been closed for further deliveries. "We had elevators in Alberta that had been closed and stayed closed for years, full of grain," Mac recalled.

One economic lever that could have broken this deadlock was more favourable freight rates for shipping from main lines, and shipping cars in multiple lots instead of one at a time. A lower freight rate might have given farmers an economic incentive to haul their grain to larger centralized elevators, but there were three impediments to this strategy.

The first was the existence of the Crow's Nest Pass Rates. Because the railways had been losing money on grain movement since the 1950s, they had virtually no flexibility to charge less than the prevailing rates, even if they had been inclined to do so. In 1975, UGG sponsored a study on the economics of large inland terminal elevators, but found "no concrete evidence that freight rate incentives would be offered by the railroads for multi-car shipments," and without them, there was "no freight rate advantages for terminals out of which we could compensate farmers for hauling that longer distance."[7]

Second, there was the CWB's control over transportation. A grain company could not have arranged the shipping program needed either to sustain the larger elevator, or to gain the lower rates, even if they had been available, because of the predominant role the CWB played in managing transportation. In fact, because of the CWB's control of "car allocation" and delivery quotas, the companies had only slight management control over their elevators and were reduced to little more than warehouse operators whose businesses were confined to individual grain delivery points.

The third factor was the restriction on farmers' deliveries. With the farmers being required to nominate a shipping point at the beginning of the crop year, grain companies had only one chance per year to attract business into a central location.

Closure of elevators from the farmer's perspective meant only a longer haul and less storage space to deliver grain into, not lower costs or improved service. For a grain company, closing elevators not only meant loss of storage revenue and shipping, it also meant loss of market share because farmers could not, and had no incentives to, deliver to newer centralized facilities. Unilateral consolidation of elevators was therefore suicidal for an individual grain company, whose customers would be irate over losing "their" elevator. Mac still has bitter, bitter letters from UGG customers over the elevator closures that did occur at that time.

The net effect of all these forces was that an elevator company's commercial success was achieved by maintaining the elevators they had with their associated storage capacity rather than by running fewer and more efficient elevators. Competition at each delivery point was fierce, but competition between delivery points was almost nil, and the best competitive strategy was simply to fight a war of attrition. The company that could hang on until the competing elevators finally closed down would be assured of picking up a good measure of the vacating company's business, and keeping the remaining elevator profitable for a while longer.

Elevator companies were slowly closing the smallest and most uneconomical of their facilities, but were forced into a slow, painful, lockstep progression toward a consolidated and modernized system. With elevator rationalization proceeding at a snail's pace, branch line abandonment became impossible. The slow closure of the least economical plants rarely translated into sufficient closures along an entire branch line to permit abandonment.

All in all, it was not one of the finest periods in Canadian transportation and agricultural policy.

Arguably, however, the most profound impediment to change was the attitudes among the farmers and residents of smaller towns, who vigorously opposed any changes to the elevator or rail line system. The sources of this resistance were several. The perverse economics described above was one, preventing farmers from seeing the full costs of maintaining the system as it was. The desire of small towns to retain the tax revenue from elevators and railway property was another. The cooperative nature of the elevator system was a third, with farmers seeing the local elevator as being "theirs," and feeling betrayed by the company when closures occurred. Local pride, often mixed with nostalgia, was a fourth, with community residents looking back to the time when local families had built the town and the elevator only a few decades before.

The resistance to consolidation of elevators was probably less than the resistance to railway abandonment. The railways had tried to abandon costly low-volume branch lines in the post-war period, but the ensuing political outcry caused the government to forestall their efforts by establishing the MacPherson Royal Commission on transportation in the late 1950s. This was accompanied by a moratorium on line abandonment pending new legislation to follow.

Politicians were wary about abandonment because of a widespread public resentment towards the railways, which had come into being almost as soon as the railways were built. In part, this resentment was a justifiable reaction to the excesses of market power in those early days. However, it was also grounded in the mistaken belief that, since the railways "got half of western Canada" when they were built, every community was owed rail service in perpetuity. At one time it was said that every farm boy and girl "was brought up to love God and hate the CPR." This hatred of the railways is legendary in the west, and is exemplified by the old joke of the farmer shaking his fist at the sky after a hailstorm had wiped out his crop, and cursing the CPR. By the 1960s, this suspicion of the railways had given rise to a belief in a railway plot to do away with the Crow Rates, abandon all the branch lines, and force farmers to haul their grain miles and miles to main lines.

Mac described an encounter with these attitudes, which bordered on being both rude and embarrassing:

> There was a community luncheon connected with some function at Russell, Manitoba, that [CP vice-president] Russ Allison attended. CP had contributed quite generously to some project in the community, and one of the things Russ did to help them out was that he took the vice-president's car up, and he had some of the dignitaries of the community in for lunch in the car, which was always a nice experience. Later, at a big community dinner, a woman at his table asked him who he was and what he did, and when he told her, she said, "Well, aren't you ashamed of yourself for working for a company like that?" Then she went on to ask, "How did you get an invitation to this function, anyway?"
>
> This is the hate you were supposed to have for anything that was CP and anything that was not "co-op." You had to be anti-railway and a dedicated cooperator to live in a rural community.
>
> I think that has gone out the window very, very much in recent times, but then, it was just part of their way of life.

Compounding the animosity towards the railways was a concern over the future of local communities, as post-war trends saw smaller towns shrink and disappear. Concerned citizens often saw the railway as an economic lifeline, without which their town would surely die. While there was some truth in this up to the 1940s, closure of elevators and abandonment of branch lines were not the prime reason why small towns were disappearing, and their retention was not going to change the fate of smaller communities. Centralization of both commercial and public-service activities was a fact of life as schools, hospitals, and post offices consolidated.

Moreover, studies repeatedly showed that it was the level of retail shopping services offered by towns that was the chief factor in determining their survival. Farmers and residents of smaller communities, just like city dwellers, were demanding a wider range of goods and services than smaller centres could support. The mobility of the automobile allowed them to shop at larger stores in larger towns and cities, leaving the smaller centres without a viable commercial life. Larger farms also meant a declining rural population base. A smaller and more mobile populace, with more elaborate and sophisticated tastes, all added up to the emergence of a new culture in which the small, rural town no longer had a place.

Many residents of small towns recognized the broader forces that were at work in shaping the demise of their communities, but they were also caught in a dilemma. The economic forces that led them to buy household goods and automobiles and farm equipment in larger centres were not operative in the grain handling and transportation system. So it made economic sense to fight to preserve the convenience of local facilities.

Collisions between the new realities and the resistance to elevator closures and rail abandonment occurred even before Mac became president, and he recalled the amusing resolution of these conflicts in Abernethy when the railway proposed removing the local station agent:

> CP had sent someone out to Abernethy to tell them they were going to close the station. Of course, there was a big protest meeting in the village and everybody turned out, and it was just going to be the end of the world if the Abernethy station was closed.
>
> At the end of the evening the railway people said, "Well, let's do a study on how much freight is being brought into town by rail. We'll come back in a month and check it."
>
> So they came back in five or six weeks, and in the month between, four spools of barbed wire and two cartons of toilet paper had come in by rail. Well, when they read the list, a roar of laughter broke out around the hall. The absurdity of it was just so bloody self-evident.

The real sense of loss felt by many as smaller communities shrank manifested itself emotionally when the grain elevator and rail line – often the last thing left in the town – were threatened. Farmers did not have the same economic incentive to shift grain delivery patterns that they had for changing their other shopping practices. So when elevators closed or rail lines were abandoned, there was a much greater sense of loss. Consolidation of the grain handling and transportation system often seemed like an arbitrary decision, made in faraway head offices, sacrificing local services in order to enhance corporate profits. Thus, elevator closures and branch line abandonments became lightning rods for concerns that had much broader causes.

Even allowing for all the forces that caused such distress to many rural residents, the defense of small communities was often taken to extremes. Mac found it frustrating, and remembered "being rapped over the knuckles by a chap from the Alberta government who was some kind of rural development officer for twenty-three communities somewhere in south-central Alberta. I forget his exact title, but he was out to build a rink and a this and a that in every community. And I raised the question one time, 'Have you ever thought of having a curling rink in one town and a skating rink in another town and some other facility in another town, and so on?' And in a stern voice he told me, 'Mr. Runciman, my role is to maintain those communities and see that they all have the facilities they should have, not to destroy them.' He told me off, you see."

But Mac knew that all communities could not be saved, and, moreover, he knew that elevators and railway lines were not the major determinant of a town's survival. When discussions of system rationalization turned to the emotional minefield of community viability, he would often refer to one of two contrasting examples to illustrate his points.

> I used to use Steinbach as a measuring stick. Steinbach never had a grain elevator. Steinbach never had a railway line. Yet Steinbach is the core of one of the most concentrated production areas of agriculture in western Canada. Why? Because they had to find ways of getting rid of their grain when they didn't have an elevator and a railway. They had the initiative to find ways around the fact. Instead of becoming a backwoods because they didn't have a grain elevator, they determined to do something about it. So they produced poultry and eggs as cheaply as anybody in Canada. They used to export eggs to Saskatchewan, to Ontario, and even to North Dakota and Minnesota until the supply management system came in and said, Oh no you don't! You'll stop at the borders and Saskatchewan will produce broilers over here and Ontario will producer broilers over there and you will reduce production.

> And one of the other things they did was to set up trucking firms, and on top of that they became the automobile capital of Manitoba, as well. The business acumen of the people was a big component of the town's success, I'm sure, right from the beginning.

The second example he often cited came from the other end of the spectrum from Steinbach. It was a small community he had first visited just after he had joined the UGG board of directors and was examining the problems with Harper Construction. "I remember on my trip with Fred Dickinson," he said, "he took me to a hamlet called Dumas on the Reston-Wolseley line. There were two houses and one elevator. There were the elevator manager, his wife, and two children living in one of them; there was a section man living in the other. They both had to drive into Wawota to get drinking water. And that's all there was left at Dumas.

"Now, I used to raise the question, 'Was society better off or worse off by the disappearance of those two houses?' And yet this is an example of what they were trying to protect."

As described earlier, the Wheat Pools had adopted a usually hostile attitude to market economics, and generally favoured a regulated and centrally controlled system. On this basis, it was natural for them to oppose railway abandonment, and to support these attitudes at the local level. However, their survival as grain handling businesses also required them to recognize the economic necessity of consolidating the system. The result was considerable tension between the politically acceptable thing to say in public, and their corporate behaviour.

"The area around Yorkton provided a classic example," said Mac. "The Pool had a number of elevators in that general area, with probably ten, at one time, on the Wroxton to Parkerview branch. They had closed all but one of these on the part of the line that ran east from Yorkton to Wroxton when the line was proposed for abandonment, but they opposed the abandonment anyway. These decisions were just incomprehensible to me, but it wouldn't have been politically popular to support abandonment of the line. You've got to fight the railroads!"

Of course, UGG faced the same concerns from their own members and customers, but the company tried to be more forthright about the need for change, and did not express this kind of intransigent opposition to branch line abandonment. In fact, Mac was not too far behind Bert Baker and Donald Gordon in talking about the need for change. In March of 1963, he made his own assessment of the transportation and handling problems, in a talk to the Kiwanis Club in Saskatoon.

> Everyone foresees in the future, larger elevators at larger shipping points taking the place of those on abandoned lines and of small outmoded elevators at sidings and smaller centres, which will not be rebuilt when they reach the end of their useful life. ...
>
> [However] to develop [the consolidation process] logically and effectively without knowing what the rail pattern of the future will be, is a virtual impossibility. ...
>
> Many of these branch lines are the lifeline of the Communities they serve and are well worth defending. However, I don't mean by this that all branch lines should be defended. Some are obviously inefficient and of little value or benefit to a Community. We will only weaken our case

and that of the railroads on the abandonment issue, if we follow that policy.[8]

Mac had the integrity and courage to speak openly about the problem, not only to urban audiences, but in rural areas where the message was less welcome. In a talk to a branch line retention committee in Carman, Manitoba, in February 1964, he said: "We should be as firm and fair in saying no to the defense of a very low volume line as we are firm in defending lines we consider to be defensible."[9]

Mac was always quick to point out that he could not have spoken out as he did without the full support of UGG's board of directors, and without an able staff that helped him to analyze and articulate the nature of the problems and the need for change. "It wasn't just me," he used to tell me repeatedly, "because the board was always behind me 100 percent when I spoke on these issues."

Despite the desire of the board to be frank about what had to be done, the attitudes of farmers caused both the board of directors and the staff to be cautious in their statements out in the country, where they had to be cognizant of the opposition they would get, and not only from farmers, but from other organizations and politicians, as well. As Mac admitted:

> Actually, we were struggling to be two-faced. We wanted to get the job done, and we didn't want to turn massive blocks of customers against us. It was as simple as that. There was the economic side of it, and there was the political side of it, and we wiggled away at it as well as we could.
>
> I don't think we were ever backward in our thinking about what had to be done in the future, but just try to do it fast when (a) you don't have the money, and (b) you can't muster farm organization support. Because every step you might have coaxed the Pools to take, the National Farmers Union would oppose right down to the last branch line and the last country elevator.
>
> And the politician of course would defend the Farmers Union position: "We've got to keep the farmers on the land," and all this sort of garbage. So these are the sort of things that held up the rationalization of the system.

While it was true that the attitudes of farmers helped to shape the grain handling and transportation system, it is also true that grain marketing policies helped to shape the attitudes of farmers that made system rationalization so difficult. Mac believed that the "ignorance of the end use of the products of the farms of western Canada was a serious obstacle to doing intelligent things. And it was a by-product of the Wheat Board system, and the pooling system, and so forth. I've said it in speeches: their view of marketing stopped, and they thought they had done their job, when they dumped their load of grain into the pit. It was the Wheat Board's responsibility then, and the Wheat Board would sure do a good job."

Because farmers did not, in general, know what was happening beyond their local elevator, the high stock level was quite often blamed on a lack of railcars, rather than on market forces and marketing policies. Mac became frustrated by this seeming ignorance at the farm level. "I would go out to country meetings," he told me, "and the only thing they felt they needed to cure the problem was a supply of boxcars. No realization of the fact the world market was not buying, that every bit of storage capacity was plugged with wheat, and there was no place to take it if there had been boxcars, and boxcars weren't being placed because there was no place to take it. And yet the attitude was, 'If we just had boxcars, there would be no problem.' "

The deficiencies in the system were brought home dramatically to the industry during the early 1960s, as it struggled to move grain for the first large sales to the Soviet Union and China. "We had that period where we couldn't move the crop because it wasn't being sold," Mac pointed out, "and then the grain started to move and we couldn't move it fast enough because we had old, outdated elevators. In some respects, we had allowed the system to run down almost to the point of being inoperative."

These events slowly forced the industry to come to grips with the problems. Faced with seemingly insurmountable barriers to unilateral closures, elevator companies had to develop other strategies to move the consolidation process forward, and so they developed a program of what they called "saw-offs": a negotiated trading of facilities. Thus, a company would trade its elevator at one point for the other company's at a second point, where both were located. Later, saw-offs came to involve multiple trades: several elevators of one for several of another. A large number of these trades were concluded in the 1960s.

The second major approach by the elevator companies to the rationalization of their facilities was a process of corporate consolidation and buyouts. Starting in the 1920s, and continuing almost unabated until the 1980s, there was a steady decline in the number of companies involved in grain handling as smaller enterprises were sold up. The number of companies operating five elevators or more declined by almost a third during the 1920s (from sixty-four to forty), probably reflecting the maturing of the industry during and after the initial building period. After 1930, the number continued to decline to twenty-three by 1950 and to thirteen by 1970.[10]

UGG had participated in this corporate consolidation, with its major purchases being Reliance Grain in 1948 (the move that brought Mac into contact with UGG in the first place) and Canadian Consolidated in 1959. In 1968, they also acquired the elevator facilities of McCabe Grain.[11] "I remember my sense of satisfaction," said Mac, "when I shook hands with [McCabe president] Charlie Kroft over the acquisition of McCabe. It was a bit traumatic for Charlie, and it was nice for us, and yet it was done in great spirit. I had a great deal of respect for the McCabe people, and Charlie was happy because it was going into what he thought were good hands."

During Mac's presidency, two very significant purchases took place by other companies: the purchase of Federal Grain by the three Wheat Pools, and the purchase of National Grain by Cargill. In both cases, these companies had been in talks with UGG and, had UGG been the buyer, the structure of the western Canadian grain industry might be very different today. He recalled the story of UGG's involvement in the sale of National Grain as being particularly interesting.

> George Heffelfinger had approached me and we had talked a few times about us taking over National Grain, and I can remember him and me going over to the Old Spaghetti Factory restaurant, and having lunch and talking about it there. He was looking for approaches.

> All of a sudden one day the phone rang, and it was George. "Mac," he said, "this business of talking about the sale has got to stop. There has been too much loose talk. I'm getting things on the street, and we've got to cut it out."

> It shocked me, because I had never mentioned it to anybody - not even within the company - because he had asked me not to. The next day, it was announced that Cargill had bought National Grain. What had happened, I guess, was that the word got going in Minneapolis that the company was for sale.

> But one of the amusing things that happened when Cargill bought National was the way the Farmers Union rose up in indignation to condemn them as a multinational company coming into Canada. About a month later, Cargill held a big reception marking their 50th year of business in Canada.

The sale of Federal Grain to the Pools was a much larger transaction. Federal was by far the largest of the private companies, larger even than UGG itself. Nevertheless, when Federal first decided it wanted out of the business, it began to discuss the possibility of a deal with UGG.

> [Federal Grain's chairman] George Sellers came and started talks with us, and while these talks were underway, the Grains Group was formed and they were going to run the elevator system in western Canada, and decide where companies could build a country elevator and things like this. So we decided we'd better halt the process. And that was around 1969.

> Well, when the dust settled about forming the Grains Group, Federal had gone to Sask Pool instead, or, for all I know, maybe Sask Pool came to them. And it was a bit of a shocker to some of our directors. They knew we had been dickering with Federal, and when we didn't get it, oh boy, this was the end of the world.

> But [UGG general manager] Bill Winslow said to them, and he would say to me, that he wasn't that sure that we could have absorbed Federal Grain. I guess it was trying to salve our wounds, but Bill and I used to say that, if the consolidation goes as far as we think it has to go, all we're going to be doing for the next ten years or so is closing elevators. It would have left us with an awful lot of work to do. We would have had places where we had four and five elevators on one market, and things like that, and it cost money even to tear them down.

UGG also missed the opportunity to buy another, but much smaller, private company called Interocean Grain. Mac was not happy with the way UGG lost the deal.

> One of the things I didn't accomplish – and it was one time I felt I was a bit weaker than I should have been – was the acquisition of Interocean Grain from Bob Purves. [UGG Manager of Country Operations] Jim Mants was a very good friend of Bob's, and Jim was very much in favour of the deal.

> The management people came in one day with a review of the economics of acquiring Interocean. They had some nice properties in good locations, but they were asking a pretty stiff price, and the analysis showed that it was going to take a long time for the properties to pay for themselves. So their recommendation to the board was not to do it, and so we didn't.

It was small potatoes – not more than fifteen or twenty elevators or something – but I wakened up one night and got thinking about it, and started to realize that what they had left out – and what I should have seen immediately – was the residual value at the end of the pay-back period. And some of those elevators were going to be good for another twenty-five years.

It was the only time I could say that personal feelings within the company affected a transaction of any significance, because Jim and John Wachal and Bill weren't getting along too well at that time. Jim left shortly after, as a matter of fact. I still wondered why on earth I didn't recognize that, even if the pay-back had been fifteen years, there was still going to be ten or more years left in the property. I always felt badly about that one.

The saw-offs and the acquisitions still did not give the companies the means to consolidate and modernize the system to anything like the degree required, and Mac addressed the difficulty of meeting the planning and rationalization challenge repeatedly in his reports to his board of directors. In July 1967, he wrote of his frustration that a hearing, scheduled in Winnipeg to consider the abandonment of the rail line from Boissevain to Lauder in Manitoba, had been cancelled:

It seemed that after years of uncertainty some indication might now be obtained of the pace and pattern to be expected as the long delayed process of branch line abandonment got underway.

However, the hearing was postponed indefinitely following protests to Ottawa by various groups. No hearings will now be held until after a "pre-hearing conference" ... to develop procedures to deal with future rail line abandonment hearings.

In view of this development it will be necessary to firm up our policy with regard to rail abandonment and abandonment procedures. This has not been possible in recent months, owing to the many uncertainties which have prevailed.[12]

The hearing was eventually held, but did not lead to resolution of this issue, as Mac had hoped. Two years later, he devoted a very lengthy section of his president's report to the difficulty of planning the elevator system. This section of the report sounds much like a man thinking out loud about a subject where the problem is apparent but the solution evasive:

Quite frequently, [we] are forced to recognize the extreme difficulty of providing ... long range planning.

The grain business is affected by such a welter of influences ... that long range planning, a difficult process in any industry, becomes well nigh impossible. ...

At the same time, with the increasing scale and cost of elevator facilities, long term planning is more essential than ever to companies intending to continue the commitment of resources to this low-return industry. ...

Adherence to a 1920 concept of elevator operation could be crippling or fatal for any company. ...

What use to project super terminals and vast capital expenditures in country facilities if the future finds western Canada engaged in the production of meat.

It may be that the best that can be done is to keep in step with change by being as alert as possible to new developments and then moving on the basis of short- or medium-term adjustments to conform to the new pattern.

This may be feasible as far as country facilities are concerned but the concept leaves much to be desired when it is applied to consideration of a multimillion dollar ... terminal elevator.[13]

What was not widely understood or appreciated during the 1960s was that the conundrum of too many elevators on too many branch lines was not the problem in itself, but merely the symptom. However, the next decade was one of intense debate on transportation and handling, and out of it emerged new understanding. It was eventually realized, but, despite much debate, not universally accepted, that consolidation and modernization were so difficult because of the complex interplay between the forces described above: marketing, storage, subsidies, freight rates, regulation, and farmer attitudes.

Over the course of his presidency, Mac and the UGG board of directors became increasingly outspoken about the industry's transportation and handling problems, and it is interesting to follow the evolution of their thinking. In the early 1960s, the public debate on transportation was just beginning, and most of the farm public was simply not ready to listen to anything other than unqualified support for the status quo. Mac's speeches at this point tended to reiterate the beliefs of the day. In his March 1963 speech to the Kiwanis Club in Saskatoon, in which he discussed at such length the difficulties of planning, he also addressed the Crow's Nest Pass Rates and gave what was the standard view of the time: "Retention of the Crows Nest Pass Rates is vital, if we are to continue to produce grain for export in Western Canada. We must never lose sight of this fact and should avoid any action which would strengthen the case of those who would like to see the rates abolished."[14]

As his views on this issue changed, his comment about the need to be "two-faced" on branch line abandonment became even more true about the Crow. As he admitted, "It was politic to support the Crow at that time, I think, and you could hurt yourself by saying the contrary. There are times when it is best not to make a point, even though you are perfectly right. When you are responsible for the business of a company, the last thing you wanted was an elevator manager phoning his superintendent to say, 'I lost a customer because the company's doing this or that.' So there is always that moderating influence."

The company had always to balance the need to see the transportation problems understood, against its desire to lead its customers and members without alienating them. This was made considerably easier in the early 1970s after the government stepped in with its purchase of railcars. While this was, as Mac said somewhat acidly, "an exact example of ... government creating a crisis and then magnanimously stepping in with a remedy,"[15] it had a positive result. He pointed out to another farm audience a few months later that "when I first left the farm to work in Winnipeg, we weren't supposed to talk about ... the Crow's Nest grain rates. ... It was taboo. The reason? We wanted no tinkering with Crow's Nest rates.

"And that taboo lasted until a few years ago when we found the railways were quickly running out of boxcars [because] there wasn't enough money in the business."[16]

By the time he retired, Mac had seen through many of the old arguments for retaining the Crow, and had lost patience with those who continued to use them.

> One of the big arguments — and I still hear about those who will not bend on this — is that the Crow was a sacred trust, given to western Canada to ensure development. It was nothing of the sort. It applied on a small number of lines to take grain to Thunder Bay from points that existed then, and I think the really terrible move that was made was in 1925 when they made it apply to all grain on all railways. How on earth can anybody talk about it being a sacred trust to develop the west when

it didn't apply to the Canadian Northern and the Grand Trunk and all those lines that became the Canadian National? I can't believe the way that people think, and talk about it.

But you can get away with that in the political arena. It's the way to talk and think, I suppose. But I bet there wasn't one person in a thousand on farms in western Canada who had a clear understanding of the Crow agreement, what it meant, what it said, and why all the grain came under it. It wasn't done by agreement, it was done by legislative fiat.

Mac's position here misses the argument that the Crow Rates were seen, to some extent, as a part of a national bargain which gave eastern businesses a protective tariff, and western agriculture a legislated freight rate. But he is quite right about cynical political statements deliberately inflaming an already woefully ill-informed debate. Continual repetition of the myth that "the CPR got half of western Canada for the Crow," by people who knew it was false, was perhaps the most extreme example.

Although the federal government had tried, through the Grains Group, to come to grips with the transportation problems, it had overplayed its hand with an arrogance that alienated the industry. Nevertheless, some progress was made in the early 1970s.

Otto Lang had tried unsuccessfully to repeal the Temporary Wheat Reserves Act in about 1972, much against the wishes of the defenders of the status quo. However, the legislation was designed to die as soon as the CWB's year-end grain stocks fell below 178 million bushels. On August 1, 1973, they did, and government-subsidized storage came to an end.

At about the same time, the Grains Council's *State of the Industry* report led the Canadian Grain Commission to reclaim its authority over elevation tariffs from The Canadian Wheat Board, and, in a constructive move, the commission began to bring handling and storage tariffs back into a proper balance. These developments largely ended the elevator companies' dependence on storage revenues, and thus broke one of the major constraints to rationalization. However, the Crow remained the major impediment to change, and the responsibility for resolving this dilemma fell squarely on the government's shoulders.

In 1974, the government seized the initiative back from the industry, and Otto Lang, who was the minister responsible for The Canadian Wheat Board from 1968 to 1979, caused an enormous public stir in the fall of that year when, at a Canada Grains Council meeting, he suggested the possibility of a public debate on the Crow. Despite the protests, he followed through on his audacious suggestion, and established two major commissions of inquiry to examine the most pressing transportation issues: prairie branch lines and the Crow's Nest Pass Rates.

The first of the two commissions was placed under the leadership of former Supreme Court Justice Emmett Hall, and was asked to make recommendations on the fate of a number of prairie branch lines. The second, under an American transportation consultant, Carl Snavely, was to settle the question of whether the railways did lose money carrying grain under the Crow Rates, and if so, how much.

As minister of transport, Mr. Lang had already taken the first step in resolving the uncertainty about the branch lines by defining a "permanent rail network." The National Transportation Act of 1967 gave the minister the power to prohibit the railways from abandoning specific lines, and Lang exempted over 12,000 miles (about sixty-five percent of the entire rail network in western Canada) from abandonment consideration until the year 2000 (a prohibition which did not survive, but was repealed during the 1990s in conjunction with other changes in grain transportation legislation). Abandonment applications were permitted on a handful of trackage, leaving about 6300 miles to be examined by the Hall Commission.

UGG played an important role both before the two commissions and, later, in determining how the issues were ultimately resolved. The company's stance towards transportation issues had attracted support from farmers who wanted reform and, as president, Mac was thrust to the forefront of the debate. It was an outstanding example of Mac's unique leadership skills, where, as he put it, "if a good cause came along that I could believe in, then I was willing to help the thing along."[17] Supported by the UGG board, Mac became a spokesperson for those who wanted change.

The work done by the Grains Group, and the review of that work by the Canada Grains Council, had given Mac and the UGG board of directors a thorough understanding of the grain transportation and handling issues, and their interconnections. Specifically, they knew – and were prepared to state publicly – that the branch line issue was inextricably linked to freight rates, and however much Hall may have wished to avoid addressing the Crow, he could not look at branch lines in isolation.

The reason for the linkage between the two issues lay in the provisions of the 1967 National Transportation Act. The MacPherson Royal Commission on Transportation had recognized that the railways were losing money on grain and recommended that they be compensated. When the Act was first presented to Parliament, it contained a provision that would have provided subsidies for the losses, but the defenders of the Crow saw an acknowledgement of financial loss as an attack on the rates themselves, and were not prepared to allow such heresy to be voiced. The opponents of change therefore managed to remove this section of the Bill.

The Bill also provided for subsidies for uneconomic branch lines, but the level of these subsidies was calculated by factoring in the costs and revenues of traffic moving on the line. The result was that, if the traffic on the line was losing money, so would the line itself the branch line subsidy would actually cover the loss occurring on the traffic as well as the losses associated with keeping the line. The net effect was to confuse the entire branch line issue. No one could tell which branch lines were "uneconomic" (and therefore candidates for abandonment) solely because of low traffic volume, and which suffered losses solely because of the depressed rates.

One consequence of this situation was that the branch line subsidies to the railways acted much like the TWRA storage subsidies did to the elevator companies: reducing their incentive to abandon inefficient operations. Grain traffic moving from low traffic density branch lines was inadvertently subsidized; traffic from efficient lines was not. It was that simple, and the result was obvious.

The company's first submission to the commission described how the entire grain handling and transportation system had evolved, and how the disparate forces previously described prevented the players from rationalizing the system. It then explained how the branch line subsidies were confusing the issue put before the commission, because losses on branch lines could not be distinguished from losses on the grain freight rate.

The initial submission was presented privately, but UGG made no secret of its contents. It contained three major elements, each of which represented a bold stance for the company to take. First, it recommended that the Crow issue be dealt with, and put forward a proposal for solving it. This position was described in the 1975 UGG annual report in Mac's "Report of the President." This part of the report was the directors' most important statement each year to the company's customers, shareholders, and members, and it was the first major public statement by UGG in favour of freight-rate reform. The following is a precis of material in the annual report, containing the key points which UGG had made on this very controversial matter:

> The existence of branch lines is a function of freight rates. The statutory rate (Crow's Nest) issue must be resolved and the railways made financially whole in the carriage of grain.

> The statutory rate issue should be resolved on the following basis:

★ The net amount that the producer pays for transport of his grain must *not* increase. The federal government has a commitment not to increase this rate.

★ There must be iron-clad guarantees that the railways provide needed facilities for grain.

★ Incentives for change must be introduced so that if rail economies can be achieved by changes in the elevator system, the elevator companies can realize the benefits and pass them back to farmers.

★ Branch line subsidies should no longer provide compensation to the railways for losses under the statutory rates.[18]

The annual report went on to describe the company's proposal. Fix grain freight rates at the level of the Crow for farmers, it said, allow the railways to charge higher freight rates to elevator companies, and then compensate the elevator companies for the difference. This proposal was put forth as a way of allowing market forces some play, while at the same time retaining a fixed rate for farmers. As Mac put it: "We just feel that it is better than a straight subsidy to the railway which would offer no incentive to the railroads or the grain companies to modernize their systems."[19]

Even in 1975, although the "taboo" had been broken, most of the farm community still had much to learn about the Crow, and so Mac saw the statements in the annual report as a bold but risky step. He said the "annual report was approved by the board of directors before it went to the annual meeting, and it was approved by the delegates before it was distributed to shareholders. So this was a real stepping stone into the deep water."

The second element of the UGG submission was a map classifying the 6300 miles of branch lines into four categories: those that could be considered for abandonment within one year; those within five years; those within ten years; and those that should be added to the "permanent network."

The third major element of the UGG submission was a forthright statement that "the grain handling and transportation system should not be used as an instrument to preserve local communities, or otherwise to serve for the fulfillment of social goals."[20]

This position was quite consistent with UGG's philosophy and its focus on the economic, as opposed to social, goals of cooperation. Nevertheless, to express these views as forthrightly and unequivocally as they did was risky as long as the fate of small towns was believed to hinge on the continued existence of elevators and rail lines.

The company's second and "supplementary" submission to the commission was made early the following year. Mac told the UGG board that it had presented "an analysis of the costs and revenues on the subsidized lines with a view to determining whether added revenues to railways would be likely to render any of the 6300 miles of line profitable and thus remove them from consideration of abandonment."[21]

The UGG annual report for 1976 described how, in its second submission, "UGG showed the Commission that even quite moderate increases in the railways' grain revenues would make many lines profitable ... and therefore would destroy the railways' case for abandonment. For this reason, deciding to abandon branch lines before knowing what the federal government is going to do about railway grain revenues is putting the cart before the horse."[22]

The contrasting positions taken by UGG and the Pools on branch lines were a vivid example of the two divergent philosophies in the farm community that had so paralyzed the Canada Grains Council. To the Pools, line abandonment was a thing the government should decide; to UGG, it was a decision that should be made by economic forces. Saskatchewan Wheat Pool believed that the commission could define the rail network for the foreseeable future, and was prepared to specify exactly which lines should be abandoned and which kept. UGG, on the other hand, put forward its classification of lines and time frames only as guidelines. Mac spoke out publicly about the difference in view, telling the Regina Chamber of Commerce that while "I respect Saskatchewan Wheat Pool for coming out and saying that 1400 miles of branch lines in Saskatchewan could be abandoned ... UGG wants continuing review of branch lines ... not an arbitrary decision right now.

"In conclusion, this whole question of a future grain handling system will depend on the real cost of the system. As far as possible, a farmer should see these costs as a charge against his cash ticket."[23] This latter point was important, because UGG continually pressed for the costs of the system to be shown openly to farmers so that market signals, rather than government decrees, would determine the shape of the branch line network.

UGG's third submission was a "summary position" presented in Saskatoon on September 2, 1976, and it showed how strongly the company believed that the transportation and handling system should serve economic and not social goals. The shape of the system, it said, should be governed by the market, not by some central planning body. That this position was not just Mac's, but was supported by the UGG board of directors, is confirmed by the fact that it was reported in the company's annual reports. An appendix to the 1976 annual report quoted from the submission: "Underlying every argument and every proposal which United Grain Growers has put forward to your [the Hall] Commission is this principle: the grain producer must be the one to choose the grain handling and transportation system he wants. Others cannot and should not be structuring the system for him.

"Only if the farmer is free to take his grain to the elevator of his choice – small or large, conventional elevator or inland terminal, on a branch line or a main line – and if he knows the cost of his decision through a tariff structure which honestly portrays the costs and the value of the service, will he be able effectively to make that choice."[24]

UGG's views were criticized on several fronts. First of all, its proposal for dealing with the freight rate issue garnered almost no support from any other organizations. However, as Mac noted in his board report of November 1975, "While it is not difficult to find weaknesses in the suggestion, and some organizations and individuals have already made a point of doing so, it is not easy to find ways of discrediting the principle involved and apparently even more difficult to come up with alternative suggestions as these, to date, are conspicuous by their absence."[25]

Second, "there was some understandable criticism [from our members and customers] of our position in some cases where we advocated reconsideration of a line after 5 or 10 years." This, of course, gave considerable concern to the company's operating people, who were always apprehensive about the impact of unpopular policy positions on the business. However, on balance, Mac thought, "it appears that to date we have managed to avoid any serious reactions to our statements."[26]

Third, and perhaps most seriously, UGG was criticized by the Hall Commission itself – much to Mac's consternation at the time. Justice Hall was populist in his attitude and interventionist in his economic views, and very little of what UGG said was welcome to his ears. In fact, the UGG delegation that made the presentation to the commission was taken aback at the reception they received at the commission's Saskatoon hearing – so much so that Mac quoted extensively from the transcript of the hearing in his report to the board on September 29. The UGG appearance, he said, "provided two very surprising exchanges."

In the first exchange, Justice Hall questioned UGG's contention that the commission should not make decisions about the 6300 miles of branch lines until the actual economic position of each line could be determined after eliminating the effects of the depressed statutory grain freight rates. This upset the commission because of what they saw as the implications of

UGG's position for its timetable. "It has concerned the commission when this suggestion is made as to whether we would take a holiday until Mr. Snavely has reported, if your view is a correct one," Hall said, rather sarcastically.[27]

The second exchange took place as Mac was replying to a long list of questions that the commission had asked all the grain companies to answer at the Saskatoon hearings. As he was reading UGG's answers into the record, Hall interrupted him. "Mr. Runciman, it seems to me that you resent questions being asked," he said. "These are issues that have come forward, we haven't dreamt them up to irritate grain companies."[28] Even twenty years later, Mac still had trouble believing that Hall would have made these remarks. The following words don't convey the emotion in his voice as he reviewed this event in our interviews.

> It was one of the most extraordinary things that happened to me in all my twenty years as president of United Grain Growers. We had been asked to respond to their questions, and we thought this was great to have a second run at it in the light of what had happened since our first presentations.
>
> I was making my presentation and all of a sudden Emmett Hall made his comment about us resenting having to answer these questions. Well, I couldn't believe what my ears were telling me! Here I was gloating over the fact that we had a chance to add these extra comments we wanted to get on the record, and the guy tells me I resent having to do it. I felt so strongly about that, that I ended my presentation that day by going back and referring to his remarks and reassuring him that we welcomed the opportunity. Right to this day I still wonder what triggered the old guy to make that observation.

In his subsequent report to the board of directors, Mac suggested that the real reason for Justice Hall's testy reception was that UGG's submissions had posed him a conundrum: "We picked up the feeling among a large group of people involved in the hearings that Mr. Hall does not like some of the UGG suggestions because they conflict with the sort of things he would like to recommend, and yet he finds it difficult to avoid the logic of UGG's arguments and the fact of its existence as a large and influential farmers' organization."[29]

In retrospect, it seems there were three points on which Hall's views differed from UGG's. The first was on the virtue of developing a "master plan" for the grain handling and transportation system. The commission had been insistent that the elevator companies reveal their plans for the future of their systems, and the direction they wanted to take with this information was well known. However, Mac thought they were going down a blind alley in trying "to form 'long term plans' by seeking the long term plans of involved groups and fitting them together. I am sure they will find the long term plans of most companies sketchy or non-existent."[30]

UGG had told the commission that no "master plans" existed, but the commissioners were reluctant to believe it. More importantly, Mac thought that the commission ought not to try to develop such a plan, and was apprehensive about the implications for the industry of the commission's thinking. In his July 1976 report to the board, he said one of his major concerns was "the apparent desire of the Commission for the establishment of a body to determine where and when grain companies can build and operate primary elevators and where and when they can close them."[31]

Publicly, he was more blunt. The central question before the commission, he told the Palliser Wheat Growers Convention in 1978, was whether "government control and regulation of the grain handling and transportation should be stiffened or relaxed." Increased control, he thought, would not be good for anyone in the business, and he warned that "while trampling on the rights of railway management and shareholders doesn't gain much sympathy in western Canada, don't be fooled into thinking the process would stop at the railways. In the name of efficiency, and following the tendency of every individual to increase his own influence, the bureaucracy would soon set to work to control the whole industry."[32]

Hall, on the other hand, as well as some of the people appearing before him, saw a master plan, administered by government, as being exactly what was needed, and he did not appreciate being told that his ideas on central planning were neither feasible nor wise. It was probably this that lay behind his feeling that UGG "resented" being questioned.

The second bone of contention arose when the commission began to expand its mandate beyond the 6300 miles of line assigned to it. In the spring of 1976, it announced that it was planning two other hearings to deal with new rail lines, extended use of Prince Rupert, and the Churchill line. "In my opinion," wrote Mac, "the Commission is ranging far beyond the original concept of its purpose [and its] study will become so broad, and its report and recommendations so comprehensive, as to render their implementation impossible. This would be an unfortunate outcome [when] the study had so many possibilities for improvement to the system."[33]

A third point of disagreement was over the company's insistence that economics, and not social considerations, ought to govern the development of the elevator system. Hall saw no reason why a community's concerns should not be addressed through the transportation and handling system, nor why elevators and railway lines should not be kept in order to preserve communities. Moreover, he seemed to believe that social and community considerations should be central to the activity of a cooperatively owned elevator company, and to see UGG's endorsement of market-driven solutions to the problems as a betrayal of the movement's ideals.

In the end, the commission's report confirmed Mac's fears. It failed to deal with all of the 6300 miles of line, and recommended the establishment of a new body – a Prairie Rail Authority – to deal with lines on which it had not made decisions. This Authority was not only to administer these lines, but would approve all elevator construction on them. It also made recommendations which went far beyond the issue of branch lines, proposing an Arctic railway to the Northwest Territories, which would open "a veritable cornucopia of heretofore undiscovered attractions."[34] It also failed to deal with the rail rate issue, and basically ignored the relationship between rates and branch lines that UGG had brought forward.

The commission's terms of reference had also required it to examine economic development and agricultural processing issues, and it had heard a great deal from the livestock industry about the impacts of the Crow Rates. Mac was particularly upset about the way the commission dealt with this issue. Mac was very rarely sarcastic or ill-tempered in his comments, but on this occasion, his frustration showed through. He told an audience of cattle producers: "I want to read you what the Hall Commission recommended," he said. "It's short, and I quote: 'The Commission recommends that freight rates on livestock and meat be set at levels which do not discriminate against the natural locational advantage of prairie livestock and processors.' End of quote.

"Thanks a lot. That was the problem: to get rid of discrimination."[35]

The UGG proposal for resolving the rate issue had not received industry support, and most of the discussion before the commission centred on whether a subsidy for losses under the Crow should be paid to the railways or the farmers. The division of opinion followed the traditional lines: those who favoured regulation and control thought it should be paid to the railways; those who favoured market solutions wanted it paid to the farmers. Hall favoured paying it to the railways, but the reason he gave for his position was almost embarrassingly trivial. "The very idea of mailing out cheques to 160,000 farmers is appalling," was the full extent of his reasoning.[36] "One wonders how they think The Canadian Wheat Board pays out farmers each year," Mac noted dryly.[37]

Despite the shortcomings of the Hall Commission's report, it still provided a basis for some movement on the branch-line problem. Otto Lang, who at this time was both transport minister and Minister Responsible for The Canadian Wheat Board, took three steps. First, he added the 1800 miles recommended by Hall to the permanent network. The Prairie Rail Authority concept was not widely endorsed, and his second move was to appoint another special group, called the Prairie Rail Action Committee, to examine the lines Hall had left in limbo. Third, he released about 500 miles of line for abandonment action.

UGG participated more fully in the Snavely Commission than Mac had originally anticipated, but because of the highly technical nature of the commision's task, the company's appearance was handled by the staff. In its participation in this commission, UGG tried to offer constructive suggestions in a process that threatened to turn into a confrontational legal wrangle, with the railways on one side trying every ploy to maximize the levels of railway loss, and lawyers and costing experts hired by the three prairie provinces trying to minimize them. Truth is not always well served in such an environment, and the railways' claims would have been as unfair to the government and farmers, who had to pay the costs, as the provinces' suggestions would have been to the railways who had to supply the services. While the Pools and a number of left-wing farm organizations supported the provinces, UGG sought a compromise.

The main hearing took place on June 25, 1976, in Regina. Mac had not intended to be at the hearing, but unforeseen circumstances intervened. "My presence at the hearings," he wrote, "was a result of the air strike which had caused me to drive to Saskatchewan for regional board meetings that week and an appeal by our delegation that I be present, if possible. The most that can be said is that my presence may have afforded moral support, but it also gave me an opportunity to assess the effectiveness of our presentation and the respect with which it was received by all participants."[38] His report on the hearing described just how effective the company had been:

> Our document was written on the assumption that ... the federal government will be attempting to balance three potentially conflicting objectives:
>
> 1. To make the railways financially whole in the carriage of grain.

2. To avoid loading the Federal Treasury with an overly burdensome subsidy.

3. To develop a revenue level for the railways which can be judged as fair and equitable.

Accordingly we made recommendations which, if adopted by the Commissioner, would make his findings acceptable to United Grain Growers for the development of policy and would, we believe, provide a suitable balance between the objectives listed above. ...

Many complimentary remarks were made to me afterwards about the quality of our submission and the worth of its contents. Mr. Snavely personally thanked me for [UGG's] valuable assistance. ...

This whole subject is highly technical. The main participants are represented by sophisticated consultants and legal specialists yet our material withstood the harshest cross-examination. It may well provide middle ground between the cases put forth by the railways and the provincial governments on which Mr. Snavely can base his report and recommendations.[39]

The Snavely Commission proved beyond doubt that the railways were losing money moving grain, and had developed costing techniques for grain traffic, but the government still had no solution to the Crow Rate dilemma. It was a problem not just for the minister of transport. On January 10, 1979, Mac and a number of senior staff members met with finance minister Donald Macdonald, who, said Mac, "will soon be faced with financing the recommendations of the Snavely and Hall Commissions" and wanted to familiarize himself with "the branch line - primary elevator - statutory freight rate - political and economic quandary.

"In many ways, the meeting reminded us of a previous session with Mr. Lang in which he was quite obviously seeking some way to cope with the statutory grain rate difficulty which is so insoluble politically and could so easily be resolved in economic terms."[40]

By this time the government was within a year or so of an election, and it was plain to everyone that grain transportation and handling issues were not going to be dealt with soon. In fact, the 1979 election resulted in the defeat of the Liberals, to be replaced by the short-lived Conservative government of Joe Clark. This government appointed a Task Force of three parliamentarians to examine a number of grain transportation problems.

UGG was asked to prepare a brief for the Task Force, and subsequently met with them, ostensibly to discuss UGG's proposals. There is a note of weariness - bordering perhaps on exasperation - in Mac's report on this meeting.

> [They] opened the meeting by indicating that they wanted to discuss the terms of reference for a car co-ordinator not whether one should be appointed. That decision had already been made. At the end of the meeting there had been no discussion of our brief which outlined our thinking on the role of the co-ordinator. ... As a consequence a good deal of preparatory work on our part seemed to have gone for naught. ...

> Discussion then moved on to possible ways to speed up grain movement. ... I told the committee that we didn't feel particularly pregnant with ideas along that line. In our opinion, many able and knowledgeable people had been applying a lot of thought and effort to the same question over a long period of time. It was probable that any easy or obvious improvements had already been made but no doubt other things could be done and we were willing to help in the search for and implementation of such ideas.

> Following discussion of the role of the co-ordinator two pet ideas of the committee members ... were introduced. One was for a mass program of trucking from low volume lines to main line elevators in order to dramatically reduce car turnaround time. This proposal appears to have dragged to a standstill as assessment of its feasibility raises more and more doubts about its practicability.

> The other idea ... was to have a complete inventory of all on farm grain by kind, grade, quantity, and its bin location on the farm. When certain grain was required the co-ordinator would simply call upon the farmer to deliver X bushels from bin Y to the elevator on a certain date and it would be there exactly when it was wanted and when the rail car for it arrived. There was some resentment of our questioning of the administrative practicability of such a plan so we let the discussion drop. Not much has been heard of the idea since and we understand it was severely criticized and turned down flat by Conservative party advisors when it was aired for approval.[41]

"I can remember," said Mac, "how aghast we were at these suggestions."

It must appreciated, in assessing the tone of this report and Mac's recollection of the meeting, that by September 1979, grain transportation issues had been under active study by government for ten full years. And yet Mac and his staff found themselves discussing trivial and jejune ideas while the basic issues remained unresolved.

Hugh Horner, former minister of agriculture and deputy premier of Alberta, was appointed to the position of coordinator that the committee had recommended be established, and the Grain Transportation Authority (GTA) was formed to work under his direction. Mac was not hopeful that this organization would be very useful, but over the following year, he changed his opinion. By this time, the Liberals had regained power, and on October 16, 1980, Mac met with transport minister Jean-Luc Pepin on "a number of matters relating to western grain handling and transportation with particular reference to the Grain Transportation Authority." In November he reported to the board on the meeting: "I explained how I had originally been unimpressed by the need for a Grain Transport Co-ordinator, but ... went on to say that we approved of the manner in which [Horner] had set up and run the Authority and that we now felt the position could be justified and that it had made a contribution in the past year to an improvement in the atmosphere in the grain industry."[42]

Mac wrote that, over the course of the meeting with M. Pepin, "I had many opportunities to introduce ideas that I thought were of significance," and "urged that the government should proceed with action on the Crow Rate issue as soon as possible." However, the conversation took its most interesting turn as it drew to a close, for it then became clear that Pepin had a further agenda.

By the time this meeting took place, Mac was sixty-five years old, and on the verge of retirement, and Pepin wanted to recruit him to help resolve some of the vexing issues the government was facing with the grain industry. "The discussion became a bit more difficult," Mac wrote, "when Mr. Pepin asked for specific recommendations for a person to succeed Dr. Horner." But then, Mac went on, "I felt even more trapped when he asked if it was correct that I was going to stay on with United Grain Growers for another year rather than retiring as had once been my intention. He said this was a pity because he wanted to ask if I would consider serving on a Grain Freight Rate Negotiating Committee which he had in mind to establish in the relatively near future. I did not give him a clear response, citing my job and my association with Canadian Pacific, so we left the matter there."[43]

Mac subsequently learned that he was one of two people who had been suggested for the task.

It was not just behind closed doors nor to public inquiries like the Hall Commission that UGG called for reform of the Crow's Nest Pass Rates.

Supported by the board of directors, Mac said it publicly in speeches, and both he and the board said it in UGG's annual reports to its farmer members and shareholders. The company's views came a long way between 1963, when Mac defended the Crow as "vital," and 1979, when he spoke to the Palliser Wheat Growers (now the Western Canadian Wheat Growers Association) on the topic, "Should Freight Rates on Grain Be Boosted?"

He began the speech with a review of the history of the Crow, and went on to list the pros and cons of retaining it. The cons he cited had become a fairly familiar list by that time: the railways were losing money and consuming the system because they weren't reinvesting; the rates were discouraging secondary processing, livestock production, and agricultural diversification; the rates actually decreased income stability by encouraging exports and keeping farmers tied to the more volatile international commodity market, rather than to a more stable secondary processing market; and the rates distorted production, marketing, and transportation decisions.

But the disadvantage he elaborated most fully was that the grain industry had no power to negotiate with the railways precisely because rail rates on grain were a losing proposition. Accordingly, said Mac, "as shippers of grain, we cannot walk into railway offices and demand that things be done properly."

He went on to illustrate his point by describing a case where UGG wanted to have a new elevator serviced by Canadian National because the Canadian Pacific line was being abandoned. A new interchange would have had to be built, and UGG officials went to Edmonton to discuss the matter with the railways. "CN made it quite clear from the start," said Mac, "that they were reluctant participants in the whole proceedings. They certainly did not want to handle our grain." CP, he explained, might have paid for the connection because then they could get out of handling the UGG grain. "But," he went on,

> perhaps most significant was our own position in the proceedings. Any idea that we as the shipper – as the man who pays the piper might call the tune – was totally absent. Any notion that we should be able to demand the service we were paying for was considered laughable. Our people were like beggars at the table. We asked politely if just maybe, please and thank you sir, the railways might build the connection as quickly as possible.

> The fact of the matter is, that under the current situation, we, as your representatives, can speak with no authority to the railways on such matters.

> What can you do when the railways come to view grain traffic as a burden? Well, you can regulate. You can set up a "boxcar czar." You can call indignantly for the railways to live up to their obligations or, by God, be forced to.

> But these solutions don't work. They don't work because so much of our system is built around the central necessity of forcing someone to do a job he doesn't want to do. And the resulting regulation fastens itself like a cancer onto the efficiency of the system and slowly destroys it.[44]

As long as Mac was president, UGG never advocated a complete end to freight-rate protection for farmers. Indeed, as we have seen, the proposal put before the Hall Commission entailed holding the freight rates for farmers at the level of the Crow. But what the company was saying – and saying repeatedly and forcefully – was that "it is time to talk about them; to begin negotiating."[45] The board of directors had seen the central importance of the rate issue, and late in 1979 Mac had carried their message to a number of UGG locals, telling them at their annual meetings that "once Crow is taken care of, our other difficulties will sort themselves out."[46]

Mac and the other members of UGG's board of directors were among a handful of farm leaders who were willing to talk publicly at meetings with farmers in the country about the need for change in the Crow Rates. Jim Deveson, who had been elected president of Manitoba Pool Elevators and, nearing retirement age, was not expected to take any bold moves, surprised the industry by supporting Mac's position. Together they became probably the most outspoken people in the grain industry on the need for change. As Mac pointed out, Deveson was a cattle producer as well as a grain farmer, and he had had experience dealing with the open market. He did not, therefore, share the negative opinions about it that were so deeply rooted in most of the cooperative movement. In fact, without Deveson's voice coming from the Pool side of the debate, which to that time had presented a solid face in defending the status quo, it is unlikely that the log-jam would have been broken.

Following Otto Lang's speech to the Canada Grains Council in 1974, it took a further five years of speeches and public pronouncements like Mac's and Jim Deveson's to bring the government to the point of taking action. It was M. Pepin who finally summoned the courage to get the ball rolling to resolve the Crow, and he appointed a distinguished agricultural economist from the University of Manitoba, Clay Gilson, to lead the negotiations he had asked Mac to conduct. But it was not until 1984 that the Western

Grain Transportation Act was passed, ending the Crow Rate regime and making the railways "financially whole" on grain movement.

What is as remarkable as Mac's leadership on the Crow issue was his perceptiveness about the other major transportation problem: the loss of management control over assets because of the role played by The Canadian Wheat Board in transportation. UGG had told the Tories' Parliamentary Task Force that "car allocation" was a problem, and the UGG annual report for 1979 outlined why.

> The present management of the block shipping system places a large amount of *discretionary* power in the hands of the Canadian Wheat Board [and we believe that] a system which allows one organization or group of people to dictate to another is wrong in principle and in practice. ...
>
> The objective of the block shipping system is to get the right grain from the country to the right terminal at the right time. Elevator companies [have the appropriate skilled staff] to do precisely that. Yet the elevator companies' role in car allocation and block shipping management is minimal. Accordingly, UGG has pressed the view that elevator companies should have a larger responsibility in the management of the block shipping system than they now do. ...
>
> UGG believes Dr. Horner's long term goals ... must be [to] decentralize the management of the block shipping system in order to use the management strengths of the elevator companies to do the job of moving grain.[47]

Mac returned to the issue in his 1979 speech to the Palliser group. He noted that the CWB "is responsible for managing the system" to bring grain forward from the country to meet sales. And while he praised the Board staff for their performance, to him, "the system is wrong - the Board shouldn't be doing it."

"I am going to argue," he said, "that the strength of the Board, and its ability to do the selling job it must do, would be immeasurably increased by giving the transportation job to the organizations which are best suited to do the job. And here I mean the elevator companies - the Pools, UGG and the private companies."[48]

Horner and the GTA never did achieve the long-term goals UGG had identified for them, and the issue remained to fester.

A narrative thread runs through the second decade of Mac's presidency of UGG, a thread that reveals the kind of unique leadership style he exercised, as a bundle of very complex issues was exposed, discussed, and pushed slowly towards resolution. In 1970, the grain industry faced some exceedingly difficult problems with its transportation and handling. The government tried, through the Grains Group, to mount a frontal attack on these problems, using a technocratic, centralized approach, which failed. However, to its credit, the Grains Group did provide a body of useful research, and it might be argued that its ham-fisted tactics were needed to start things moving. If nothing else, it gave the industry a common enemy in that no one wanted to be controlled and managed from Ottawa.

However, the industry was (and remains) fractious: split along ideological lines, controlled by powerful organizations with competing views, and always facing farmers who, as stakeholders, customers, voters, and lobbyists, possess an enviable independence that allows them to speak out. In this environment, it was difficult for the government to formulate policies that would be acceptable within the farm community.

It was Mac's particular skill to function in this environment in a way that earned respect from all quarters, but which, as he said, continually "nudged things in the right direction." During the period that he chaired the Canada Grains Council, when it was studying the Grains Group's reports, many people in the grain industry learned a great deal about the transportation problems: their historic roots, their interconnections, and their complexities. The UGG board judged correctly that the time was right for an organization like theirs to come out in favour of change, and to begin public discussion of issues that had long been forbidden topics of conversation.

In countless meetings in the country and in grain industry forums, Mac and the other board members challenged farmers to reconsider their attachment to the Crow Rates and their local branch lines, continually asking them whether there was not a better way. Through the material the UGG staff put together, the company challenged the Hall Commission to consider whether more centralization and control was what the industry needed, and whether the traditional view of grain elevators and rail lines as instruments of social purpose to sustain small towns really served farmers' interests. As president of a large cooperative, both speaking for its farmer members and running a commercial enterprise, Mac had to be listened to.

But, as president of a large co-op, and thus subject annually to election as president, and triennially to election to the board by UGG delegates, he had to listen to farmers, as well. No matter where he and the board thought the industry should go, if they could not bring their constituency with them, they could be stopped in their tracks. And while the election of co-op directors and presidents is not without its politics, as far as Mac was concerned, it was a tough audience to sell.

"The delegate body was usually pretty darn good," he said, "and I never tried to hornswoggle a meeting. Don't ever try to pull the wool over the eyes of those guys out there in the country, because there are lots of them who are smarter than you are. Able, able people, who are doing what they consider the right thing, and putting their chips against the people who think they are wrong. And you have to convince them that you are right."

Throughout the second decade of Mac's presidency, the company continued to push for reform of the Crow Rates, to seek an intelligent and realistic approach to ridding the system of redundant branch lines, and, at the same time, to convince farmers that these were "the right things to do."

How far did things progress over the fifteen years or so, between roughly the early 1960s when the need for modernization and renewal began to be felt, and 1981 when Mac retired? It depends on what is measured, and on your standards of progress.

Despite all the impediments, rationalization of the elevator system, at least, made some progress. UGG reduced its elevator system from 609 in 1961, to 534 in 1971, to 359 in 1981 when Mac retired – just over a forty percent reduction. This was about typical for the industry at large. The number of grain delivery points across western Canada fell proportionally.

The rail system, however, remained almost totally static. The long series of studies, commissions of inquiry, committees, and task forces produced almost nothing. Even as late as 1980, Mac was able to tell a class of agricultural diploma students at the University of Manitoba that "the process [of system modernization] is confounded with an outdated rail system. United Grain Growers has tried to take a balanced view in this matter. On the one hand it weighs the needs and desires of farmers for convenient and accessible rail and elevator service. On the other, we recognize the need to develop an efficient transportation and handling system not burdened with costly and redundant facilities."[49]

However, the ground had been laid for dealing with the rate issue, with no small credit due to Mac's and UGG's leadership. The Western Grain Transportation Act, which finally set up a new rate regime to provide the railways with adequate compensation, was passed in 1984 – a task that had proven impossible in 1967 when the Crow was so sacred that legislators were not even allowed to provide a subsidy.

The logistics management issue was not addressed, and it is only now that the wisdom of UGG's vision is being rediscovered. The idea of getting the CWB out of the business of controlling grain transportation finally, in about 1995, took root and gained widespread support - except within the CWB itself, and among a number of die-hard supporters of a tightly regulated and centralized system.

Mac mused on whether all the things that he and UGG did to advance these issues had any real efficacy at all. "I find it hard to believe," he said, "that if I hadn't been there doing and saying these things, we wouldn't be about where we are today anyway. I'm a great believer in the inevitability of the ultimate success of economics. And whether it takes ten years or thirty years or fifty years, economic forces will finally prevail."

Others, however, have a different view of his contribution. Two years after he retired, Jean-Luc Pepin left the transport portfolio, and Mac wrote to him, congratulating him on his leadership on grain issues and wishing him well in his new portfolio. He received a reply which he still has and is one of his proud possessions. The letterhead reads "Minister of State (External Relations)" and its full text reads as follows:

September 15, 1983

Dear Mr. Runciman:

One assesses his performance in public life by the judgements of a very small group of people he admires and respects. Since my appointment as Minister responsible for the Canadian Wheat Board in 1968, you have been one of that select body!

At the time, you and a few others, such as Parker pere[50] and MacNamara [sic], welcomed the young French-speaking Quebecer interested in understanding the West and the wheat economy, and guided him with great kindness.

You can consequently imagine my pleasure at reading your letter on the occasion of my "transfer" out of Transport Canada to External Affairs, not a promotion... but a convenient political move to which I was a "consenting adult."[51] Of course, you underestimate your own role in the Crow debate. You and a few others gave my efforts the credibility without which they could not have succeeded even partially.

I hope everything will turn out well and that those of us who believed from the beginning that the Crow change was in the best interest of the West will be amply rewarded in heaven and will receive a little bit of recognition on earth!

I am sending a copy of your letter to Arthur Kroeger. As you know, I worked hand in hand with Arthur and officers of Transport Canada on this project and I share with them the compliments I get.

My best to you for a continued healthy and fruitful half-retirement.

Yours sincerely,

[signed] Jean-Luc Pepin[52]

Mac reached the "normal" retirement age of 65 in 1979. But, somewhat to his own embarrassment after having insisted on normal retirement age for the company's staff so many years ago, the board was reluctant to let him go. "The first year," he said, "was not so bad, because I was finishing out my term as an elected director." Following that, he had to seek re-election for a new term, and he was persuaded, not entirely willingly, to stay on until 1981.

And thus his time as president of United Grain Growers came to an end, and he went on to what M. Pepin so aptly called a "half-retirement," which was as full a professional life as some people have during their working careers.

The Retiree: 1981 – 2000

8

This account of Mac's life has covered only a small part of the professional activities he undertook during his time as president of United Grain Growers. In addition to the roles covered in this account, he managed to find time for a host of other responsibilities. A partial list of the more significant of these illustrates the major role he played in business, government, and the community.

To begin with, his presidency of UGG automatically made him president of a number of UGG subsidiaries. Later, it also led him into directorships in several companies with which UGG was involved. From 1970 to 1974, he was a director and vice-chairman of XCAN Grain, a grain export company formed by UGG and the three Wheat Pools, but from which UGG withdrew in 1974. Between 1974 and 1977, he was president of United Oilseed Products, a venture jointly owned, one-third each, by UGG, British Columbia Packers, and Mitsubishi Canada Limited and Nisshin Oil Mills Limited.

Mac was also involved with a number of other companies and organizations outside UGG but still within the grain industry. Specifically, he was a member of The Canadian Wheat Board Advisory Committee from 1961 until the Committee became an elected body in 1975, and a vice-president of the Western Agricultural Conference from 1974 to 1976. He was a director of Prince Rupert Grain (the company that operated the grain terminal at Prince Rupert, in which UGG was a shareholder) from 1979 to 1982, and a director of Ridley Grain (a holding company for the assets of the Prince Rupert Grain consortium) from 1980 to 1982. He also sat as a member of the policy committee of the Winnipeg Commodity Exchange from 1971 until his retirement.

He served as a director of a number of Canadian companies, the larger of which were Canadian Pacific Limited (1969 to 1985), the Great West

Life Assurance Company (1967 to 1985), Massey Ferguson and Varity Corporation (1975 to 1987), and the Royal Bank of Canada (1976 to 1985). He was also invited to become one of the founding directors of Power Financial Corporation in 1984, and was a member of its board until 1990.

He was asked to sit on several government committees and advisory bodies, both federally and provincially. Among the more prominent of these appointments were: governor of the Agricultural Economics Research Council of Canada; a member of the Economic Council of Canada; a member of two separate committees of the Science Council of Canada; and a member of the Manitoba Marketing Board.

He served with various industry and industry-government groups, including the Great Lakes Waterways Development Association (twice: as a director from 1976 to 1982, and as Chair from 1984 to 1986), and the C.D. Howe Institute and the C.D. Howe Institute Foundation as a director in both cases.

Within a year of his retirement, he was elected to the board of governors of the University of Manitoba, and in 1983 was elected Chair, a post which he held until 1988 when he stepped down from the board.

He was also active in the community, performing a public service role with organizations ranging from the United Way to Rainbow Stage (a Winnipeg performing arts group), Victoria General Hospital, and The Wildlife Foundation of Manitoba, for which he was both a director and a trustee. His most active involvement with the hospital occurred from the 1972 to 1992, during which time he filled a number of roles, including chairman of the finance committee, chairman of the board of trustees, and president of the Victoria Hospital Foundation. In 1992, he stepped down from the hospital board, but remained on the board of the hospital foundation.

He was Honourary Colonel of the Queen's Own Cameron Highlanders of Canada from 1979 to 1993, chaired the Cameron's Regimental Foundation from 1991 to 1993, and continues to serve on the regiment's advisory board.

Mac was honoured with a total of twenty-two awards and distinctions, including two honourary doctorates (from the universities of Manitoba and Saskatchewan), membership in both the Saskatchewan and Canadian Agricultural Halls of Fame, and appointment as an Officer of the Order of Canada. For his various contributions to agriculture, he received honourary life memberships in (among others) the Canola Council of Canada, the Agricultural Institute of Canada, and the Canadian Seed Growers Association.

By condensing each of his professional accomplishments to a single line, his complete curriculum vitae can be squeezed down to six pages, and for the interested reader, it is found in full, with all the relevant dates, in the Appendix. The one thing not listed – because he refused the honour – was the invitation to become Minister Responsible for The Canadian Wheat Board. It occurred after the 1980 election when the Trudeau Liberals were returned to power, but had virtually lost the west.

> One evening, [Trudeau's principal secretary] Jim Coutts phoned me from the prime minister's office to ask if I would become Minister Responsible for the Wheat Board. I said, "Jim, how on earth can we do that? I'm not even a member of parliament, let alone in a position to become a minister."

> "Oh," he said, "we'll make you a senator."

> So I turned it down and the next day Marj and I sat and watched on TV as Hazen Argue was sworn in as minister of the Wheat Board. I said to Marj, "Would you believe if I had said yes to Coutts last night, that would be me up there today instead of Hazen Argue?"

> And you know, when I think about what Hazen Argue did when he was in charge of the Wheat Board – But no. I just wouldn't take it under those circumstances at all.

Mac's account of how he began his career as director of a number of large Canadian companies reveals a good deal about his character: his modesty coupled with a touch of fatalism, by which he attributes his success to chance as much as to ability.

> These are the sort of things that absolutely turn your life around. I don't know if you remember the name of Red Foster in connection with an advertising agency in Toronto – a big one. He had a mentally handicapped child and he was head of the mentally handicapped children's association in Canada and he came out to Winnipeg one time to get Lou Driscoll to run a campaign for fundraising here.

> This was back in the 1960s, and the amount of money put by the government into the education of mentally handicapped children at that time was practically negligible. The parents themselves had to pay for most of the services.

> I hate fundraising, but they came to me and asked if I would go to Great

West Life and ask the company for a donation. So I made arrangements to meet their vice-president, John Morrison. Very shortly after going to see them, a cheque arrived for $10,000.

Within a month or six weeks after that, I got an invitation to have lunch with Joe Harris and Dave Kilgour – Joe was the chairman and Dave was the president of Great West Life – and they asked me to go on the board. And I had never contacted Great West Life before at all, except for the interview with John Morrison. Well, once I got on the Great West Life board, it seemed to put me into a different category, and other people started to pick me up.

So it was being asked to do something I hated to do – this fundraising – that I think opened the door and made the rest of it possible. So you're really not master of your own fate.

At the same time, when Mac told me about his invitation to sit on the Great West Life board, he introduced the story with reference to a business acquaintance who, being possessed of both a commerce and law degree, aspired to a career as a corporate director, but seemed unable to get his foot in the door. The implied contrast between himself and his acquaintance was obvious, and it was clear that Mac felt a certain pride that the farm boy from Saskatchewan with a grade eleven education could take his place in the most powerful business councils of the nation.

Mac was also quick to note, quite rightly, that "United Grain Growers' reputation was also a strong factor in these other organizations picking me up. The banks knew that United Grain Growers was a well-managed company with excellent accountants and treasury people, and the railways, locally at least, knew that our operations were well managed. I think the middle-of-the-road policy position taken by our board was also important because those people knew about the National Farmers Union and they knew about the Pools.

"I strongly feel that it was the respectability – the acceptability – of United Grain Growers and their standards of business procedure and business ethics that had something to do with it."

After such a full and active career, it would not be expected that he would merely sit back and relax. Consulting work would have been an obvious step, but his response to this suggestion was characteristic: "I used to say, 'Look! I haven't got enough confidence in my own knowledge and wisdom to be sure I made the right decisions for myself, let alone pry into other people's affairs and try to tell them what to do.'"

As events transpired, hanging out his shingle as a consultant was not required. Most of his company directorships continued for some years, as did his work with Victoria Hospital, and, at the same time, he took on major responsibilities with the university. The invitation to sit on the Power Financial Corporation board came three years after he left UGG, and came in a way indicative of the esteem in which he was held.

"Paul Desmarais Senior was in Winnipeg for a Great West Life board meeting," Mac recalled, "and when the meeting was over he asked me to speak to him. He said, 'We're starting up a new company, Power Financial, to hold Montreal Trust, and Great West Life and some other companies, and I want you to be on the Board.'

"I said, 'Paul, for goodness sake, I'm at the age for retiring from boards, not going on new boards.'

"'Oh,' he said. 'Well, we'll *grandfather* you. You can stay until you're seventy-five.'

"I was seventy-five in 1989, and you're not eligible to run for re-election after reaching that age. But I was entitled to continue until the end of my term, and dropped off the board at the annual meeting in 1990."

In 1990, at the age of seventy-six, he became president of his condominium complex, a post he occupied until 1999. This may seem a fairly minor responsibility in a life as full as his, until one knows that, just as the writing of this book was coming to completion, he was scheduled to appear in court as the prime witness in legal proceedings the condominium had been party to for nine years. The case centred on precisely who was responsible when a storey-high section of stone cladding fell from the building. Fortunately, no one had been injured.

The case was an important one, which had been before the courts more than once to deal with its different aspects. At one stage, the Supreme Court of Canada granted the condominium leave to appeal a decision of the Manitoba Court of Appeal because the case involved a controversial area of Canadian law on which clear precedents had not been established. Previous rulings had provided for compensation to plaintiffs in damage suits against contractors or architects only when they involved bodily injury or injury to property, but not if only economic loss was involved. This Supreme Court ruling established the right to sue for economic loss, a new concept in this area of Canadian jurisprudence. Mac had to answer more than 900 questions through the examinations for discovery and cross-examinations related to the case, and had to be on top of details that would have daunted some people many years his junior.

By the end of 1998, Mac had largely set down all his corporate and community involvements, and, just as he enforced retirement on senior

UGG employees in 1961, it was his intention to enforce it on himself: "I was appointed to the Victoria Hospital Foundation board for a three-year term which terminated in 1999. I served notice when I got the last three-year appointment, that there would be no more re-appointments because by the time that expired, I would be eighty-five years old, and I refused to serve on any boards after I turned eighty-five."

In fact, 1999 marked the end, not only of the last of Mac's service on any boards, but the end of his residency in Winnipeg. His older daughter, Dorothy, her husband, and their son Graham – Mac and Marj's only grandson – moved to Red Deer, Alberta. Since a number of Marj's relatives are also in Alberta, Mac and Marj decided to join them there.

As remarkable as Mac's career was, there were other matters that were of greater interest to me. What were the values by which he lived in his working career? How, in his life and work, did he come to command such respect and admiration? How was it that, despite his list of accomplishments and honours, he remained, in everyone's judgement, so "down to earth"? And at the same time, how did he stand the years of frustration as the need to modernize the grain handling and transportation system was so evident, and the ability to do so was so constrained?

These were not easy things to determine. As he himself said, "It bothers me to think of myself in analytical terms," and he found my direct questions on such matters both embarrassing and difficult. I was not the first person to try to quiz him in this way. In 1975, he received a letter from Pat Motherwell, the wife of W.R. Motherwell's grandson, and a former Saskatchewan schoolteacher then working in Calgary. She was compiling a "Famous Persons Historical Library" for the Calgary Public School board, and wanted to gather information about Mac as a prominent Saskatchewanite. A long questionnaire accompanied the letter, which he never got around to completing, but he told me about the questions she had posed:

"What took you to the top so swiftly in UGG?"

Well, how do I know? I just went along for the ride.

"What is a man's key formula for staying on top?" and "If you were to speak to a body of students, what fundamental principles would you suggest they employ in order to reach their objectives?"

None of these questions are answered at all. To me, they were too hypothetical altogether. Anyway, there are few elements of my life that were decided on the basis of long, careful thought, based on philosophical attitudes or anything like that. It just seemed to go on day by day and you made decisions as you came to them.

Despite his reticence, he dropped a number of hints throughout the many months that we worked on this project which point towards the answers. To begin with, he referred more than once to the values he had absorbed from his own family, and how these had been a lifelong foundation for him.

By the time I was ten or twelve years old, my thinking was amazingly similar to what it is today, and I have to attribute that to my family and background. I have no recollection at any stage of my life of having suddenly changed attitudes or directions or beliefs. Always, what I was putting forth was what I believed, and it must have been simply ingrained in me that this is my attitude towards life.

It goes back to my father and grandfather, and also to Mr. Downey, one of my teachers in Scotland. My grandfather was a highly principled sort of an individual. Dad did not have my grandfather's Victorian high-mindedness, but still, he was absolutely honest. But basic to them all was fair play – justice and fair play.

It seems awfully self-righteous to say I built a whole lifetime's philosophy on a basis of fair and equitable treatment, but the more I look at it, the more it seems to be the case, and I don't think it has ever led me to do things that I want or need to apologize for. It's funny to talk about yourself in these terms, but I think these have always been overriding principles in my life.

His commitment to justice and fair play was not merely an intellectual concept, but something he demonstrated through the major decisions in his life. His decision to enlist during the war was, as we saw, driven by his "sympathy for the underdog and the absolute injustice of what Hitler was doing to Poland and all the various countries in Europe." To Mac, this was no joking matter.

"I remember," he said, "the doctor who examined me when I went into the army, saying, 'Is that a Scottish accent I detect?' And I said, 'Yes. I was born in Scotland.' 'Oh.' he said, 'You found a good way to get a cheap trip back home, eh?' which didn't please me too much. I said to him, 'No, I think it goes quite a bit deeper than that.'"

Mac's fundamental concern for the welfare of others showed up in his command during the war. "I met so many different types in the army," he said, "and never really had a severe personality clash with anybody. Even when I put a man on orders sometimes they would take it in the best spirits and maybe it was that they understood that I was trying to help them. I was three, four, five, six years older than a lot of them, and I had a lot of sympathy for those guys. To push them around was the last thing in the world I wanted to do."

The same sentiment lay behind his involvement with UGG, he said. "A lack of fair play and decent treatment for everybody just raises my hackles, and I had this feeling about farmers vis a vis the rest of society, and agriculture vis a vis other industries. It just came naturally as part of my make-up. I wouldn't have come to United Grain Growers if I hadn't thought, If I do the right thing at the right time perhaps I can make farming a little better in western Canada, because I had real sympathy for the people out there on the farms."

Politically and economically, Mac was a laissez faire liberal, although it was a long time before he learned the language to describe these beliefs. It is clear that he became increasingly critical of the heavy regulation of the grain industry and of the central marketing regime, and, simultaneously, he was favourably impressed with the way the rapeseed industry had been developed under the open market system. However, Mac's laissez faire liberalism was not solely – or even predominantly – concerned with commercial freedoms. Historian Ed Rea, in his recent biography of one of Mac's predecessors as UGG president, Thomas Crerar, speaks of Crerar's "life-long commitment to the sturdy liberal values of independence, self-reliance, thrift, and voluntary association."[1] It is these values that lay at the heart of Mac's liberalism, and these values that he bodied forth and championed in his own life.

Much of this part of his philosophy appeared in a short talk he gave in November 1981 to the St. Andrew's Society of Winnipeg. As a former president, he was responding to the toast to "Canada, The Land We Live In," and his notes for the occasion reflect not only his political and economic beliefs, but also how they were shaped by his own life experience. He began by observing that Canada is "the largest country in the western hemisphere ... about 3,850,000 square miles of land inhabited by about 25 million people."[2] However, he went on, "numbers tell us nothing of the qualities of our people. ... Little of what has been achieved was done without hardship, but the toughness and tenacity of our predecessors laid the foundation for today's bountiful production. This was especially true of those who undertook agricultural production in what was initially a harsh and hostile environment."[3]

He asked what had brought the pioneers to such a difficult land and, while recognizing there were many factors, he singled out "freedom and opportunity" as of primary importance: "Freedom to live as they wished in pursuit of their own beliefs and opportunity to earn by their own efforts success beyond what could possibly be expected in their native lands."[4] Both Canada and the United States, he said,

> are, or at least have been, unique in providing conditions so that no one man could lord it over any other.

> Well over a century ago, Alexis de Tocqueville in his work, "Democracy in America," described the situation. He said, "No novelty in the United States struck me more vividly ... than the equality of conditions."

> The equality that De Tocqueville wrote about was the equality of opportunity. It implies conditions that allow each man or woman whatever their origin to make their way on the basis of ability. But to make this possible, freedom of the individual is essential.

> The same conditions De Tocqueville saw in the United States certainly applied to Canada in the early years of its development. We had no feudal system here. With plenty of space, a venturesome society of immigrants and a capitalistic order, Canada soon had a rising standard of living and the promise of plenty for all.[5]

However, he thought that individual freedom was threatened as governments sought to replace equality of opportunity with equality of condition. How far, he asked rhetorically, "is government going to go in order to achieve - not equal rights - but equality for all."[6] Mac held Crerar in high regard, and often acknowledged his debt to him. In this speech he quoted words Crerar had used in the 1920s.

> "There is a growing tendency on the part of many of the Canadian people ... to throw upon the institution we call 'government' a multiplicity and complexity of duties. It is very questionable how far this will in the long run work out successfully. In the end it will probably be found that people can do most things better for themselves through the medium of co-operation than can possibly be done by government agencies.

"What people want is more freedom, freedom from the exaction of special privileges in any of its forms, freedom to buy and sell when they
please, freedom to order their daily lives as they wish so long as they do
not overstep the boundaries of the rights of others."[7]

In one of our earliest interviews, he read these quotations from the St.
Andrew's Society talk and told me how Crerar's words summed up what
he had stood for during his life. Mac's fear of excess government control
was not driven by a simple ideological aversion to the public sector. It was
founded in a moral concern - suggested by his comment about the "feudal
system" - about the arbitrary exercise of power by one person over another,
whether that power came from monopoly control in the private sector, or
regulatory control in the public sector.

In 1976, Mac was called upon to reflect deeply about his laissez faire
beliefs when he was asked to address a local church group "on the issues
and challenges facing me in my field of endeavour as a result of the exercise
of my Christian conscience."[8] The group he addressed was an adult lenten
study group at Knox United Church in Winnipeg, and some of those involved, both as participants and organizers, were prominent Winnipeggers
engaged in both business and the law. With most of the speeches Mac
delivered as president of UGG, about two-thirds of the work, he estimated,
was done by UGG staff, primarily by the man responsible for UGG's public affairs functions, John Clark. This one, however, was written solely by
his own hand.

It was not an easy task for him. Early in his talk he said that he really
should have been a bricklayer because "my natural inclination is to deal
with tangible, visible, concrete things." As a bricklayer, he would have been
able to see quite readily how many bricks he had laid each day, how his
bricklaying project was progressing, and much work remained to be done.
In contrast, "the numerous non-tangibles encountered in the preparation
of this talk created many problems for me."[9]

It is an important speech, and worth considering at some length, because it contains his personal answer to why a free enterprise society (and
a commercial grain marketing system) was not the immoral proposition
the cooperative movement portrayed. It also conveys the kind of balance
Mac thought had to exist between the private and public sectors, and between free enterprise and regulation, in a healthy society.

His answer to the question he had been asked to address was simple and
unequivocal: "In my carefully considered opinion the exercise of my Christian conscience does not pose a single issue or challenge that cannot be

accommodated in the normal working pattern of the businesses with which I am associated. That's it."[10]

This conclusion, he said, would not be accepted readily by some in his audience because it had become popular to see business as "selfish and soulless ... stalking the fringes of civilization alert to every opportunity to snatch money from the unwary [and] prepared to turn to dishonesty and sharp practice as long as there is a dollar at the end of the road."[11] But Mac rejected the accuracy of this view completely.

To begin with, he pointed out, business had brought immense material benefit to society. It had, he said, made possible "the most comfortable, enjoyable and free state of society the world has ever known"[12] and he invited his listeners to compare today's world with past eras on these points. Moreover, he asked, what would be the consequences of shutting business down completely? What kind of society would it be where there was "neither food nor clothing, transportation or shelter, nor a tax base to provide the great good that is done, and should be done, and must be done, by public funds. What then?"[13]

He then raised three arguments to explain why he felt no conflict between his business activities and his conscience. First, he said, "the moral standards of Canadian business are high."[14] He himself, he implied, had seen little evidence of "dishonesty and sharp practice," nor had he experienced his colleagues as "selfish and soulless."

Second, he said, "we live in a time when much has been accomplished for the improvement of the lot of mankind [and] we live in a relatively kindly society by comparison with any standards of the past [and there is now] much more concern with the freedom, and rights, and welfare of the individual than ever before."[15]

Finally, he said, "Today's businessman typically pays more attention to his social responsibilities than did his predecessors of a century, or even a generation ago. ... The view that the businessman is responsible only to himself or that the maximization of profit should be the main consideration in business decision-making is firmly rejected by responsible business people as out of date and unrealistic."[16]

He raised one further point.

> It concerns the age old charge ... that greed is the motivator and money the goal of business. Certainly a man's job may well be to make money for owners, shareholders, or even governmental agencies, but money is not always the prime reward that is sought. ...

I suspect that the average young person goes into business because they like it just as other young people may select law, or medicine, or teaching, or the civil service as careers. Once committed to business the business person does indeed look for profits. That is their job. But it is too simple to equate profit with personal gain. Profit includes other factors - salary for services rendered, and reserves for depreciation and new investment.

On the whole, I would accept that in the traditional professions the ideal of the social good had been and will remain more in control of self-interest than is the case in business. But this does not mean that business is inherently evil. It simply means that some of its procedures are different. It also means that external regulation of its freedom is likely more necessary than control of freedom in other areas. But business cannot be run as a charity. Business must be technically efficient and financially solvent. These requirements are not necessarily inconsistent with the idea that business must recognize the human rights of employees and the public.[17]

If Mac's defense of free enterprise seems to be excessively vigorous, it must be appreciated that he was describing his ideals for the business world. He readily conceded that these ideals were not always met, that the world had more than its share of serious social problems that needed to be addressed, and that "there is plenty of room for improvement." However, he said, "We are making progress. I can live with that."[18]

More importantly, Mac was describing the values by which he lived and conducted himself in his work. For himself, there was no conflict between his business career and his conscience because he would not countenance greed, sharp practice, and dishonesty in any endeavour in which he was involved. At the same time, he recognized that UGG – and the companies on whose boards he served – had a wider responsibility to the public and to their employees than the balance sheet alone would dictate.

It was also certainly true that Mac did not equate profit with personal gain, where he himself was concerned. On one occasion, he absolutely refused a salary increase which the UGG board had recommended. He wouldn't take it, he said, "because by that time I was drawing money from Great West Life, I was drawing money from Canadian Pacific, and there were others. And as I said to them, 'Well look, guys, I can't be working all the time for you, if I am getting paid this much for time for somebody else.'"

Moreover, Mac was well aware that love of money is decidedly not the root of all the world's evils. He recognized that love of power itself, apart from any material rewards that power might yield, presented its own temptations. More than once, he told me a story about a grain industry meeting where someone, speaking about the growing use of computers and information technology, had said, "One day, we will have a little black box that will control the whole industry." Mac felt he gained an insight into the corrupting nature of power when one participant responded, in all seriousness, "Yes, and wouldn't it be wonderful to have control of that black box."

It emerged clearly in his talk to the Knox United Church study group that Mac's embrace of laissez faire and individual freedom was married with – and subservient to – a commitment to "fair play and decent treatment for everybody." These values, implanted during childhood, had found fertile ground in his character. They emerged in his sympathies for people who suffered the worst ravages of the 1930s, guided him in enlisting in the army, and were part of his attraction to UGG. His desire to make "farming a little better in western Canada" informed his actions as president of UGG, and was more compelling to him than making UGG a more profitable agri-business enterprise for its shareholders. While he was not blind to the dictates of the balance sheet, the cooperative nature of the company permitted a happy resolution if these two goals came into conflict.

Even later in his life, he found himself reacting angrily when people sought special privileges or power at the expense of others. In the condominium, there was "a group in the building that wanted to run the show, but they didn't want the chore of serving on the board. They actually introduced a motion that all matters had to be referred to a building committee, by the management, and get the committee's opinion before it was passed to the board. It was passed by the board once, and I simply told them I wasn't going to stay on the board or be the chairman if that motion stayed on the books. I said, 'I'm not going to sit on a board that is a residuary of a committee's findings.'"

The raw thirst for power and the misuse of authority were things that he abhorred and fought against all his life.

Ironically, despite his obvious admiration for "the opportunity to earn success," Mac was not an aggressively ambitious person himself. As we have seen, he actively sought neither the presidency of UGG, nor his place on the boards of the large corporations where he was a director. But with the wisdom of maturity, he came to recognize this part of his character as a strength: "I've never been an ambitious person, and that may have been part of my salvation, because when you look at the downfall of so many people - particularly in the political field - it is just sheer raw ambition that drives them. I was always happy to be doing whatever I was doing.

"A great deal of my success was lack of ambition and an element of laziness. I couldn't be bothered getting out there and doing things that lead people into trouble when they try to do too much. I've seen so many of them just fall down on things when they tried to perform beyond their ability, you might say."

"Lazy," of course, is a self-deprecating judgement, which few of those who knew Mac would support. However, that he was able to be "happy doing whatever he was doing" is a key part of his character, and is perhaps why he remained so "down to earth." It is also the ideal expressed in a famous prayer that was originally written by the theologian, Reinhold Niebuhr. The prayer has been paraphrased different ways in a number of renditions, but its best-known version runs like this: "Lord, give me the courage to change the things I can change, the serenity to accept the things I can't, and the wisdom to know the difference." Those who have tried to apply this principle know it is a good deal easier to recite than it is to live, but Mac seemed to find the balance for which Niebuhr so wisely prayed.

Had he been a man of driving ambition, it is likely that he would have found it much more difficult to live with the frustrations of trying to create a modern elevator system for UGG, when achieving that goal faced so many insurmountable hurdles. However, his was the approach that, as Jean-Luc Pepin so perceptively observed, eventually prevailed and led towards resolution of the issues. His own assessment of what I describe as wisdom is, as always, more straightforward and simple: "I suppose gradualism probably describes me as well as anything else. A hundred years from now, it won't matter much, but in the interests of those people who had to adjust to change, I believe gradualism was right. When you think of a million light years, an extra ten years to do it are not very long. And maybe my slow, deliberate way suited the grain business."

I came to United Grain Growers in 1975 as a relatively young man, and shortly after being caught up in the reforming zeal of the Grains Group. I often found Mac's "gradualism" to be a source of frustration, and there were many times I wished he would take a stronger and more aggressive line in promoting the kind of changes for which the company stood. However, the impatience of youth is not the better part of wisdom, and while I did not know it at the time, Mac often shared my frustrations. We now both realize that Mac's "slow deliberate way" was one of the reasons why he came to be held in such high regard. As he put it, "If I have a weakness, I know it's that I'll avoid an issue rather than create a confrontation. Time after time, and meeting after meeting, I came away with the thought, I wish I had stood up and said this, that, or the other thing. But today, I know it wouldn't have improved the situation a bit – it wouldn't have advanced things. A great deal of it was just the desire to stand up and say, 'I don't agree with you.'"

Others did not see Mac's aversion to confrontation as a weakness. When he stepped down as chairman of the Great Lakes Waterways Development Association, he received a letter from Frank Shearstone, a vice-president of one of the lake shipping companies, Halco Incorporated, and Halco's representative on the association's board. The letter is handwritten on a fine quality paper meant to be used for communication of a more personal, rather than purely business, nature. It is dated October 7th, 1986:

Dear Mac,

I have just received Don Rothwell's letter advising us of your retirement from the G.L.W.D.A. This is indeed sad news; your gentle leadership and patience will be missed greatly.

I do however, recognize that nothing is forever and, inevitably the torch must be passed on. Suffice it to say I have enjoyed the short period of our acquaintance and hope that whatever you are retiring to will afford you the greatest of satisfaction. Many thanks.

Sincerely yours,

[signed] Frank Shearstone[19]

"Gentle leadership" is a more apt description than "weakness" and Mac came to recognize this.

Sometimes you can get further if you avoid antagonism. I can think of different cases along the way where people actually came on-side with me, and if I had treated them disparagingly, or pulled some one-upmanship on them, they would have wanted to get even some day.

I think of someone like Jim Deveson. He was a typical Manitoba Pool director at one time, and he would take shots at Grain Growers, and shots at me, and that sort of thing. But as time went on Jim and I drifted into a common understanding, because we could see a common objective.

It was the same with Bill Parker. Bill took some shots at me in the early days because he was an old hand at Manitoba Pool and I was a greenhorn at United Grain Growers, but I never tried to put Bill down and as time went on, we became real allies on some projects.

Does Mac have any regrets about his life? Just two. The first is that he never learned to sail. The second grew out of his love of farming. One of the questions in Pat Motherwell's questionnaire was, "Why did you become interested in agriculture?" Although Mac never completed the questionnaire for her, he read me the notes he made as he contemplated his reply to this question: "'I was born and grew up on a farm, and agriculture has been a part of my life for as long as I can remember. There is something very basic about the industry. It produces many of the necessities of life rather than the frills or luxuries. I always loved the outdoors and animals and farm people, and the independence of action, and the self-reliance and freedom of decision and action. It is still a wonderful way of life, in spite of hardships and frustrations, which has to be experienced to be understood and appreciated.' So I guess my major regret is that I didn't end up farming as I wanted to do, but damn it all, I had enough satisfaction in other things, and you can't do everything in this world."

By the late 1990s, as this book was being completed, the western Canadian grain industry was in the midst of a near-revolution. Major organizations were abandoning philosophical positions they had held for decades, and the prairie grain industry was being changed out of recognition with new construction, new entrants, and new corporate alliances. The end of The Canadian Wheat Board was openly debated and, in some quarters, eagerly anticipated. The resolution to a number of long-standing transportation issues was quite widely assumed to involve greater deregulation, and the issue of railway market power, which led to many of the controls in the first place, was seen as less important than the need for commercial flexibility. All these things, of course, represent merely the latest in the long series of upheavals and transformations which, as noted in Chapter 7, have been the rule rather than the exception in western agriculture.

Throughout all these upheavals, leadership appropriate to the occasion has arisen. United Grain Growers was fortunate in being headed by people who stood out among their peers – T.A. Crerar and John Brownlee are obvious examples – but the early leaders of the Pools, A.J. McPhail and Henry Wise Wood, were also men of great vision who led the grain industry through these periods of change with dignity and courage. Under their leadership, new institutions were forged to meet the demands of the day. In the 1970s, as the industry struggled with such badly needed reform of its marketing, transportation, and handling arrangements, it was Mac

Runciman who led the industry through the dissension and argument, and it is to this great company of past leaders in western agriculture that he belongs.

And, yes, to those of us caught up in the latest chapter of this ongoing drama, his gentle leadership and patience are most sorely missed.

Mac looking every inch the Scot in the uniform of the
Honourary Colonel of the Queen's Own Cameron
Highlanders of Canada. The man in the foreground is Bud
Jobin, then lieutenant governor of Manitoba (courtesy UGG).

Appendix: Summary of Mac Runciman's Major Positions and Awards

Business, Government, Industry, and Community Service

1953–1955, Secretary, Abernethy Local of United Grain Growers

1955-1981, Director, United Grain Growers Limited

1961–1981, President, United Grain Growers Limited (As UGG President, Mac also served, for varying terms, as President of a number of other UGG enterprises, including United Feeds and United Livestock Feeds Limited, UGG Insurance Services, Grain Growers Export Company, UGG Terminals, The Public Press and Country Guide.)

1970–1974, Director and Vice-Chariman, XCAN Grain Limited

1974–1977, Director, United Oilseeds Products Limited

1974–1977, President, United Oilseeds Products Limited

1977–1981, Member, Management Committee, United Oilseeds Products Limited

1961–1968, Director, The Canadian Federation of Agriculture

1961–1975, Member, Canadian Wheat Board Advisory Committee

1961–1974, Member, Winnipeg Commodity Exchange

1971–1981, Member, Policy Committee, Winnipeg Commodity Exchange

1967–1972, Director, Rapeseed Association of Canada

1967–1971, President, Rapeseed Association of Canada

1968–1969, Member, Advisory Committee on Agriculture, Targets for Economic Development, Government of Canada

1968–1969, Member, Manitoba Marketing Board, Government of Manitoba

1968–1970, Member, Committee on Agricultural Research and Development, Science and Development

1969–1972, Governor, Agricultural Economics Research Council of Canada

1969–1982, Director, Canada Grains Council

1969–1972, Chairman, Canada Grains Council

1971–1972, Member, Palliser Wheat Growers Association

1974–1975, First Vice-President, Western Agricultural Conference

1975–1976, Third Vice-President, Western Agricultural Conference

1974–1980, Member, Economic Council of Canada

1976–1982, Director, Great Lakes Waterways

1984–1986, Director, Development Association

1984–1986, Chairman, Great Lakes Waterways Development Association

1976–1980, Member, Committee on Canada's Contribution to World Food Supply, Science Council of Canada

1977–1978, Chairman, Agriculture and Rural Development Review Team, Task Force on Government Organization and Economy, Government of Manitoba

1979–1982, Director, Prince Rupert Grain Limited

1980–1982, Director, Ridley Grain limited

1985–1986, Member, 1986 Census, National Advisory Committee

1986–1990, Member, National Statistics Council

1965–1968, Trustee, Canadian Hunger Foundation

1969–1970, Governor, Canadian Association for Latin America

1969–1972, Trustee, United Way of Greater Winnipeg

1970–1976, Member, United Way of Greater Winnipeg, Administration Committee

1970–1973, Member, Advisory Board to the Prairie Regional Laboratory of the National Research Council of Canada

1971–1973, Member, The University and Community Council, University of Manitoba

1972–Present, Mac's most extensive public service involvement was with the Victoria Hospital in Winnipeg, where he served in many roles: Trustee, 1st and 2nd Vice Chair, and Chair of the Board of Trustees; member or chair of various committees (Finance, Executive, and Planning and Services Review committees); and Director and President of the Research and Services Fund Inc. (which later became the Victoria Hospital Foundation)

1985–1989, Director/Chair, Victoria Health Guard Inc.

1973–1976, Director, Rainbow Stage Inc.

1976–1985, Member, Rainbow Stage Honourary Advisory Board

1973–1975, Counsellor at Large, Canada West Foundation

1973–1982, Member, Army Benevolent Fund, Manitoba Committee

1974–1983, Member, The One Hundred Club

1976–1978, Member, Advisory Committee, Agriculture and Food Marketing Forum, University of Manitoba

1980–1983, Director, C.D. Howe Institute

1982–1985, Director, C.D. Howe Memorial Foundation

1982–1985, Member, Advisory Council, Children's Hospital of Winnipeg Research Foundation Inc.

1983–1988, Member, Special Awards Committee, Manitoba Chambers of Commerce

1982–1988, Governor, The University of Manitoba

1982–1983, Vice-Chairman, Board of Governors, University of Manitoba

1983–1988, Chairman, Board of Governors, University of Manitoba

1982–1988, Member and Chair, Executive Committee, University of Manitoba

1982–1984, Director, Alumni Association University of Manitoba

1985–1991, Member, Advisory Board, University of Manitoba Transport Institute

1982–1984, Director, Ducks Unlimited (Canada)

1963–1966, Director, Robinson Little and Co. Ltd.

1965–1980, Member, Winnipeg Advisory Board, Crown Trust Company

1970–1974, Director, Crown Trust Company

1967–1985, Director, The Great West Life Assurance Company

1969–1985, Director, Canadian Pacific Limited

1975–1987, Director, Massey Ferguson Ltd./Varity Corporation

1976–1985, Director, The Royal Bank of Canada

1981–1989, Director, Fletchers Fine Foods Limited

1981–1989, Director, Atlas Lance Travel Limited

1984–1990, Director, Power Financial Corporation

1983–1984, Member, Winnipeg Advisory Board Central Trust Co.

1984–1986, Member, Winnipeg Advisory Board Central Trust Co.

1988–1990, Dirirector and Chair, Springhill Management Co. Ltd.

1982–1992, Trustee, Wildlife Foundation of Manitoba

1979–1993, Hon. Colonel, The Queen's Own Cameron Highlanders of Canada

1968 onward, Advisory Board, The Queen's Own Cameron Highlanders of Canada

1991–1993, Trustee and Chair, The Queen's Own Cameron Highlanders of Canada Regimental Foundation ·

1990–1999, Director and President, Winnipeg Condominium Corporation No. 36

1983–1988, Member, Winnipeg Clinic Research Institute and Paul T. Thorlakson Research Foundation

1986–1987, Member, Ad Hoc Committee on Nursing Education, Health Sciences Centre, University of Manitoba Schools of Nursing

1982–1985, Founding Trustee, Manitoba Historical Society Heritage Foundation Trust

1988 onward, Founding Partner, Partnership for Sustainable Development

1988–1991, Charter Member, Manitoba Round Table on Environment and the Economy

1988–1995, Member, Council of the Developing Countries Farm Radio Network

Honours and Awards

1967, Awarded Canadian Centennial Medal

1967, Awarded, Honourary Chief Flying Eagle, Blackfoot Tribe, Cluny, Alberta

1971, Awarded Manitoba Centennial Medal

1974, Honourary Degree: Doctor of Laws, University of Manitoba

1977, Honourary Degree: Doctor of Laws, University of Saskatchewan

1977, Awarded, Queen's Silver Jubilee Medal

1982, "Golden Award," Canadian Feed Industry

1983, Appointed Officer of the Order of Canada

1984, Award of Excellence, Fiftieth Anniversary of the Canadian Excellence Agricultural Outlook Conference

1969, Honourary Member, Agricultural Institute of Canada

1969, Honourary Member, Manitoba Institute of Agrologists

1972, Life Membership, Rapeseed Association of Canada (now the Canola Council of Canada)

1972, Honourary Member, Canadian Seed Trade Association

1974, Honourary Life Member, The Canadian Seed Growers' Association

1976–1980, Honourary Counsellor, Winnipeg Chamber of Commerce

1982, Member, Saskatchewan Agricultural Hall of Fame

1982, Member, Canadian Agricultural Hall of Fame

1984, Honourary Member, C.D. Howe Institute

1984, Honourary Member, Board of Directors, C.D. Howe Institute

1985, Honourary Life Member, Saskatchewan Canola Growers Association

1991, Honourary Life Member, University of Manitoba Transport Institute

1993, Awarded, 125th Anniversary of Canadian Federation Medal

Notes

Preface

1 Mac Runciman, "The Strait Straight Way," School of Religion - 1976, Knox United Church, Winnipeg, Manitoba, March 18, 1976, p. 17. Note that the description of his audience here as a "school of religion" is not accurate. It was actually a lenten study group composed of members of the Knox United congregation. See Chapter 8 for more details.

2 For the reader who is unfamiliar with this term, the Crow's Nest Pass Rates were the rail rates on grain, whose levels were retained by legislation until the early 1990s. See footnote 5, Chapter 5, for more details.

3 C.F. Wilson, *A Century of Canadian Grain: Government Policy to 1951* (Saskatoon, Saskatchewan: Western Producer Prairie Books, 1978); also *C.D. Howe. Howe: An Optimist's Response to a Surfeit of Grain* (Ottawa, Grains Group, 1980).

Chapter 1

1 Mac produced several short, written, biographical pieces, some of which were titled, and some of which were not; some of which were paginated, and some of which were not. This is from a piece called "Foreword To the Life and Times of Alexander McInnes Runciman." These biographical fragments are found in either Mac's personal papers, or the papers from the preparation of this book. This quote is from "Foreword," p. 1.

2 Ibid., p. 1.

3 Ibid., p. 3.

4 "Sasines" is a word peculiar to Sottish Law, referring to the granting of legal possession of feudal property. The word itself is a Scottish variant of the word "seisen," meaning feudal possession of an estate in land.

5 "Foreword," p. 1.

6 Ibid., p. 2.

7 Ibid.

8 Ibid.

9 Handwritten addition to "Foreword" (unpaginated).

10 "Foreword," p. 3.

11 Ibid., p. 2.

12 Ibid., pp. 4, 5.

13 Letter, no salutation, signed by R.H. Bone, Chairman of the Easter Ross Commitee, and J. Munro, District Clerk, Runciman papers.

14 "Foreword," p. 6.

15 Ibid., p. 5.

16 Ibid., p. 6.

17 A "stint" was the name applied to a kind of work unit in potato-picking at the time. A child or woman was given "half a stint"; a man, normally one "stint"; and a large man, "a stint and a half."

18 "Grieve" is a Scottish word for farm manager or overseer.

Chapter 2

1 Breechings are the straps that pass behind a horse's haunches and allow it to back up and push whatever load it is pulling. It is pronounced "britchings."

2 Grain pickling was the process of treating grain with formaldehyde to prevent the development of a disease known as smut, which forms on the heads of the grain and turns good kernels to a black powder. This lowers yields and grades. In the process, the chemical, diluted in water, was sprinkled on the grain, which was then turned over and over by shovel until all the kernels were wet. The grain was then heaped up and covered with a horse blanket to keep the fumes in overnight. Today, problems like this are handled through disease resistant varities and by seed treatment with powdered chemicals, and grain pickling is a thing of the past.

3 Information provided by Mac; grades are taken from his report card from his personal papers.

Chapter 3

1 Those readers familiar with military ranks will recognize that in this chapter these terms are used somewhat loosely. The Ordnance Corps uses a unique terminology for some of its ranks. Mac was actually appointed to what is here called the highest non-commissioned officer rank in the Canadian army, "Subconductor of Ordnance (Acting)" in March 1944. "Subconductor" is the equivalent of Regimental Sergeant Major, or Warrant Officer I. There was, in fact, one higher rank: Conductor of Ordnance. However, there is only one individual who holds this rank, and that person is the absolute highest non-commissioned officer in the entire Canadian army. Neither Mac nor I were certain whether the ranks and titles used in this chapter are still used today, but we tried to be as accurate as we could about the terminology of the wartime,

while at the same time using the most familiar terms, and without intruding into the flow of the narrative with too much explanatory detail.

2 The term "tough" refers to the moisture content of grain. The levels vary between grains, but for wheat to be dry, it must have less than about fourteen percent moisture; between about fourteen percent and seventeen percent, it is referred to as "tough"; if the moisture content is still higher, it is referred to as "damp."

3 From an untitled and unpaginated biographical fragment on Mac's war experience (hereafter referred to as "War Account"; this account had two sections, the second of which carried the subtitle "Vinchiatura").

4 "War Account."

5 Ibid., augmented by material from an interview (April 24, 1994).

6 Ibid., augmented by material from an interview (April 17, 1994).

7 Ibid.

8 Ibid.

9 Ibid. ("Vinchiatura").

Chapter 4

1 "The Postwar Years" (hereafter "Postwar"), a short piece written and entitled as we prepared this chapter, p. 1.

2 Ibid., p. 2.

3 Ibid., p. 1.

4 Ibid., pp. 1, 2.

5 Ibid., p. 2.

6 Ibid., p. 2, augmented by material from interview (June 23, 1994).

7 "Postwar," p. 2.

8 Text and following table from "Postwar," p. 3.

9 "Postwar," p. 3.

10 "Postwar," p. 4, augmented from material from interview (April 13, 1994).

11 "Postwar," p. 5.

12 Ibid., p. 4.

13 Since the company became publicly traded, three of their directors are elected by the shareholders. The remaining twelve are still elected by farmers.

14 All material on Abernethy-Balcarres Local Board from UGG local board history files, prepared by Don Fraser, retired UGG employee.

15 Letter, Dickinson to Brownlee, March 4, 1955. The letter is in Mac's private papers.

16 "Postwar," p. 6.

17 The "annex," in older wooden elevators, is a building sitting beside the elevator, which contains a number of grain storage bins. It is filled through a spout from the top of the bucket elevator that elevates the grain, and emptied by dropping the grain

out of the bottom of the bins in the annex, down to an auger or a conveyor that hauls the grain back into the elevator itself.

18 Quotation from Mac's notes, read by him during interview (April 24, 1994).

19 Letter, Fred Dickinson to Mac Runciman, Nov 12, 1956. The letter is in Mac's private papers.

20 "Postwar," p. 6.

21 Memo, from P.C Watt to J.E. Brownlee, August 19, 1955. A copy of this memo is in Mac's private papers.

22 Franklin Foster, in his book, *John E. Brownlee: A Biography*, says that Brownlee had a series of operations, but this conflicts with both Mac's recollection and records. According to Mac, he underwent surgery only in 1957 and 1961. The account of his Vancouver trip and forced return to Calgary is recorded in the UGG board minutes of June 6, 1961.

23 Board Minutes, June 6, 1961, p. 144.

24 Ibid.

25 Foster, p. 312. According to Mac's recollection, Driscoll accepted the position sometime in early June. Foster's date, therefore, must have referred to an official announcement, but Mac had no record of it. A telephone call to Foster was unable to unearth any detail. We assumed the date to be correct, and did not check further.

26 Letter, December 15, 1961, Watt to Runciman, p. 3. The words quoted are attributed by Watt to Brownlee. The letter is in Mac's private papers.

27 Ibid.

28 Ibid., p. 2.

29 Foster records (p. 312) that Mr. Brownlee submitted his resignation on June 21st. However, Mac has no recollection or record to indicate that this was so. In fact, it is at odds with what occurred at the meeting of the board on June 30. Had Brownlee resigned, that would have been known at the outset of the meeting, and the board would have immediately been able to consider the selection of a new president. However, they did not and, in Mac's recollection, the board had a very confusing and confused day before the matter of the presidency was settled.

Chapter 5

1 Since the company went public, the annual meeting is in two parts: the members' meeting, which is still approximately as described here, and the shareholders' meeting, which is indistinguishable from the annual general meeting of any public company.

2 "Report of the President to the Board of Directors, United Grain Growers Limited, Vancouver B.C., July 18, 1967," p. 15. (Hereafter, these reports are simply cited as "President's Report.")

3 Ian MacPherson, *Each for All: A History of the Co-operative Movement in English Canada, 1990 - 1945* (Toronto: MacMillan of Canada, 1979), pp. 46, 47; 106.

4 Vernon Fowke, *National Policy and the Wheat Economy* (Toronto: University of Toronto Press, 1957), p. 191.

5 The Crow's Nest Pass Rates were, of course, legislated rail freight rates that applied to grain. They had first come into force through the Crow's Nest Pass Agreement between the Canadian Pacific Railway and the federal government, providing for the construction of a railway from Lethbridge through the Crow's Nest Pass to the Kootenay area of British Columbia. The Agreement also provided for the rail rates on grain to be reduced by three cents per hundredweight. Grain freight rates went through a complex series of changes between 1897 and the 1920s, sometimes being lower than the Crow levels and sometimes higher. However, grain interests always supported them, and in the mid-1920s rail rates on grain were legislated to be at the level of the Crow Rates for all railways, on all lines, with no possibility of their being revised upwards. From this point on, they would be more accurately called the "statutory rates," but they were almost universally referred to as the "Crow's Nest Pass Rates," reflecting their origin. They were the subject of a long and bitter debate in the 1970s, discussed in Chapter 7, and were eventually repealled in 1984 by the Western Grain Transportation Act.

6 The Rochdale Principles, which were named after the British town of the same name where the cooperative movement started, are a set of precepts that are supposed to be followed by all cooperative enterprises, and while there are various versions, they include: democratic control; open membership; fixed or limited payment on capital; distribution of profit in proportion to (for consumer co-ops) purchases from, or (for producer co-ops) sales to, the organization; cash trading; dealing only in pure goods; education of members; and political and religious neutrality.

7 Mac Runciman (Untitled), Notes for Talk to Eastern Division Construction Department Luncheon, Winnipeg, Manitoba, January 9, 1967, p. 6.

8 E.B. Nourse, "The Economic Philosophy of Cooperation," *American Economic Review*, vol. xii, no.4 (December, 1922), pp.577,594.

9 Quotations from letter, October 15, 1990, read by Mac during an interview, March 14, 1999.

10 Feed Freight Assistance was a federal government program to subsidize the transportation of grain for animal feed from the prairies to eastern Canada and British Columbia.

11 "President's Report," January. 18, 1966, p. 6.

12 "President's Report," April 5, 1966, p. 2.

Chapter 6

1 (Untitled), Notes used by Mr. Runciman to address the Dufferin Agricultural Society, Carman, Manitoba, November 24, 1966, p. 12.

2 A.M. Runciman, "Markets Unlimited (And Limited)," to Ontario Soil and Crop Improvement Association, Toronto, Ontario, January 25, 1967, p. 3.

3 "President's Report," January 1969, p. 6.

4 "President's Report," July 1969, p. 10.

5 "President's Report," July 1971, p. 20.

6 Vernon Fowke, *The National Policy and the Wheat Economy* (Toronto: University of Toronto Press, 1957), p. 221.

7 Mac Runciman, "Government Support of Wheat Prices" (location and audience unknown), September 28, 1967, p. 2.

8 A.M. Runciman, "What's Wrong With Canadian Wheat Markets? - A Farmer's Viewpoint," Regina Chamber of Commerce, Farm Forum, Regina, Saskatchewan, March 5, 1968, p. 12.

9 Ibid., p. 14.

10 Ibid., p. 11.

11 Mac Runciman (Untitled), Notes for a talk to a Delegate Report Supper Meeting, High River, Alberta, February 12, 1969, p. 6.

12 Mac Runciman, "Some Notes on the Role of the Canadian Wheat Board and the Canada Grains Council in Marketing Western Canadian Grain," Young Men's Section, Dufferin Agricultural Society, Carman, Manitoba, February 24, 1970, pp. 6, 7; see also Mac Runciman (Untitled), West Winnipeg Rotary Club, Winnipeg, Manitoba, March 26, 1970 p. 9.

13 Mac Runciman, "A Look at 1970 Adjustments in Agriculture," A Balanced Adjustment Program for Agriculture - Components and Coordination, seminar, University of Alberta, Edmonton, Alberta, March 10, 1970, p. 4.

14 "President's Report," January 1971, p. 4.

15 Mac Runciman, "The Wheat Economy: What Wrong - What Can Be Done?" Saskatchewan Association of Rural Municipalities Convention, Regina, Saskatchewan, March 18, 1970, p. 4.

16 "A Look at 1970 Adjustments in Agriculture," pp. 1, 2.

17 Ibid., p. 2.

18 Mac Runciman, "Domestic Feed Grain Marketing," Canadian Barley and Oilseeds Conference, Winnipeg Inn, Winnipeg, Manitoba, February 14, 1974, p.10.

19 Ibid., p. 10.

20 "Domestic Feed Grain Marketing," p. 12.

21 Mac Runciman (Untitled), Rapeseed Marketing Seminar, Winnipeg, Manitoba, November 20, 1972, p. 3.

22 "A Look at 1970 Adjustments in Agriculture," p. 3.

23 Note that "rapeseed" was the name used for this grain until developments in plant breeding resulted in a new strain which is called "canola." The term "rapeseed" has now largely disappeared. I use the term "rapeseed" throughout this section, because it was the term used to describe the product during the time that Mac was involved.

24 "Chairman's Remarks ....A.M. Runciman," Barley and Oilseeds Conference, Winnipeg, Manitoba, March 14, 1967, p. 3. (The apparent ellipsis points are in the actual title of the talk.)

25 "President's Report," July 1967, p. 3,4.

26 "President's Report," September 1967, p. 2.

27 Letter, Jim McAnsh to A.M Runciman (date uncertain), quoted by Runciman in interview (April 24, 1994).

28 Mac Runciman, "Market Demands for Grain Through the 80s," Annual Meeting of the Western Canada Fertilizer Association, Richmond, British Columbia, August 28, 1979, pp. 17, 18.

29 Mac Runciman, "Let's Not Solve Farm Problems by Doctrine," annual convention of Unifarm, Macdonald Hotel, Edmonton, Alberta, December 12, 1973, p. 1.

30 Mac Runciman (Untitled), Rapeseed Marketing Seminar, Winnipeg, Manitoba, November 20, 1972, p. 6.

31 Mac Runciman, "Three Things One Shouldn't Talk About When One Is Asked to Talk About Rapeseed," High Energy Grains and Oilseeds Industry Conference, Palliser Hotel, Calgary, Alberta, January 17, 1973, pp. 9, 10.

32 "Three Things One Shouldn't Talk About When One Is Asked to Talk About Rapeseed," p. 10.

33 Quoted in: Mac Runciman (Untitled), Fall Social of the Western Manitoba Farm Business Association, Shoal Lake, Manitoba, November 17, 1972, p. 11.

34 "President's Report," October 1968, p. 5.

35 "President's Report," April 1969, p. 5.

36 Ibid., p. 2.

37 "President's Report," April 1972, p. 2.

38 "President's Report," July 1973, p. 37.

39 "President's Report," October 1969, pp. 1, 2.

40 "President's Report," November 1970, pp. 3, 4.

41 "President's Report," January 1970, p. 9.

42 "President's Report," April 1970, p. 10.

43 Ibid., p. 10.

44 "President's Report," July 1970, p. 4.

45 This story was related to me by a railway executive who had been part of the GTTG at the time.

46 "President's Report," July 1971, p. 5.

47 "President's Report," September 1971, pp. 20, 21.

48 "President's Report," July 1972, p. 5.

49 Mac made this remark to me in 1973 when the *State of the Industry* report was in its final stages of completion.

50 "President's Report," July 1973, pp. 31, 32.

51 The Grains Institute is a body established in Winnipeg to assist with market development and liaison with overseas customers. It is primarily an educational body, and runs courses for representatives of buyers to teach them about Canadian grains and the Canadian grain system. It also runs courses for domestic purposes, of which the most notable is probably the "Farm Leaders" course, teaching farmers who are interested in becoming involved in farm organizations and agriculture policy about both the Canadian and international grain industry.

Chapter 7

1 Reference is made to the Gordon speech in a letter from E. Baxter, Chief Statistician of the Board of Grain Commissioners, to Chief Commissioner G.N. McConnell, November 5, 1962; the Baker talk is documented in a column by John Schmidt in the *Calgary Herald*, March 14, 1964, p. 42. Copies of both the letter and the column are in Mac's personal papers.

2 Mac Runciman, "President Years," biographical fragment, (n.d.); edited in April 1997.

3 Mac Runciman (Untitled), Notes for 1976 Delegate Report Meetings (no places or dates given), p. 9.

4 Mac Runciman, "The Future Grain Handling System as United Grain Growers Sees It," Regina Chamber of Commerce, Regina, Saskatchewan, March 2, 1976, p. 3.

5 UGG internal report entitled "Purchases, Sales, Saw-offs, Closures and Consolidation," September 1970. A copy of this paper is in Mac's personal papers.

6 These two sentences are taken from two speeches. The first paragraph is from Mac Runciman, "Costs and Revenues in Handling and Moving Grain," 8th Annual Meeting of the Palliser Wheat Growers Association, Saskatoon, Saskatchewan, January 3, 1978, pp. 3, 4; the second is from Mac Runciman "The Issue of Too Much Government over Farmers and the Grain Industry," Annual Meeting of the Hudson's Bay Route Association, Red Oak Inn, Brandon, Manitoba, April 13, 1977, p. 5.

7 UGG Annual Report for 1975, p. 15, quoted in speech, "The Future Grain Handling System as United Grain Growers Sees It," p. 8.

8 Mac Runciman (Untitled), Kiwanis Club, Saskatoon, Saskatchewan, March 25, 1963, pp. 3 - 7, passim.

9 Mac Runciman (Untitled), Notes for Carman Branch Line Retention Committee, p. 2. Note that the speech is undated, but the index to the file folder containing this speech shows the date as February 21, 1964.

10 Data taken from the *State of the Industry report*, Table 4A.

11 UGG purchased most, but not all, of Reliance Grain's elevators, but it was the major purchaser. UGG purchased only McCabe's elevators. McCabe's feed and seed division was purchased by Peavey about a year later, and the McCabe's merchandising division was sold to National Grain in 1971. (See Charles W. Anderson, *Grain: The Entrepreneurs* [Watson & Dwyer Publishing Ltd.], Winnipeg, Manitoba, 1991.)

12 "President's Report," July 1967, p. 14.

13 "President's Report," October 1969, pp. 6, 7.

14 (Untitled), Kiwanis Club, Saskatoon, Saskatchewan, March 25, 1963, p. 7.

15 "The Issue of Too Much Government over Farmers and the Grain Industry," p. 17.

16 Mac Runciman, "Prairie Cattlemen and Rail Freight Rates," Annual Meeting of the Saskatchewan Stock Growers Association, Kenosee Lake, Saskatchewan, June 3, 1977, p. 4.

17 See Chapter 6.

18 UGG Annual Report for 1975, p. 16; this material is a precis of selected paragraphs, not a direct quote.

19 "The Future Grain Handling System as United Grain Growers Sees It," p. 10.

20 UGG Annual Report for 1975, p. 16.

21 "President's Report," March 1976, p. 17.

22 UGG Annual Report for 1976, p. 61.

23 "The Future Grain Handling System as United Grain Growers Sees It," p. 11.

24 UGG Annual Report for 1976, p. 61.

25 "President's Report," November 1975, p. 9.

26 "President's Report," March 1976, p. 18.

27 Hearing transcript, quoted on p. 15 of the "President's Report," March 1976.

28 Hearing transcript, September. 2, 1976, vol. IV, p. 760.

29 "President's Report," September 1976, p. 14.

30 "President's Report," July 1976, p. 14.

31 Ibid.

32 "Costs and Revenues in Handling and Moving Grain," pp. 17, 18.

33 "President's Report," July 1976, pp. 13, 14.

34 *Grain and Rail in Western Canada* (Report of the Grain Handling and Transportation Commission of Inquiry), April 18, 1977, p. 128.

35 "Prairie Cattlemen and Rail Freight Rates," p. 8.

36 *Grain and Rail in Western Canada*, p. 337.

37 "Prairie Cattlemen and Rail Freight Rates," p. 12.

38 "President's Report," July 1976, pp. 27.

39 Ibid., pp. 26 – 28.

40 "President's Report," January 1977, p. 4.

41 "President's Report," September 1979, pp. 6, 7.

42 "President's Report," November 1980, pp. 8,9.

43 Ibid., pp. 11, 12.

44 Mac Runciman, "Should Freight Rates on Grain Be Boosted[?]," Palliser Wheat Growers Ninth Annual Convention, Regina, Saskatchewan, January 4, 1979, pp. 4, 5.

45 Ibid., p. 8.

46 Mac Runciman (Untitled), "Notes for 1979 Delegate Report Meetings" (no places or dates given), p. 6.

47 1979 Annual Report, pp. 16, 17.

48 "Should Freight Rates on Grain Be Boosted[?]" p. 9.

49 Mac Runciman, "United Grain Growers' Role in the Canadian Grain Business," Diploma Agriculture II Grain Marketing Program, University of Manitoba, Winnipeg, Manitoba, 1980, p. 19.

50 "Parker pere" refers to former Manitoba Pool President Bill Parker, who by this time had to be distinguished from his son, Lorne, who had became active in farm policy debates.

51 Note that what appear to be ellipsis points in this sentence do not indicate an omission. This is the text as M. Pepin wrote it, and he used them as punctuation exactly as they are shown.

52 Letter is in Mac's personal papers.

Chapter 8

1 E. Rea, *T.A. Crerar: A Political Life*, Preface, p. vii.

2 Mac Runciman (Untitled), "Notes in reply to the toast [to "Canada The Land We Live In"] at the St. Andrew's Society dinner, November 27, 1981, p. 1.

3 Ibid., p. 2.

4 Ibid., p. 3.

5 Ibid., pp. 3, 4.

6 Ibid., p. 5.

7 Ibid., pp. 5, 6; the source from which Mac quotes Crerar is not specified. Note that it is likely Crerar used the phrase "Special Privilege," and perhaps capitalized it, rather than "special privileges." The phrase was in common use in the 1920s.

8 Mac Runciman, "The Strait Straight Way," School of Religion - 1976, Knox United Church, Winnipeg, Manitoba, March 18, 1976, p. 6. As noted in the Preface, the identification of the audience as a "School of Religion" is not accurate. The audience was as described here.

9 Ibid., p. 2.

10 Ibid., p. 7.

11 Ibid., p. 8.

12 Ibid., p. 12.

13 Ibid., p. 11.

14 Ibid., p. 13.

15 Ibid., pp. 13, 14.

16 Ibid., p. 16.

17 Ibid., pp. 17, 18.

18 Ibid., pp. 13, 14.

19 Letter, Shearstone to Runciman, October 7, 1986. The letter is in Mac's personal papers.

Index